The
CONTROVERSIALIST

The CONTROVERSIALIST

ARGUMENTS WITH EVERYONE, LEFT RIGHT AND CENTER

MARTIN PERETZ

WICKED SON

A WICKED SON BOOK
An Imprint of Post Hill Press
ISBN: 978-1-63758-227-5
ISBN (eBook): 978-1-63758-228-2

The Controversialist:
Arguments with Everyone, Left Right and Center
© 2023 by Martin Peretz
All Rights Reserved

Cover Design by Hampton Lamoureux

Interior Design by Yoni Limor

Post Hill Press
New York • Nashville
WickedSonBooks.com

Published in the United States of America
1 2 3 4 5 6 7 8 9 10

To Tom Williamson, Eric Breindel,
Fouad Ajami, Marie Syrkin, Charles Krauthammer,
and Henry Rosovsky, who have passed on.

CONTENTS

Vantage Point, 2022:
The Ballad of My Life

And this is the ballad of my life: that I mumble strange
syllables before the people of silence.

That's a line from Avrom Sutzkever, a Yiddish poet. It captures, better than any other words I know, what it feels like to be eighty-three. I know some syllables that matter, in case anyone wants to listen.

You should want to—not so much because of who I am, though most people would say I'm a psychologically interesting character, but for where I've been, what I've seen.

A collection of snapshots are scattered in front of me on the coffee table. Here's me, at thirteen, speaking before a crowd of ten thousand Yiddish Jews on the Lower East Side, dedicating I. L. Peretz Square to my famous relation, a literary hero of this poor but thriving community. Here I am, ten years older, in a Harvard seminar room, during my second year of teaching, grinning and sticking it in old Harvard's eye: "Freud plus Marx equals truth," I tell my students. Here I am in the crowd at the March on Washington in 1963 watching Josephine Baker wonder at the sight of a salt-and-pepper crowd like one she'd never seen before, saying it gave her hope for America. I see what she sees, or at least I think I do. Five years later, I am speaking at Harvard Memorial Church to an almost all-white crowd of 1,200 people, some of them my students, about Dr. Martin Luther King, Jr.'s death: "But we may take whatever slight hopes we can," I say, "from the fact that it was the young who eagerly sought him out. They know, as this beautiful man did and had tried to tell us, that it is now five minutes before midnight. Not earlier. Five minutes before midnight."

In this snapshot, dated October 1973, I am in Henry Kissinger's office with a group of Harvard colleagues, urging him to send arms to Israel, quick. Henry ribs me for my dovish politics a decade before. "Dovishness," I tell him, "stops at the delicatessen door." Here's one from ten years later: I'm sitting at the editorial table of the *New Republic* with Mike Kinsley, Leon Wieseltier, Charles Krauthammer, and Rick Hertzberg. We're arguing over a tricky topic, one that's sure to cause grief. This week it is "should we arm the Contras?"; last week it was "should gay people have the right to marry?" A few years later, here I am at Kramer Books in Washington, D.C., offering Andrew Sullivan, a pugnacious, young British conservative, the editorship of the *New Republic* and making him the first editor at a major American periodical who is openly gay. Here's a shot of my sixtieth birthday under the Brooklyn Bridge, and Yo-Yo Ma is playing the "Tennessee Waltz" for Al Gore, my friend and former student, who we are all sure is going to be the next president of the United States.

And then, a last snapshot. It's eleven years later—the invasion of Iraq, which I backed, is a disaster; the financial system that my friends helped build has crashed; my wife and I are divorced; the *New Republic* is sold after I feared going bust—and here I am in my white suit walking across Harvard Yard, surrounded by students: "Harvard, Harvard shame on you, honoring a racist fool." The racist fool is, apparently, me. It's a sodden coda, one I don't quite grasp, or believe.

These snapshots are from the last two eras that shaped American life: the postwar era and the neoliberal one. They were thick eras, and I was in the thick of them. America became a national, consumer, finance-based nation and a new elite came into consciousness to govern it. I knew many of the players, and, at the time, I stood for the assumptions of both of these eras. Some of what we hoped for came to pass; some turned out not to be; some turned out to be a fantasy. The subject of this book is how that happened; the question it poses is why. I should say at the outset that I don't have an "answer," a broad concept or overarching theory of the past seventy-five years that can explain all these events. But if I look at them long enough, I can discern the outline of a pattern of shifts.

For us—by which I mean the people I came up with, the middle classes of what's now called the Silent Generation, born between the two great wars—the logic of things was obvious, self-explanatory. We were the only generation to grow up with the old America, a country of ethnicities grounded in local, traditional authority and the new, a country of movers and consumers grounded in distant institutional structures. By "us" I also mean American Jews: the first immigrant ethnic group to be allowed inside the old Protestant class. America was changing in the postwar period: its political, financial, and educational institutions were receptive to new blood in a way they never had been before. My friends and I made a place for ourselves in these institutions—Harvard, the Democratic Party, and then, after I had bought it, the *New Republic*, which in its time was the most influential political magazine in Washington. We had a hand in shaping them and saw them change up close. The America we came up in was one of neighborhoods and ethnicities and creeds and unions; the America we helped grow, the one we have now, is one of PhDs and interstate systems and investment portfolios.

But what I didn't envision was that the institutions we helped construct would become divided between specialists and ideologists, experts and deconstructionists, with very little of the breadth—the passion for applying expertise and ideas to real life, and letting real life inform expertise and ideas—that characterized the educated leaders we imagined.

The equal society I hoped for in the sixties has not materialized; if anything, it has gotten more unequal in the intervening years. Consumption, not cultivation, seems to tie America together. Politics are divided, with a media making those divides into cartoons: between a multicultural statism that doesn't ring true to the complexity of life on the ground and an antistate conservatism that feels misplaced, grafted onto an era that no longer exists. Even the news, which once provided a reliable supply of factual information that could be argued over by reasonable people, is now relayed to the public via attention-grabbing takes on social media and on channels like Fox News and MSNBC, so that the warring parties cannot even refer to a shared reality. My grandchildren's generation, which knows only this sort of shallow, hyperbolic commentary, expresses less trust of institutions than any cohort in recent history.

All the assumptions I held at the millennium, at the apex of my influence, when Al Gore seemed to be on the verge of the presidency and the *New Republic* was still in the center of American political discourse, are upside down: a global America, a stable society at home, compromise politics in Washington, benevolent or half-benevolent institutions, and a manageable debt. The logic I grew up with and operated on was sound, until the point when it wasn't.

✻ ✻ ✻

There are a few things to know about me before I have my say. I offer them not in the spirit of justification or concession but full disclosure, just so you know that the Martin Peretz who will tell you this story, through whom the events of the last eighty years and two eras will get filtered, is such-and-such a man, with such-and-such limitations and preoccupations, at least in his own mind.

I am a marginalized man. Politically, I'm a Democrat. But even within the party of the historically marginalized, I'm on the side of the margin. Part of the marginalization is psychological: I don't mind feeling attacked; it makes me comfortable. Part of it is political: everything I have believed always turned out to be somewhat on the margins; people who are held up as paragons have never been my people. Even at the apex of whatever influence I might've had with the Gore campaign, I felt like an outsider. It says something about my self-conception that the modern Jew I've always had the strongest connection to is Kafka: the prototypical marginal man and a Zionist until his death.

My own marginality, or sense of it, is partly hereditary, a matter of my childhood community in the Bronx, a partly Yiddish enclave on the tip of America, which was to outsiders a black box. We were foreign and self-referential, confident in our heritage, and fearful for our future; we embraced politics not in the American sense of a pastime—like baseball or the stock market—but in the émigré sense of an absolute commitment; we were emotionally fractured like all communities from someplace else, one eye to our past, one eye toward our people, both eyes on the big American unknown. My character is a convergence of these inherited qualities, and they interlink and reinforce and justify each other.

I'm publicly known as a controversialist: someone determined to stir the pot and who answers to his own emotions and instincts and to not much else. That reputation for heedless controversy has, to a certain extent, swallowed me, creating a kind of polarity where you either approve of or dismiss me and is abetted by the fact that I never, ever relent or leave the ring. My own sense of myself is more tentative, more complicated than my reputation. But then it would be. Still, part of my story is of controversy: throwing myself into the fray, arguing for the sake of clarifying, holding others to account, asserting my grudges and loves with vigor. And my story is of mistakes that come with that—things I didn't think about when I said them, things I didn't say that I should have.

The career I staked out for myself says a lot about my sense of my own marginality. I was never an institution man because institutions couldn't hold me or my passions. But I was a supporter of institutions because they were a way in for my people and, after the sixties, institutions were the only things I trusted. So I fashioned a place for myself as a kind of catchall, on the borders of different establishments—financial, intellectual, journalistic, political—as a connector of their different practitioners, with an ear to the street. I've always had a gift for friendship. I love good company and good conversation, and the dinners my wife and I gave in Cambridge were famous. I'm always interested in talking to strangers, to see what I can learn from them.

Finally, my heritage, my Jewishness, is another cause of my marginality. But it's something deeper. It's a force in me—not a belief, a force—so strong, so roughly and deeply sensed, that it obviates contradictions with which other people grapple. Jewishness spans three thousand years, between antiquity, with its rigors and abstractions, and modernity, with its difficulties and contradictions. To me, there are no divides between the eras: *Jewishness bridges them.* In that sense, I am not a modern man at all, or I'm modern only to the extent that I see myself as part of a people that modern life gives the chance to mix with others.

There's one last thing to bear in mind. People aspire to different things: I aspired, from the beginning of my life, to be in the thick of things, and that aspiration I've achieved. But for all of my success, for all the success of my people and my cohort and some of my causes, I am a dissatisfied man: the society we tried to create in this country, a humanized technocracy, has stalled; the project of my life is incomplete. I don't know *why* things have gone so wrong in the way of a theory—but having lived at the center of so much history, I do know *what* happened, what triumphs occurred, and what mistakes were made. My observations are those of an insider, but my perspective is that of an outsider. This is a late act in a long life story: an offering up of this tale of failure in the hopes that it may help point the way to what I and my cohort couldn't achieve and, maybe, to gain some late garlands along the way.

CHAPTER ONE

Postwar: Inheritance

When I was three, maybe four, my mother bought me a canary and named it *Faygeleh*, Yiddish for "little bird." One day it flew away. I was heartbroken, and so my mother told me it had gone to spy or fight against the Nazis. I vaguely knew I had cousins who were somewhere in a war, and I imagined them fighting together with my canary, which they would certainly feed. I could not quite imagine the war. I wondered how far Europe was and how far canaries could fly. *Faygeleh* is also Yiddish slang for a gay man: it was the first *faygeleh* I fell in love with. But in those years, love did not come first. It was always the war.

On September 1, just a month after I was born, Adolf Hitler's Wehrmacht rolled over Poland, through the towns and villages where my parents and their friends were born. From my small point of view, the war came through the radio, looming in my mental landscape over my toys and my model railroad, a nifty Lionel set whose tracks covered my bedroom. My mother, Elka, had a little radio on a shelf over the kitchen table. She got upset almost every time news came of the war. My mother had lush hair and fine features. She spoke a French taught to her in the shtetl when it was the language of Europe. She always read *Der Tog* (*The Day*), the most literate and literary of the Yiddish newspapers—she was, in every way, a product of the old country we could hear being destroyed on the radio. Sometimes, when the news was especially bad, she would cry.

At night we listened to the news on my father Julius's radio in the living room, a gigantic Germanic-looking Stromberg-Carlson that seemed built to deliver bad news. My father never cried. He got angry. He was not a soft man, and he didn't sympathize with softness. He was short, he was old—in his midforties when I was born—and he was angry all the time. The atmosphere he created in our home was a frightening one: he was cold and then he'd go hot. It seemed like he wanted the rest of us around just to bully us. But my little brother, Gerry, was seven years younger, so my father's rage, when it came, came at me and especially at my mother. When the storm passed, I would go to my room and read, and my father would leave me alone because he respected learning: that was my out. Fighting was a form, the only form, of bonding for my father. When you grow up in an atmosphere of anger and fear and mistrust, it seeps into you in ways you're never really able to trace but that you're likely to imitate later. Certainly, it gave me a thick skin: if I had been sensitive, alive to his complexity, it would have paralyzed me, sucked me in.

The news my mother and father heard was not just bad in the abstract, for the Jews of Eastern Europe who were being destroyed were not just our people but our family. My father had nine brothers and sisters and, aside from my uncle Jake, who lived in Brooklyn with his wife and owned a candy store, they and their families were all in Europe. My parents had a list of the people who they were close to, and they were always waiting for them to write. Most of them never did. In the end, my father counted about forty-five nephews and nieces dead. On my mother's side, our only survivor was her only brother, who escaped east. The Soviets sent him to Siberia with his wife and daughter, my cousin Chava, who survived and came to America.

My father had a special—but natural—obsession with those who'd stayed alive. Every Sunday or every other Sunday after the war, he went to the Lower East Side where the refugee organizations had their headquarters. The Joint Distribution Committee, the United Service for New Americans, and HIAS: the Hebrew Immigrant Aid Society would post lists of survivors in some displaced persons camp in Europe or on other refugee lists. My father would scan them looking for people from Levertov, the townlet in Poland where he had met and married my mother before he came to America in the mid-1920s. He'd give money to help those people come to America.

Many of these landsmen accepted his invitation and came. Some were nice, some not. Some were crazy from living through the war. Some were almost transparently trying to forget or lay away reminders of their suffering. We had a tiny summer place in Hopewell Junction, upstate in Dutchess County, where some of them came, traumatized by their experience with history. My mother's cousin Heska came with her husband and son to live in an apartment my parents had for them in the Bronx, on Walton Avenue. This boy, exactly my age, had spent the first four years of his life hiding from the Nazis behind a barn door. He didn't talk much. In 1950, when we were both eleven, he threw himself from the fifth-floor fire escape. Another relative, Charlie, a big, strong, handsome guy, went back to Germany in 1946 or maybe 1947, found out the identities of some ex-Nazi soldiers who had been in a unit that had occupied Levertov, and killed three of them. Then he came back to America, where he proudly told everyone what he had done.

It was a community in mourning. In the millions of homes transplanted from Europe they called it the *churb'n*, "the catastrophe." Yizkor books, after a prayer for the dead, were made by survivors and named for entire towns—Warsaw, Vilna, Cracow, Vitebsk, Klesiv, Turek. They were palpable cartographies of the slaughter: who died and how, who survived, who resisted. The books were all we had to remember—almost every family had one. Levertov's said that 3,300 Jews lived there before the war, more than half the townlet's population. By November 1939, 2,500 were deported and the remaining 800 assigned to forced labor and by 1945, the community and its inhabitants were essentially wiped out.

It was a genocide of people that was also a genocide of a culture. My father's cousin was I. L. Peretz, one of the masters of Yiddish literature. Peretz was an intellectual—an arbiter, a convener of culture—and his project was to create a distinctive identity for Yiddish Jews, a national culture like other peoples had. In the Europe of his day, Peretz saw a world old and new, universal and particular: ethnicities representing their complicated heritages in their schools, clubs, synagogues, and churches, mixing and separating. Peretz thought these cities were models for how modern peoples could be.

But Peretz's vision, and the social order that had allowed the Yiddish Jews to thrive, was under siege from two sides: the reactionary anti-Semites who unleashed a wave of pogroms after the assassination of the tsar in 1882, and those dedicated to their overthrow, a cohort of European intellectuals, mostly Jews, who saw states themselves and the rules of private property that undergirded them as the problem. It was a German Jew who rejected his Jewishness, Karl Marx, who called for the overthrow of the propertied class and their states by the new industrial workers. That many property owners were Jews, since that was one of the few activities allowed them by custom and prejudice for hundreds of years, did not trouble Marx. In the hands of Vladimir Lenin—a quarter Jewish from his mother's side—Marx's dream found a state to host it, and within twenty years the Jews who had helped Lenin set up the state and proselytized it to the world were being killed by their erstwhile comrades. By the time I was born, people like my father could listen and read about both atavistic and levelling hatreds destroying our people from the west and the east, Germany and the Soviet Union. In Germany we were scapegoats; in the Soviet Union some of us, many of us, colluded in our own destruction.

In both cases, the result for Yiddish was the same: Peretz's civilization became a civilization of refugees, shattered at the point of its greatest density and development. When I was thirteen, I spoke in Yiddish and in English to a crowd of thousands at the dedication of I. L. Peretz Square, a tiny footprint at the point where Houston Street meets First Avenue on the Lower East Side. In those days, in 1952, there were still Yiddish theaters and newspapers and tens of thousands of people who read, spoke, and wrote in the language. Zionism, shmayism. There were very few Hebraists.

The people who made this new world, our parents and their friends, were solidly middle class through unrelenting effort, and they had all kinds of contradictions and complexes. They wanted to master English, but many didn't want to lose Yiddish. They were proudly Jewish but almost totally secular. I was bar mitzvahed only because Tanta Zlateleh, a "great aunt," which was short for close friend of the family, threatened to die if I wasn't, and my mother was sentimental. The next time my father went to a synagogue was for my brother Gerry's bar mitzvah, and Zlateleh was there.

They talked politics all the time: they were obsessed because politics had determined the course of their European lives. The organizations they formed reflected their politics above all. The Workmen's Circle, a fraternal organization that promoted Yiddish culture and provided services like educational and insurance programs, was probably the largest of the secular groups. It had tens of thousands of members around the country, which made it a powerful force in the labor movement. The International Ladies' Garment Workers Union and the hatters union were democratic socialist. The American Labor Party in New York was under the discipline of the Communists. They had one Jewish congressman, Leo Isaacson, whose slogan was "Peace, Prosperity and Palestine," meaning Jewish Palestine and also Vito Marcantonio from Harlem and its environs, who drew his support from a lot of Communists and who, if not himself a Communist, was as close as it ever came for a congressman.

Folk schools were other important instruments of politics. When I was probably eight, my parents put me into Sholem Aleichem Folk Shul 45, an afternoon school for when I was done with classes at P.S. 28. Instruction was in Yiddish, and it was carefully pro-Zion in only the most moderate left-wing sense. Zionist organizations came in different political stripes. They all would collect coins in the blue and white boxes, *pushkas*, to send to the *chalutzim*—the "pioneers" in the land that would soon be Israel. A dollar and a half bought a tree; many trees would make a forest in the desert. The Jewish National Workers Alliance, the labor Zionist organization, ran a summer camp where only Yiddish was taught, which made no sense since Hebrew was the language of Zion. But the Yiddish Zionists made them coexist, like a lot of other things in our world that didn't add up.

The Left and Zionism seemed to add up, at least for a while. In 1947, I remember attending a left-wing rally for Israel at the Polo Grounds, the old Giants baseball stadium across the river in Manhattan. Albert Einstein was the event's big draw, the great Jew of our time, "with his saintly politics," as Allen Ginsberg said. With him were Henry Wallace, the former vice president, who thought any conflict with the Soviet Union was a result of us misunderstanding them, along with Vito Marcantonio. This was the last time I remember Communist-affiliated Jews coming out for Israel. Once Britain left Palestine, the Zionists lost much of their anti-colonial enthusiasm.

Zionism was never complicated for me—it went naturally along with my Yiddishness however much it reasonably didn't. It was not just because of the Folk Shul but because of my summer camp. Boiberik, named for the shtetl in *Fiddler on the Roof*, was a summer colony of the Sholem Aleichem Folk Institute, located in Rhinebeck from 1923 until its closing in 1979. The place was beautiful—there were little forests, meadows, a lake. The director was Leibush Lehrer, a real intellectual who believed very strongly that Yiddish was a culture, not simply a language, and there was no reason that the culture and Zionism couldn't coexist. At Boiberik, I met kids from the Middle East and even North Africa. Most of them understood Yiddish, most notably Asher, the first boy I fell in love with, or lusted for, when I didn't really quite know what those feelings were. One of the things that attracted me to him was that he was so exotic, a Jew from a different part of the world. He was brown, light brown. His parents came from Bessarabia, which was a romance to me, and his mother had beautiful, luxurious hair pulled back into a chignon.

The Jews I knew went to the city's elite public schools: Brooklyn Tech, Stuyvesant, the High School of Music and Art, Hunter College High School, and the Bronx High School of Science, where I went. You had to take a test to get in, and I would say 80 percent of the students were Jewish. Many of the teachers were Jewish; most had PhDs. They'd studied at City College and Brooklyn College, the public colleges that were hotbeds of Trotskyites and Stalinists in the thirties. Because of the Great Depression, their Jewishness, and their politics, they couldn't get jobs at universities, or lost their jobs at other high schools. Naturally, there was much political talk in class.

The students were mostly democratic socialists, social democrats, or just plain Democrats, and not many of us understood the differences. But there was a cohort of Communist kids who made me see what my father always talked about at home: the reality of people believing lies. I see them now, seated together at the Science Forum, our debate club, on Thursday at four in the afternoon: Bob Williamson, son of Robert, who was indicted and convicted under the Smith Act, a federal law enacted before the war that the McCarthyites used to target Communists and their sympathizers; Sally Belfrage, daughter of Cedric, who cofounded and edited the *National Guardian*, a loyal fellow-traveling weekly; and Jacob Rosen, my best friend, truly—but with anxieties.

Jacob and I met when we sat next to each other in homeroom. We both spoke Yiddish, he was very funny, and we grew to love each other. He and his brother Chaim went to a communist-leaning folk school, and in 1953, the day Stalin died, Jacob came into class with a black armband. When it came to Stalin's purges of Jewish Communists in Eastern Europe, Jacob took the Communist line that reports were misinformation, Western propaganda. But once, at the Science Forum, when I pushed him, he went further, and burst out: "Well, of course there are some Jews on trial! They're bourgeois Jews—like you!" My father, the most zealous anti-Communist you could ever hope to meet, never minded our friendship. Maybe because he had faith in America. He owned a pocketbook factory and was also a landlord, with five- and six-story buildings in Washington Heights rented by blacks and whites alike. He saw everyday how capitalism and democracy smoothed things out. They let you keep your inheritances but lose your politics. That's why America, unlike Europe, would keep us safe. That's why he loved it.

During the war, my father was an air-raid warden, which my mother called a *narishkeit*, "a silliness"; what could really help us if the German planes came? But the air warnings would sound, everyone would douse the lights, and he would go around the neighborhood with his flashlight, meeting other Yiddish Jews out in the night, defending America.

Of course, America was not, had not been, a perfect place for Jews. We had just lived through a war filled with enormous ambiguities: the Japanese internment and Franklin D. Roosevelt's failure to do anything specific to stop the Holocaust or help the Jews. But I never heard my father say a word against FDR or the Democratic

Party, which was the party that accepted us and, through Harry Truman, helped us get a state of our own.

I think my father ignored the ambiguities because he couldn't take them; he ached to belong, and he needed to see America and Israel as places that were unequivocally his to belong to. He looked like an immigrant: high pants, white shirt, fat tie. He talked like he came from someplace else—he had good grammar but his pronunciation was off. He said "veg-ay-tables" or "ly-ving room" all his life. But he was a patriot. He had a big chest and good voice, and he would sing, or shout, "My country 'tis of thee…land where my father died." I'd say, "What do you mean? Your father didn't die in America." And he'd say, "But *I'm* gonna die in America." Which was true; you couldn't argue. That was the one thing I had from my father, the thing I could always rely on: I was Jewish and American at all times, and there was no contradiction between those inheritances.

❋ ❋ ❋

New York in those days was not really a melting pot: it was more like a TV dinner, and the clearest delineation of all was between the Jews and the goyim. Jews lived on the west side of the Grand Concourse in the Bronx. On the east side were the Irish and Italian Catholics. The Catholic diocese under Francis Cardinal Spellman was a culturally and politically powerful force, and we sensed that Catholics held mysterious immediate power over us. The Irish Catholics "went parochial" more than the Italians, many of whom we knew from P.S. 28. The Italians were often our protectors; they took the dogma less seriously than the Irish, who acted like they really thought the Jews killed Jesus. They used to threaten Jewish kids, and when there were snowstorms—which was often, not like now—they threw snowballs at us. To get to P.S. 28, I had to pass St. Margaret Mary's, the church and the school, and I would always cross the street to avoid it.

On some level they had reason to resent us. The Irish had been here longer. They had the police and the political machines—that was their way up and out. We were interlopers newly arrived. But we had brains, and we seemed obviously upward bound, educationally, even if that wasn't true of all of us. When I was at Bronx Science, we'd see the Irish kids from other high schools every so often at political forums held by the Hearst-owned *New York Daily Mirror*, one of the multitude of papers that were then circulating in the city. Kids from the different high schools would come to give political speeches, and the Jewish students would always win.

My ancestors had never lived in a country where Jews weren't persecuted, and now, in America, there was Catholic Joe McCarthy on the airwaves every day telling Christian Americans that people who swam in the waters of socialists and Communists were enemy agents. One day, at the height of McCarthy's power, the Yiddish Communist newspaper *Freiheit* was accidentally delivered to our apartment, and my mother was hysterical at the idea someone might think we were Communists. It was funny—and yet it was not.

Mostly I was not afraid of the goyim but curious, a fact I realized when I was eleven. My parents had a friend from Levertov, Uncle Benny, who owned a barbershop on 98th Street between Madison and Fifth Avenue. Benny wasn't actually my uncle, but my family was very close to his. Benny and Esther lived with Esther's mother, Zlateleh, the bar mitzvah guest. She was in her nineties and spoke only Yiddish, but she was fascinated by American television. One weekend we were at the apartment watching a show about the Cloisters, the outpost of the Metropolitan Museum of Art built by the Protestant Rockefellers and filled with relics from Christendom. Zlateleh looked at me sternly and said: "Don't ever go to the Cloisters. The Cloisters are a church where they convert Jews."

I was already a contrarian, so the next day I went straight to the Cloisters, at the peak of Fort Tryon Park by the George Washington Bridge, and saw all the treasures the Rockefellers had collected. I loved the iconography, and I fell in love with the image of Jesus— his suffering was so real. But I felt very hostile to his mother Mary because, for me, she was a fraud: a virgin couldn't give birth! That was Catholicism for me: aggressively alluring, not quite authentic.

Besides the Catholics, the other major group in our world was black people. There might have been fifteen black kids in my class of eight hundred students at the Bronx High School of Science. At that time, there weren't many blacks in the Bronx. Most were in Harlem, which we saw as an ordered world of merchants and civic and religious leaders. It was where you could see titanic cultural figures, from Paul Robeson to Lena Horne to Billie Holliday to Louis Armstrong to Countee Cullen, beautifully dressed, out to dinner or going to church.

Jews and blacks were friendly, formal, and sympathetic since we'd both been marginalized—but there was a distance. One of the Jewish buildings in our neighborhood had a black superintendent who lived on the premises and managed repairs. Everyone knew this particular man had "a brilliant Negro boy," a boy certain to go somewhere big, a boy who knew Yiddish because his father's building was full of Yiddish-speaking Jews. Many years later I met this man, now chairman of the Joint Chiefs of Staff, for lunch in Washington, D.C. "We were both brought up off the Grand Concourse," I said. "Yes," said Colin Powell, "you in the upper stories and me in the basement."

Really the only Jew I knew who was close friends with blacks was Uncle Benny, who lived in Harlem and whose close friends were upper-middle-class Republican blacks with loyalties that went back to Lincoln. He was the only Republican I knew. Other than the Orthodox, Jews were Democrats because the Republican Party was not socially or economically attuned to poor immigrants.

Black, Catholic, or Jew, the candy store, with the drug store on one side and the kosher butcher on the other, was the center of everybody's social world. There was the standard drink, the egg cream—milk chocolate syrup and soda water, "two cents plain," though I think it was already a nickel. There were pinball machines, and there was music, mostly Sinatra. Always there was argument: political debates for the adults and disputes over sports for the kids.

Basketball, the sport of the public colleges of New York City, was a Jewish sport and, difficult as this is to picture, Alan Dershowitz, a year older than me and certainly never any taller, was the star player at Yeshiva High School. Baseball was more certifiably American, and we had less of a presence there: the only famous Jewish major league baseball player was the first baseman for the Detroit Tigers, Hank Greenberg, who had also grown up in the Bronx. This meant that on the Grand Concourse people all cheered for the Detroit Tigers, even though we hardly even knew what or where "Detroit" was.

On weekends I went down to Gramercy Park to the Sholem Aleichem Mittelshul, which was the next step up from the Folk Shul. After the Mittelshul let out, I would run the twenty-two blocks and four avenues over to the Metropolitan Opera on Thirty-Ninth and Broadway, where my mother was taking me to see whatever matinee was playing. (We once saw *Aida* with real elephants.) My father never came with us. "Why don't they perform the Jewish operas?" he complained.

The smart Jewish kids at P.S. 28 would all go into Manhattan together. The leader of our little group was Emily Cohen, who lived in our building on the Grand Concourse. Even though she herself was Jewish, her father was decidedly nonpracticing, and so Emily played the role of the Shabbos goy for some of the pious in the building, turning on the lights for them on the Sabbath, when religious law did not allow them to do it themselves. Also in the group was Lorraine Abelson, Nita Melnikoff, Charles Rabb, and Charles Wynn. The boys were quick but immature; the girls set the agenda.

As I got older, I ranged through Manhattan on my own. Everybody was still respectable, which meant that kids could roam free without fear. I used to go hear Allen Ginsberg read in the MacDougal Street cafes. Once I got stuck in an elevator at the St. Regis Hotel in Midtown with Salvador Dalí. We talked for two hours while he chain-smoked cigarettes in a long holder until the firemen came to get us. First we talked about art and then politics—at his initiative. People thought he was sympathetic to Francisco Franco during the Spanish Civil War. And he wasn't, he told me, he wasn't at all. He later painted lots of pictures of Golda Meir to prove it.

I had other adventures, quieter more complicated ones, with other friends, like Asher. We were very innocent; we slept out in the woods together a lot at camp. Years later, Asher committed suicide, and I am pretty sure it was over this desire he had that he couldn't discuss with his family. He was immensely smart and immensely handsome.

The next complicated friend I had was Roger Haloua, the editor and my fellow copresident of a French student magazine. Roger was really, really beautiful, and the birthmarks on his face just made him sexier to me. He might have played on the tennis team. I never saw him play, but I still imagine the elegance of his strokes.

When it came to love, it was never completely clear to me what I wanted, where I fell. I loved Asher and Roger, but I also had a crush on Emily Cohen. It was an enormous crush: she was gorgeous, she was thin, and she ice skated beautifully in winter. She was very bright and more mature than me, as girls tend to be at fifteen, and she rejected me, which pushed me over into the feeling I was having that I was not really inclined toward girls. I graduated high school when I was fifteen, before I could really learn how to talk to girls. It wasn't like I swore off them altogether—the first time I had sex was with a woman at a Jewish camp that next summer—but there was always something else, and I was never quite clear why that something else was there.

As I got older, I was increasingly aware of the Jewish tension between the urges to merge with America and the urge to be separate from it. The idea I got from my parents, that there was no contradiction between "Jew" and "American," was a fantasy that masked a great deal of complexity because the hearts of Jewish immigrants were torn. They loved America but they were somehow still in the old country. Their home had been eradicated forever and there was not even an urge for return. But in her heart, my mother was still *there*. And when there was a struggle for Palestine, they were ardently for Israel; it was a new home, and yet most of them had never been there, most would never visit. In the meantime, there was America, which was and was not for us—the Jews on the northwest tip of an island off the Atlantic. A country we hardly knew stretched south and west forever.

Even the postwar world order that was supposed to protect us from another catastrophe, underwritten by the United States, was riddled with complications. In our classrooms at P.S. 28, they had a poster on the wall that said "We are One" and "One World: We Believe," with the two spheres of the western and eastern hemispheres overlocking. This, I later learned, was political propaganda by well-meaning internationalist school administrators against the threat of nuclear war with the Soviets. But in it can be detected a new American model for the postwar world, one meant to correct for what its creators saw as Woodrow Wilson's vain and misguided attempt to use the League of Nations to organize states according to the ethnicities and religions of peoples—their "nations"—and to enshrine mutual protections for minority nations of peoples in each nation-state. This vision never had much of a chance at Versailles and died in the Second World War. The new United Nations was an effort to get beyond nation-states to a "Family of Man." The Edward Steichen photography exhibit of that name that opened at MoMA in 1955 celebrated a collection of individuals and their universal humanity in the face of the Cold War. The book of the exhibition was the quintessential bar mitzvah and birthday gift. I think I got three copies, and each one I cherished.

Of course, this was a pleasant fiction: there was no family of man, only human beings who were part of different families, who sometimes mixed, sometimes didn't, and often killed each other. This is true all over the world. Jews are very familiar with the incontrovertibility of tribal hate, even in a state of individuals like America, where, as I write this in 2022, we're facing an unprecedented surge in anti-Semitic hate crimes.

But for all the complications, contradictions, and falsehoods we were exposed to, we didn't lack for hope. I, at least, wanted to mix in the world, which to me meant America. If there was a universal culture in America, it was Protestantism, which was distant but also real: you could see it in stone at the Cloisters, that broad tradition of individual work for communal betterment. It had created this America that didn't just smooth out heritage and religion but could smooth out ideology and create a place that anybody could be part of. We Jewish kids were all in. As I. L. Peretz said: "Ghetto is impotence. Cultural cross-fertilization is the only possibility for human development."

The Protestant inheritance, of course, was not particularly welcoming to Jews before the war. A. Lawrence Lowell, president of Harvard from 1909 to 1933, introduced a number of policies to limit Jewish enrollment. Nicholas Murray Butler, president of Columbia University from 1901 to 1945, also didn't like Jews, which is why so many of the best students in the city went to the public colleges in Brooklyn. He once ran for vice president on the Republican ticket and was much respected, publishing a Christmas Letter in the *New York Times* every year. Here is his "Message to Columbia Men" at the close of the First World War: "You have aided, and powerfully aided, in giving to the world a peace that is to be based upon justice, and that will last so long as justice rules the hearts and guides the conduct of men. There can be no lasting peace without justice, and justice is the only sure, the safe, and quick path to durable peace."

This is a lot of bullshit. But people like Butler were ultimately hoisted on their own petard, those principles of justice he mentions. The America the Protestants had put in place was opening up. We knew it, and it seemed like they knew it too. It was my good fortune to walk up to this golden door just as it was opening up. My father loved America. But there was a limit to how American he could be. He had a shtetl mentality: he liked it where he was, he resented that he couldn't get further, and he backed into or doubled down on what he had. My mother was different: she would say "America gonif," by which she meant not that America is a thief or a crook, but more like a benevolent trickster. A better translation would be "America is strange."

That's what drove me into America. To us kids, this new world that held us and shook us up was an object of absolute curiosity, full of fascinating people you could see just getting on the subway. In those days, younger New Yorkers will be stunned to learn, you could just strike up a conversation on the train. Why did I want to talk to all these new people? It wasn't that I didn't like where I came from. I was, in my way, a little cloistered. It was simpler than any of that: it was that I wanted my world to encompass a little bit more.

CHAPTER TWO

College: Intellectual Hothouse

I think I was seventh in my class at Bronx Science, and for that I was wait-listed at Harvard and rejected at Yale. My father wanted me at Columbia, close to home. But I wanted to be as far away from him as I could. I got into Princeton, my third choice, but when I went to visit I was stunned to find that there was no proper dining hall, only "eating clubs" in old colonial houses where I knew I wouldn't be allowed because I was Jewish.

The next weekend, I went up to Brandeis University outside of Boston and met Michael Walzer. He was speaking at a meeting of the Student Political Education and Action Committee. "Education" came before "Action" because SPEAC took no action, but it was always discussing. Discussion was Michael's great strength; he had a special moral sway. He didn't assert ideas reflexively, like we did on the Grand Concourse: he spoke from a place where ideas were mapped out, abstracted, explored. It was what he'd taken from Brandeis, and it was what, listening to him, I knew I wanted to find.

Brandeis had been founded in 1948, the same year as Israel, and named for Louis D. Brandeis, the first Jewish justice on the Supreme Court and a world-renowned Zionist. American Jewry had an "edifice complex": the idea that if we built enough lasting monuments in America, distinctly Jewish yet universally tolerant, it would save us from the next Hitler.

Everything Brandeis did was in accordance with this mission. The board of trustees wanted Einstein to be the college president, but the great man wisely turned it down. Instead they got Abram Leon Sachar, a Jew, but one guaranteed to please the goyim. His voice was actually saccharine, and his wife, Thelma, always wore a cute hat and veil. Sachar was determined to offend nobody, which instinctively offended me. Long before he became president, he'd written a book called *Sufferance is the Badge: The Jew in the Contemporary World*, which, even at fifteen, was not my philosophy. But I could also see that Sachar was a showman, a talented maître d', and his talent, along with his sufferance, made him the right man to stage Brandeis's coming out into American culture. It was definitively Jewish but self-consciously open, proud of its heritage but welcoming to everybody.

The college emphasized tolerance, inviting blacks, Muslims, and foreign students until there were more of these at Brandeis, I think, than at Harvard. Still, the student body was mostly Jewish, probably 80 percent. But they were a representative slice of American Jewry, rich and poor. A tiny minority were Orthodox, and although maybe a few wore a yarmulke, none wore full Orthodox garb. The all-American window dressing was the football coach, Benny Friedman, a Cleveland Jew who had been the first great passer in professional football. But the football players themselves were Irish and Italian Catholics from Boston. My guess is that they had full scholarships. The cheerleaders were led by another classmate, Letty Cottin (later Pogrebin), one of those bright, loud, percussive people who wanted to build up the enthusiasm of the place for football and basketball. Now she is an enthusiast for...you name it.

My close friends were a microcosm of our variety. Ira Rosenberg was from middle-class Jews, not too devout, and he had a bad relationship with his father, sort of like me. He developed a kind of Beat sensibility, a Jack Kerouac outlook. Donald Cohen's family owned a bakery in Chicago, even as they became wealthy. Robert Renfield was the only person in our class with a car other than Abbie Hoffman, who would come around to the dorm rooms selling sandwiches—a hustler, even then. Bob's socialite mother, daughter of a Jewish Prohibition-era gangster, didn't give a whit about Jewishness. By our senior year, we had a group: Bob went with Gigi Chasen; Ira went with Louise Lasser, who went on to star in the popular television show *Mary Hartman, Mary Hartman* and was married to Woody Allen for a few years; and I went with Margo Howard, who was from Chicago, the daughter of the advice columnist Ann Landers. Sometimes we'd take trips to upstate New York or down to Cape Cod. Once we got lost in New York and hitchhiked our way back. Other friends were nearby: Emily Cohen attended Wellesley, and I'd sometimes visit and spend time with her and her roommate, a (to me) obviously Jewish girl named Madeleine Albright.

Most of the professors at Brandeis were Jewish, too. While Sachar was making outreach to the culture at large, he was also more quietly, on the inside, fostering an intellectual hothouse of a very Jewish character. A large cohort of serious intellectuals couldn't find jobs during the McCarthy era because they were leftists, or Jewish, or both, and Sachar saw an opportunity to get a brilliant faculty on the cheap. Like some of my teachers at Bronx Science, they had come up participating, at City College and elsewhere, in the big political struggles across the Atlantic—at least in their minds. But they were also invested in this big, strange, changing country they were living in. And Sachar protected his faculty and never capitulated to the McCarthy hysteria, which could easily have targeted more than a few Brandeis professors. No faculty members were fired, and Sachar hired Felix Browder, the son of Earl Browder, a former head of the American Communist Party, as a professor of mathematics. His son, Bill, is now a legendary zillionaire.

The faculty was remarkable. The anthropologist Paul Radin had studied under Franz Boas, and his specialty was the American Indian. For sociology you could take a class with C. Wright Mills, who'd written *The Power Elite*, or Philip Rieff, the scholar of Freud, whom you could see on campus with his much younger wife, Susan Rieff, née Rosenblatt, later Sontag. The psychologist Abraham Maslow was there: he had a big following but not as big as it got later. I skipped his class because even then his stuff struck me as too soft. Musically, the college was unusually eminent. Leonard Bernstein was the marquee name, along with Bernstein's friend Harold Shapero, Arthur Berger, and another Bernstein friend, Irving Gifford Fine, a great composer in the neoclassical style. There was also Philip Rahv, surrounded by his left-wing yet ardently anti-Communist literary crowd, who was then editing *Partisan Review*, the most influential intellectual magazine in New York, maybe also in America.

Brandeis was so remarkable because it was fulfilling a specific function: it was assimilating mostly Left-American Jewish thinkers and smart American Jewish kids who might be accepted to the University of Chicago but not to the Ivy Leagues, at least somewhat on our own terms. Once we were accepted everywhere, Brandeis wasn't needed and began to fade. But that was a long time off. When I got there, I was a month past sixteen, articulate, gregarious, with a phenomenal memory for everything. Brandeis was a carousel of dangling rings to grab onto. And I did.

❋ ❋ ❋

I was the editor of the student newspaper, *The Justice*, a hub of activism on a mildly activist campus, and Abram Sachar was our enemy. We fought him on everything, no matter how ridiculous. One fracas was over Christmas trees in the dormitories, which the college put up to be inclusive but which provoked awful pushback from religious Jews whose point was: "At least *here* we didn't think we would have Christmas facing us." My girlfriend, Margo, had a sharp tongue. "Well, just go in the back door then!" she said, which only made them madder.

The newspaper was fun. But my main purpose at Brandeis was ideas and reasoned discussion. My model was Michael Walzer, who was a senior when I was a freshman. After he graduated and went to Oxford, I sought out his mentors in the world of ideas. The first was the historian Frank Manuel, who wrote books on the French philosophes and whose specialty was utopian ideas. He was a one-legged man—he'd lost the other to cancer—and like a lot of people who have gone through enough in life to really know themselves, he could not be bullshitted. Frank never, ever said a sentence he couldn't back up. He told me, early on, that I was a "skimmer not a plumber": I would instinctively gravitate to the important points of a text but I didn't have the patience to go deep. Alas, I never forgot these words of his. Alas, they were true.

Another mentor I got from Michael was Marie Syrkin, a powerful figure in the Zionist movement. She was Golda Meir's best American friend and on the executive committee of the World Zionist Organization. Marie was a socialist Zionist. She had a love affair while still in high school with Armand Hammer, whose father, Julius, was one of Lenin's conspirators in America. Her father, Nachman, a socialist thinker who hated Communists, put a quick stop to this youthful dalliance.

Michael's political mentor was Irving Howe, who was already an eminent literary critic writing for every important publication on the Left. Irving was one of the American democratic socialists who'd turned against Stalin and then Trotsky. *The American Communist Party*, his book with Lewis Coser, a sociologist also at Brandeis, was devastating to Jews who supported Stalin. In 1956, my second year at Brandeis, he founded *Dissent*, which he edited until his death in 1993. From the beginning, *Dissent* set the terms for a decent, non-Communist Left in America, and Michael made his career a model of Irving's. He became editor of *Dissent* and a world-renowned political theorist who never deviates from his decencies. Irving was Michael's inspiration for what an intellectual should be, once telling him, "When you talk about politics, you should stand," a line Michael repeats to this day. I never fell under Irving's spell that way. He was interested in austere political morality, which didn't interest me at all, and he judged you for thinking differently from him, which Michael never did.

The two most determining people I met at Brandeis I moved toward instinctively, without Michael's guidance. Herbert Marcuse and Max Lerner were men of ideas, and they were absolutely mesmerizing. I just gravitated their way. But they trafficked in different brands of ideas and different brands of charisma.

Herbert was the most sophisticated innovator of theoretical Marxism in America. He inspired many figures of the New Left, and also me, but I'm not sure that many of us understood him. He was everything I'd been brought up to be against. But he operated on a different plane: his ideas had the power to draw you in on their own terms. He didn't have to be dogmatic. Though a short book, his magnum opus was *Eros and Civilization*, which was a break from the Marxist tradition. His Marxism was explicitly for lovers. You didn't know, unless you talked to Herbert, that Lenin had loved sex, and Rosa Luxemburg was a woman of many intimacies. Neither of them made an ideology of it—they were too busy with revolution. But Herbert did.

He came from the Frankfurt School of German Marxists, whose preoccupation was decoding why Marx's prediction—that workers in the economically developed societies of the West hadn't woken up to capitalism's accelerating contradictions, discovered their oppression, and overturned the property owners and the state—hadn't come true. The Frankfurt people took from this disappointment the insight that people's behavior could not be altogether explained by economics. To their rescue came Freud, who theorized that people's formative instinct came not from economics but from sex. Herbert's insight was to combine the part of Freud he liked, sexual individuation, with the part of Marx he liked, revolution, and bring the synthesis to America.

It was an elegant synthesis: unlike in Marx's day, when capitalism meant industrial production, modern capitalism is based on consumption, which depends on advertising, which depends on sex. The marketing logic is that whatever makes you sexually desirable as a woman or a man is what you should buy. Herbert pointed out that most of this advertising was false, which meant that capitalism was playing on people's weakness, manipulating their natural desires, and depleting their energies for revolt by creating sexual expectations that couldn't be lived up to or fulfilled. This insight led Herbert to the solution that sex—real sex, exploratory sex, sex sundered from consumer corruption—was the key to political liberation. What twenty-year-old *wouldn't* like going to class and hearing that? I read *Eros and Civilization* fully, three times, and it was a handbook, with all its arcane language, for my first real love affair with a woman.

Herbert wrote in the book, and he'd elaborate after a drink or two, that the "right" way of sex, for both satisfaction and to make revolution, is the polymorphous perverse: generalized sexual desire that makes no distinction between types of pleasure. In his actual life, he was unable to abide by his theory. He could not avoid getting married three times, and he ridiculed homosexuality, which has to be included in any reasonable definition of polymorphous perversity.

Herbert was a theorist, which made his practical choices easier when it came to politics because he didn't think specifically or even really factually: he thought in terms of ideas and how reality measured up to them. He had sympathy for the Soviets; he thought they were on the right track even if theirs wasn't the revolution he'd had in mind, so he would overlook their misdeeds without entirely endorsing them. And he was a German Jew, so it was easier for him to evade what the Soviets were doing to Jews in the east, the show trials and the purges, because he didn't feel it was *his* people suffering, except in the most abstract of senses. But he never hid his Jewishness and, like a lot of Marxists early on, he supported the Jews' new state as a step up from colonialism. He went to Israel a couple of times and the red intellectuals there idolized him.

Herbert's friends, his close friends, were mostly fellow travelers, ex-Communists, and Communists of the heart. Early on, he invited me to a party at his house in Newton with a bunch of academics and journalists whom I knew, vaguely, as very, very Left. I asked Herbert who these people were, and he responded in his deep German accent: "You've discovered a secret. Not for nothing were we called the Office of Stalin's Servants." During the war, with America allied with the USSR, Herbert had worked for the Office of Strategic Services, which later became the CIA. His friends at the OSS were Marxists. They might not all have passed information along to the Soviets like the political theorist Franz Neumann, whose widow Herbert eventually married, but their hearts were with Stalin. This party was a subversives' reunion, with cocktails served by undergraduate waiters, in a leafy Boston suburb. I don't remember all of the people who were there—but Irving certainly wasn't, nor Phil Rahv—and I wondered why *I* was there. I didn't know then, and I don't know now.

None of these people were thinking real revolution. Communism in America was a fantasy; anybody with any sense of reality knew it. And Herbert, when I knew him, wasn't a revolutionary in that way. He was frivolous and a little sybaritic: he liked his comforts, liked to be worshiped by the women students even though he didn't capitalize on it carnally, and liked being worshiped intellectually by the men. Still, I wonder whether, when he was working at the OSS, Herbert didn't have two trains of thought running in his head, one that favored the Russians who he liked more and the other the British who he liked less, and whether the favoritism affected his reports.

At least once he did stick his hand into history on the side of the Communists, from a distance, using me as his patsy. In 1962, when I was a couple of years out of Brandeis, he had me try to help Robert Soblen, who'd just been convicted as a Soviet spy in America. He jumped bail and was flying to Israel on a false Canadian passport, hoping to get asylum there. By coincidence, I was on the same plane and saw him at the gate. Herbert was convinced the case against Soblen was government propaganda, and at his direction I went to see people in Israel on Soblen's behalf. In the end it didn't matter: I had no influence whatsoever. Israel kicked Soblen out, and he ended up committing suicide to avoid prison. But it was a crazy thing for me to do, and I puzzle now over why Herbert asked me to do it and why I did.

My other mentor wouldn't have been caught dead with anyone like Robert Soblen. Max Lerner and I were, at the moment we met, almost made for each other. He was very penetrating intellectually and a deeply influential person in the American intellectual-political scene. Unlike Herbert, Max didn't proselytize for anything. But he did everything. He was in his early fifties when I met him— small, pudgy, kind of ugly, and yet possessed of a hypnotic attraction to women. During the time that I knew him at Brandeis (and beyond), he had affairs with Elizabeth Taylor, Marilyn Monroe, and a whole series of lesser starlets, including Phyllis Kirk (a very bright woman). How he did it I don't know. But there was something about his energy that captivated them or maybe overwhelmed them. He was one of the most famous columnists in the country, writing for the *New York Post*, a liberal paper in those days, with a syndication of twenty newspapers besides.

He was born in Russia to a Yiddish-speaking family in 1902, and when he and his parents immigrated to America, they moved directly to New Haven. He went to Yale and got his PhD from the Brookings Institution, where he met Harold Laski, the leading British Marxist of the day and an intellectual star of his time. In 1948, Laski came out with a big book called *The American Democracy* that framed the country squarely through his Marxist lens: *either* postwar America would use democracy to tame the inequalities created by mass industry *or* a proletarian revolution would occur. *The American Democracy* wasn't new analysis. But it was the first Marxist word by an eminent Marxist figure on postwar America, and Max saw it as a challenge. I have among my books Max's copy of Laski's book, and written in longhand on three of its back pages are Max's notes to himself, which end, "you can't criticize it by quarreling with particular descriptive details. You have to attack its central thesis." And so he spent seven or eight years developing, testing, and finally, in 1957, publishing an attack on that thesis: *America as a Civilization*.

Max's thesis was that nothing was written in life, not oppression nor revolution, and capitalist democracies survived because their core principle was adaptability, a capacity to respond to human urges. This meant that laws could change and markets could create new economic demand, giving new groups a route to power and equality. In Max's pluralist view, America was *the* capitalist democracy par excellence: because it was a land of immigrants, it didn't have a single ethnic or tribal identity, so it was a country of peoples and people, mixed and separate.

The book made a big stir when it came out. Max had married his gift for popularizing with his intellectual strength, and this meant that *America as a Civilization* had done something new— allowed educated but not expert readers to see America as a distinctive society instead of a European offshoot. Max was saying that America was producing something bigger and more lasting than itself, like ancient Rome.

I was in Max's course my sophomore year. I helped him with the book's bibliography, and I did my senior dissertation on Harold Laski. He was more than an intellectual mentor: his life was the confirmation that all the things I hoped for from America—a path for people who were brainy, even a place at the center for people who were brainy—could really be. He recognized his need for a protégé; I recognized my need for a father figure. And so I was Max's sidekick. A weekend or two every summer I'd go to his place in Southampton, when Jackson Pollock, Lee Krasner, and Willem de Kooning lived there. Weekends I might go to his townhouse on the Upper East Side, 445 East Eighty-Fourth Street, which had more books than I'd ever seen outside of a public library or university: it was his intellectual history.

He had five children and a second wife, Edna, and I was Max's excuse to Edna when he was out fucking around. He'd say, "I'm out with Marty," not that she was fooled. At the time I knew him, he was seeing Susie Black, a forty-year-old heiress from Seattle who lived in Cambridge, did nothing, and was very, very sexy. After Brandeis, we took up with each other, and it became a more regular thing while Max was off teaching in India. We met once or twice a week in her little house, and she really threw a monkey wrench into my gayness. She was a gorgeous woman.

Max came to campus every Thursday for his early morning class and nighttime forum aimed at the senior class: a weekly program of noted and accomplished guest speakers talking about how the ideas they'd developed applied to life and how the life outside shaped their ideas. Because of Max's clout, the guests were serious men and women, many of them celebrities, none of them bullshit artists. Harold Wilson, Eleanor Roosevelt, and Allen Dulles came; so did Norbert Wiener, a pioneer of cybernetics, the physicist Leo Szilard, and Mark Rothko before his paintings were worth $30 million each. Martha Graham came and told us "My companion is my body," and all of us sat a little straighter. I never missed a Thursday night, and I know why I went: to find out how serious people made important life choices.

In 1956, my sophomore year, Elia Kazan came to the forum. This was four years after he named names of Hollywood Communists to the House Committee on Un-American Activities, and I felt, even at the time, that Kazan was very brave for coming. But I had also absorbed the axiomatic antagonism to McCarthyism, so I got up and asked a question about Kazan's testimony, which was really an accusation. Immediately, people clapped for my question, and *that* embarrassed me—I hadn't been looking to make a name, just to make a move. I went up and apologized to him afterward.

That was the other thing the class allowed you to do: to assert yourself against these famous people on your own terms. In this way, too, it was very much a creation of Max, who wrote a book, really a collection of essays, called *Ideas are Weapons*. He was first and foremost an immigrant, and his main trajectory was *up*. There's a picture of him, around the time we met, and he's smiling in a way that says "I've made it." He'd come from some shtetl in Russia and now he was teaching at great universities and writing for a big newspaper and fucking movie stars and fighting for America—and what a great country this was! He was a happy man, and the implicit promise of his life was that you and I could be happy in this country in this way, too.

✻　✻　✻

In October 1956, the Hungarian people revolted against the puppet Communist government imposed on them by the Soviet Union. The uprising lasted less than a month before it was crushed by the Red Army. At Brandeis we met in Seifer Auditorium, the largest hall on campus, to learn and to protest. The main speaker was Frank Manuel. He had difficulty making it up to the stage with his one leg, but I remember the first words he said: "I have come to tell you that *a people* can be murdered."

This was not news to any of the Jews in the audience, especially the Yiddishists. But it was a reality that left-wing luminaries and students were inclined to ignore. Our biggest enemy was McCarthy, who we saw in gothic terms: not a symptom of a short hysteria in an expanding country but a reminder of the paranoid tribalisms that had plagued Jews for centuries. Whereas, to many in our world, Stalin might not have been a hero, but he wasn't quite a villain; after all, a lot of his believers were Jews.

I was completely with the Hungarians; I was never fooled by Stalin. It was instinctive to me, and it set me against Herbert, who was also acting on instinct: he couldn't, wouldn't, believe the Hungarian uprising was an indigenous revolution. Any revolution supported by William Donovan, his old boss at the OSS, was not a real revolution to him. I wondered on some level what Herbert thought of me for it.

I liked a lot of what he said, and I liked him, and yet when it came down to a life-and-death issue, we were on opposite sides.

I threw myself into the Hungarian cause; it was my first real activism. I worked with Vincent Scully, the still quite young and dazzling Yale architectural historian who was a pious Catholic. (Catholics and anti-Communist Jews were allies here against the Soviets.) Together we convened a meeting in Faneuil Hall, where Samuel Adams had spoken and where the "no taxation without representation" chant was launched, to raise money. God knows where the money went, but I received a phone call from Anna Kéthly, the leader of the Social Democratic Party of Hungary, thanking me. The phone call meant something to me—Anna Kéthly was called the Joan of Arc of Hungarian politics—and so did the activism. I remember how I felt on the podium at Faneuil Hall when I got up to speak: I felt that I was right there with Samuel Adams, taking my place, my small place, in the sweep of American history.

For some of the faculty and maybe 20 percent of the Brandeis student body, commitments like this were what got us out of bed each morning. You got in the arena and fought for what you believed, and you didn't resent anybody who believed differently for doing the same. Walk twenty steps, and you'd find an argument. Someone was always not talking to someone else over something: it was that intense. It was a hothouse, the intensity I'd grown up with on the Grand Concourse at a higher intellectual pitch. I loved it.

CHAPTER THREE

Harvard: Christians and Jews

I was twenty when I came to Harvard as a graduate student. From there, I stayed on as a teaching fellow and then as an instructor. When that title phased out, I became an assistant professor, and then a lecturer. I never became a full professor, but I was a permanent fixture. Almost from the beginning, I was a Harvard patriot. Harvard didn't need my patriotism, but I didn't care. I was taking a social leap into the domain of ruling Protestant America.

Harvard College was founded in 1636 "to advance learning and perpetuate it to posterity; dreading to leave an illiterate ministry to the churches, when our present ministers shall lie in the dust." In 1959, in an America where Protestantism was still the Establishment to aspire to, if you were any combination of intellectual, ambitious, and upwardly mobile, it was the place you wanted to be.

Harvard fascinated me. In the center of Memorial Hall, in the north of Harvard Yard, there is a lobby with a monument that lists the names of the Harvard men who died on the Union side in the Civil War. The Confederate dead, and there were many, do not have their names chiseled in stone because Harvard was a Union school and the memory of the war was fresh when they put it up. The Second World War memorial on the wall in Memorial Church in Harvard Yard lists Adolf Sannwald, a graduate student who became a Nazi, as an "enemy casualty." So a Nazi was let in but not a Confederate. The old rules were oblique but rigidly followed.

Harvard had a kind of indifference to its Americanness then: Europe was still everything, Cambridge and Oxford were *the* colleges, Britain was *the* culture. American bounty was ignored. Four Mark Rothko murals hung until they were battered and faded in the dining room of Holyoke Center, a large and absurdly ugly brutalist building just off Harvard Square; now they're in the Fogg Museum, which at the time had a great collection of nineteenth-century American painting—Winslow Homers, George Innesses, Frederic Edwin Churches—all rolled up in the attic. Harvard had an indifference to its wealth, too, which was substantial but somehow assumed. My friend Roger Rosenblatt studied literature at Harvard and got fellowship after fellowship. But eventually there was a fellowship he needed that wasn't going to come through. One of Roger's instructors said to him, apologetically, "Well, Rog, looks like you'll have to dip into capital." It was assumed a Harvard student would have capital to dip into.

The undergraduate houses in those days were class based, on the model of Oxford and Cambridge. Eliot House was for the upper class, the place for boys from Groton or St. Paul's. If you'd been to Andover or Exeter, it was Lowell House. People from New York City public schools, the few there were, went to Adams House. Winthrop House was far away by the river and for the lower classes. It was like a map of the class structure, but it wasn't axiomatic. For example, FDR had also lived in Adams House, though that was earlier, and so had John Reed, who is buried in Red Square. Alan Graubard, a very Jewish friend of mine, lived in Eliot House and was called "Mr. Israel" by his house master, John H. Finley, Jr., a classicist descended from prominent Episcopalian ministers and public servants. Finley used the nickname not to be unkind—he was a friendly man—but probably in desperation at forgetting Alan's name.

Harvard was a Protestant stronghold in an otherwise very Catholic city. Down Brattle Street, in the very center of West Cambridge, there stood a Unitarian church, a Congregationalist church, an Armenian church and, on one side of Longfellow Park, the Quaker meeting house. There was a Mormon church on the other side of the park, and if you were there on a Sunday morning, you'd see the two different groups—the Quakers, who were old, and the Mormons, who were young, big, buff, and blonde—leering at each other in distaste.

Boston was Catholic, too—sometimes nutcase Catholic. There was a priest called Father Feeney who ran an organization named the Slaves of the Immaculate Heart of Mary. On Sunday mornings, he and the Harvard students he had converted would walk from Adams House to the Boston Common with placards and crucifixes and Feeney would preach against the Jews. His favorite topic was the vaccine for polio, which was developed by Jews and, he said, killed Christian children. It was a blood libel like the one that started the Kishinev pogrom and brought out the Jewish toughs from Roxbury and Mattapan. The college students would go over to the Common to watch the fights.

Harvard's three hundred years of Protestant inheritance was in its last, most overripe stages. The old forms were increasingly minoritarian; most of the culture was actually decadent. A young man, part of a group that used to go down to New York to see Andy Warhol, died the first or second year I was there from a drug overdose. But it wasn't the kind of thing you ever talked about. Eventually, though, the rumors of rampant marijuana use in the houses became so loud even the masters had to hear them.

A distinguished sociologist, George Homans, and I were appointed to investigate these rumors in Kirkland House. We knew that they were true before we even started and George said, "We're going to have to tell Charles very gently." He was referring to master of Kirkland, Charles Taylor, an undistinguished professor of history and man of a passing era we both liked. We went into the master's office for tea, biscuits, and sherry, like they used to serve at Harvard, and before we could say anything he proclaimed: "If I find out that there is marijuana [he pronounced it with the *j*] in this house, I will cut my throat." That brought us both up short, so George took over. He began, and began, and began again, and finally the master, who could see what was coming but needed a lifeline, said, "You're not going to tell me, are you, that *so and so* does pot?"

So and so was a lovely, shy, handsome African American boy in Kirkland House. He always wore a suit and tie to breakfast, lunch, and dinner at a time when other undergraduates were meeting the jacket and tie requirement by omitting the shirt. Here was the master's escape hatch, the one reverent black boy in a house of three hundred transgressors. We couldn't let him take it. We told him we didn't really know the names of the people who smoked, but our estimate as to how many was 10 percent of the house. The master took a long breath and said, "I don't think we should do anything about it." Which was right: there was nothing to be done.

Another time, I was a teaching fellow to William Yandell Elliott, a big voluble man with a loud voice, who was an adviser to several presidents and a tutor of Henry Kissinger, famous even then. As members of the teaching staff, we had to write reports about the lectures, and we'd meet for lunch once a week to review at the Signet Society, the old social club in Cambridge. Once I came in late and he yelled, "Peretz, my field n***** could write a better brief than you just did!" Sometimes I can think of the right thing to say in the moment: "Then why isn't he here?"

Not all of the Protestant elite were like Elliott, who was a dinosaur even then. American colleges were becoming more competitive as they started to become breeding grounds for the experts who would administer the growing federal government and build the weapons to win the Cold War. This was the reason more Jews were getting into Harvard, where before there had been quotas imposed on admission in the name of "social cohesion." Perhaps with this in mind, Jewish students and even faculty were very quiet about being Jewish.

My PhD supervisor was Adam Ulam: a conservative and a patriot who cast a cold eye on international issues. For our sessions, we would meet at Hazens, a cheap cafeteria where he saw students and dated the prefaces to his books. Adam wasn't afraid of being thought a right-winger. But he was afraid of being thought a Jew. He came from Lodz, the same Polish city as Richard Pipes, the one open Zionist on the history faculty. The Pipes and Ulam families apparently knew each other in the old country, but at Harvard they barely spoke because Adam was pretending that he was a Polish Protestant, which he did so effectively that even I didn't know he was Jewish until much later.

Once I was at a formal dinner at Kirkland House, sitting with Louis Hartz, the eminent political scientist who wrote *The Liberal*

Tradition in America. He was actually crazy—he'd been in an insane asylum, and he'd end up there again—but he was also, as Norman Mailer says, "crazy family good." That night, he said to me, "I'm glad to be sitting with you. You're a real Jew." I said this was true, and he said, "My father was a cantor in Cleveland, and look at us now. We are so intimidated. We're talking very quietly because Jews are expected to talk loudly." Then, suddenly, he raised his voice: "Now George Homans over there is not lowering *his* voice!" George Homans was a very decent man and a serious scholar in the new field of behavioral sociology and his uncle was Henry Adams, grandson and great-grandson of presidents. George had a picture on his office wall of his uncle holding him on his lap. As Louis's voice boomed out and George looked over to see who was talking about him, I hissed at Louis, as quietly as I could, "Be quiet! Be quiet! Be quiet!"

Then there was a whole other cohort of Jews at Harvard, a social type I recognized but had never known. These were the assimilated upper-class Jews, most of whom were German. They weren't afraid or aspirational but simply established. The divide with Yiddish Jews went back to Europe. Under the Napoleonic Code, German Jews were gradually allowed into society by the princes and then made full citizens, in a way they never were in the Russian Empire. The deal Napoleon offered was this: they could be citizens in the lands where they lived, but they couldn't have another loyalty; their religion was their religion, but first they were citizens. They took the deal, found success in Europe on those terms, and in the late nineteenth and early twentieth centuries, they brought that value system to America. People like Felix Adler founded institutions like the Ethical Culture School that transmitted their worldview and funneled their children into Harvard.

Politically, they were much more moderate than the people I came from: German and French society was much less messily ethnic than the cities of Eastern Europe and the differences in heritage showed. They'd been in America longer, they'd seen capitalism work for them, and they'd lost interest in socialism or even social democracy and had become welfare-state liberals. When Franklin Roosevelt needed experts and intellectuals to help him fight the Great Depression, they were among the major architects of the

New Deal. After the Second World War, they helped construct the postwar order of individuals over ethnicities: ideas I first encountered in propaganda terms, a family of man.

They wanted to help new Jewish arrivals, but they were embarrassed by our Yiddishkeit: it was too old-fashioned, too anti-modern, and too unassimilated. Jacob Schiff, a Jewish German financier, raised money to send the masses of Yiddish immigrants flooding into Boston, New York, and Philadelphia on to the Midwest and West, so as not to overburden the psyches of the cities with too many unassimilated Jewish immigrants. Schiff was not a self-hating Jew. He was the epitome of what a rich Jewish liberal should be: generous, conscientious, a supporter of the Jewish Theological Seminary and the 92nd Street Y. His granddaughter Dorothy owned the *New York Post*, where she published Max Lerner. And yet there was a divide between people like us and people like the Schiffs that only deepened after the war. A significant number of established American Jews opposed Israel on the grounds that once you gave a nation to the Jews, you were putting a false ethnic category in the Kantian universalist, individual, ethical firmament. The Sulzbergers, who owned the *New York Times*, were worried it would call the patriotism of American Jews into doubt, and so supported the American Council for Judaism, a committee of socially prominent financiers and public intellectuals who rejected Zionism—and fought it.

This ideological dispute aside, several German Jews of that ilk became important to my career, none more so than David Riesman. David was "our" Alexis de Tocqueville, a star. Americans were moving to suburbs, using interstate highways and homeownership loans financed by the federal government. Corporations were growing to cater to their tastes. The Soviet Union's aggression was being challenged—not through scientific or administrative expertise but by encouraging people to buy things to keep the economy humming. Herbert Marcuse called this sublimating capitalism, sham democracy. Max Lerner thought that America was flexible enough that nothing would change its pluralist character. David and the other German Jews at Harvard weren't as committed to causes. They were more scientific: they thought America was undergoing a tectonic shift, and they wanted to examine it and understand it. And be in it.

In 1950, with Nathan Glazer and Reuel Denney, David had published the best-selling work of sociology in American history. *The Lonely Crowd: A Study of the Changing American Character* asked a big question—how did this new society shape the values of its citizens?—and answered it in a methodological way, with sociological research. David and his colleagues went out and talked to people in the middle- and upper-middle classes who worked in the new corporate, information, and government sectors—people with the money and influence to set the tone for the future. He got a clear read on their predicament: modern society allowed more freedom and created more anxiety; it allowed more choice and created less confidence about how to choose. As a result, people were more likely to behave not as real individuals but as members of a crowd. But David thought the phenomenon on balance was a liberating one because the market that created the confusion also offered a way out: people could escape from the contradictions it created by focusing on all the new choices it offered.

David's diagnosis mirrored his own life. He'd grown up wealthy in Philadelphia, and his mother was one of those people who supported Schiff's program to send Jews out West. He clerked for Louis Brandeis (in his first interview for the position he told Brandeis that Zionism was Jewish fascism), became a lawyer, got bored, and switched to sociology to explore popular culture. He loved it, I think, because it loosened him from the strictures of his background. For David, there were never risks in being unrooted by modernity: the risks were all in the other direction. And if there is an intellectual criticism of *The Lonely Crowd*, it's that it has no sustained focus on older identities and the roles they still played in the lives of Americans. Women, who were playing such a huge role in the social changes that were happening, are not considered in any great detail, nor is the working class. The book is all about the mobile middle- and upper-middle class, the creation of the contemporary consumer by the market and the state.

This was the same with David's intellectual cohort of psychoanalysts who studied personality formation in modern society:

Erich Fromm at New York University, and Erik Erikson and Robert Coles at Harvard. They were all Jews who didn't identify as such and for whom the modern sphere was all there was. Erikson developed a whole theory of stages for how modern people moved through their lives. But there was a part of his own life he never talked about: his real name was Erik Homburger, his mother and stepfather lived in Israel (his biological father, a gentile Dane, abandoned his Jewish mother before his birth), and he'd been bar mitzvahed. In a 1975 review of *Life History and the Historical Moment*, Marshall Berman writes of "his repudiation of his stepfather, whose Jewish name he should normally bear" and "the cosmic *chutzpah* of his claim to be 'Erik Erikson,' his own father, in the most literal sense a self-made man." Erikson confessed it all to me over lunch one Saturday at the Riesmans, a few years after I came to Harvard. His mother had died at a great age, and he had gone to Haifa for the funeral. But there was never a mention of the word "Jew."

These people were so different from me that we were almost speaking separate languages. But their work was what let me find my place at Harvard.

* * *

The Harvard Social Studies program was founded in 1960 and had, as its first set of teachers, a remarkable group: Stanley Hoffmann, Alexander Gerschenkron, Barrington Moore, Jr. None of them were my intimates, but they were professional friends who had an influence on me. Erik Erikson and Nathan Glazer came on board later, and Michael Walzer was the chair for a while after that. Even though he was not active in the program and was politically less radical than the rest, David was the guiding light, and his study of the American character exemplified what social studies was meant to do.

Following the method of *The Lonely Crowd*, Harvard undergraduates used specific social science methodologies to answer broad questions about society. Sophomore tutorial went through classics of theory: de Tocqueville, Weber, Durkheim, Marx, and Freud. Junior tutorial broadened the terrain to maybe fifteen subjects—nationalism, industrial society, the experiences of women, etcetera. Senior year was when students chose a subject for a thesis that ranged from the specific (multiparty exceptions in one-party dictatorships) to the theoretical (Marx and Freud: community and individual). The social studies premise was a radical one: serious thinkers were asking nineteen- to twenty-two-year-olds to see society through theory and metrics, which is not the way young people, even the most intelligent ones, see the world. It was that disconnect that gave me my Harvard opportunity: being the human glue in an otherwise intensely clinical program.

It began with a crisis. I was in the middle of my PhD thesis with Adam Ulam when one day I was asked out to lunch by the political theorist Judith Shklar. Judith—who knew Yiddish but was still no fun to talk to—began with some pleasantries and then came out with this: "You're a very smart man, but you really don't want to be here." I was shocked, but she continued: "You've never come to a faculty seminar directed at graduate students." I said, "Well I have other things to do besides being a graduate student"—I was working on a political campaign, among other things—and she said, "That's what's wrong with you. You should really leave graduate school."

She was terribly intimidating, with a chin that went up and down almost like there was a rubber band holding it together. The chin moved again and the mouth told me I should go see the chairman of the government department to discuss leaving.

Instead, I went to Louis Hartz and asked him if I should drop out. "Hey, you're very bright. Maybe you won't be a professor, maybe you'll do something else. Who cares?" I was glad Louie was in my corner. But I still wasn't sure what to do. Judith was right about my problem: I wasn't a Harvard scholar, *and* I wanted to stay.

Help came from an unexpected quarter: Barrington Moore, Jr., an odd but brilliant Marcuse acolyte. He more or less founded comparative sociology, which mapped out convergences between history and sociology to understand patterns of political change. He was also extremely rich because his grandfather was J. P. Morgan's private attorney—an adherent of the working class whose most troubled times were when the motor on his yacht was not working. He had watched me teach a seminar and, after deciding that he saw something there, he made me an early version of what became my deal with Harvard: leave me alone, I'll be a lecturer forever.

Lecturing meant teaching, and Moore was right: I *was* a teacher—it came as naturally as talking. My class, a seminar really, was called "Problems of Postindustrial Society." My style was Max's—active, engaged, intense, personal—but my intellectual lodestar was Herbert. My opening announcement to students was "Freud plus Marx equals truth": an invitation to take the rigor of the methodologies and then to personalize them, to question the bloodlessness of the universalist Kantian worldview.

I'd ditched the suits I used to wear at Brandeis and grown a beard. I wore glasses. I didn't go in much for lecturing—the lecture just always turned into an exchange. I prepared for each class, always seriously. But once I got there, I didn't think much about how I ran it: I just ran it, and it worked. And a few years later I started running the Social Studies program, choosing the fifteen to twenty people who got in every year when the program was still small.

Word got around about my freshman seminar and later that I was the person to see if you were interested in Social Studies. Relationships built from there, and being just a couple of years older than the students helped bridge the status divide. I didn't seek them out; they knew who I was and they came, all different people, because Social Studies was a program that attracted all types.

Before the Second World War, there were few women. Harvard was all men, Radcliffe was tiny by comparison, and men and women students rarely mixed. This changed a little after the war. But even twenty years later, the women I had in my seminar were really pioneers.

Sherry Turkle, a "nice Jewish girl" from Sheepshead Bay in Brooklyn and not at all elite, was one of my first firsts. She told me she spent her first college break in the Brooklyn Public Library reading Marx for my course. He was talking about sheep, and because she hadn't had a serious high school education, she had no idea what sheep had to do with anything. She did know that when she got back to class, everybody would speak. I would keep the bottom from falling out of the conversation and eventually tie it all together...to sheep, key to Marx's argument about peasants shifting property from communal to private ownership. After she graduated, I put her in touch with David Riesman who became her PhD mentor in sociology. Another of my early female students was Nancy Rosenblum, who quite quickly showed an astonishing aptitude for political theory. She was in the same class as Sherry, and they were a dynamic duo.

I wrote hundreds of recommendations for my students over the years. Of Tom Williamson, a defensive lineman on the football team and the son of a black army officer who commanded white troops, I wrote: "My letter must be couched in superlatives [since]...in seven years of teaching at Harvard College, I have not yet encountered a student as bright, as serious, and warmly imaginative as he." Other bright students I didn't like as much. Michael Kazin, the son of Alfred Kazin, the literary critic who worked with the *Partisan Review* crowd, was always chafing beneath the father-son comparison: he went activist Left as a sort of response and stayed there.

Rick Hertzberg, who would go on to run the *New Republic*, was a born journalist. Rick's father, Sidney, was a son of immigrant garment workers in the Bronx and lived his life as a peripatetic journalist and activist of the small-d democratic Left; he edited and wrote for smaller weeklies like the *New Leader* and the *New Republic*, as well as mass magazines like *Time* and *Fortune*. Rick's mother, Hazel, a distant relative of Walt Whitman, was a nice Protestant girl from a respectable Flatbush neighborhood who was radicalized to socialism and pacifism. Rick grew up prizing empathy above all other virtues, and so naturally he became an old-fashioned social democrat. He and I met in 1962 when I became a faculty advisor to the Harvard-Radcliffe Liberal Union of which he was president. At that point, I was more Left than Rick was, mostly because of Herbert, and we made it a habit to argue over it at Hazens.

Because this was Harvard, a lot of the students were still financial or aristocratic legacies. Richard Rockefeller was a wonderful boy. His father was David Rockefeller Sr., and so he could have run Standard Oil if he wanted. But Richard had too good an idea of his father's life—the interminable meetings, the self-importance—to want that for himself. He became a doctor but died young when he crashed the single-engine plane he was piloting home from his father's ninety-ninth birthday celebration. I always liked him. I also taught Donald Graham, whose mother owned the *Washington Post*. He was going into the newspaper business, no question. But he was intellectually curious and wanted to learn as much as he could before he started.

I met the inheritor with the clearest sense of purpose in the 1965 freshman seminar: Al Gore. He was the one student I had who really will go down in the history books. But Al was not one of the "dazzlers" when he was in my class: he had ideas, but he always held them to the test of empirics. He and his ally in class, Don Gilligan, whose father was a Democratic congressman from Ohio, would try to make the conversation relate to real life.

Al's father, Albert Gore Sr., was a senator from Tennessee, a "hail-fellow-well-met" kind of guy who was enough of a bullshit artist to get himself elected senator. But when he got to Washington he turned out to be a real mensch, doing all the right things—supporting civil rights, opposing Vietnam—at real political risk. Al had been raised in in the penthouse of the Fairfax Hotel, five blocks from the White House; he sat in Vice President Richard Nixon's lap while Nixon presided over the Senate. He had a sense of duty about leadership, and when he got to Harvard, he ran for freshman student government council and was elected president. But he wasn't ambitious so much as he was diligent and polite to a fault. He called me Mr. Peretz for half the year. He was also religious, a Southern Baptist, truly a believing man.

Between the students and the teachers, Social Studies was close to a lot of intellectual loci. And by virtue of these people's intellectual connections, it was close to a lot of power loci, so the students who got entranced by ideas were starting to feel that their ideas could matter. McGeorge Bundy, the institutional shepherd of the Social Studies department, had left Harvard and was national security advisor in the White House. John Kenneth Galbraith, teaching economics at Harvard, had become the president's ambassador to India. Arthur Schlesinger, who had graduated from Harvard and taught there for the past decade and a half, was the half-resident intellectual in the White House. Michael Harrington, not a Harvard man but a Left intellectual, had written *the* book on poverty, *The Other America*. It had been read by President Johnson, who was taking the ideas in the book seriously.

So the field felt wide open—for things much more radical than what these people were talking about. In fact, there was an undercurrent of conflict in the program: David Riesman was a sociological centrist, and Barrington Moore and increasing numbers of students were not. Al's class was an interesting one, not only because of the usual theorizing but because of what it showed about the way the university was changing. The class radicals took it upon themselves to sway the one conservative, James Truesdale Kilbreth III, whose family had been at Harvard for generations. Jamie, of the old aristocracy but growing disillusioned with its hypocrisies, began his conversion that year. Soon after he would take his cohort's shrug at its inheritance to the next logical stage: revolt.

Unlike many of my students, I wasn't a real radical. But outside of the seminar, Left activism was becoming my reality, too.

CHAPTER FOUR

Politics: Man of the Left

The committees of correspondence were an idea Samuel Adams had before the American Revolution. Groups of patriots would write each other letters so that when they met in Philadelphia in 1774, many of them already knew each other. In the 1960s, David Riesman and Erich Fromm started their own committee, the Committee of Correspondence at Harvard, which sent out a newsletter to a small list of colleagues. They were influential, and they had the ear of a senator from Wisconsin, Gaylord Nelson, or more probably his very young legislative director, Gar Alperovitz, who would send around their thoughts about the "issues of the day" to politicians and policymakers.

The primary issue as the sixties began was nuclear arms. When the new Kennedy administration took a hard line against Cuba, the new Soviet client state ninety miles from Florida, the threat of nuclear collision became an imaginable reality, especially to those on the Left. At Harvard, the alarm was philosophical: Kantian universalists like David saw the potential for nationalist competition that would destroy the cosmopolitan, Enlightenment world—and maybe even civilization itself. The Harvard Left saw it as a tragedy of misunderstanding, a confirmation of all their fears of state power run amok.

The antinuclear activist organization Tocsin was less decorous and more active than the Committees of Correspondence. My friend Stephan Thernstrom, whom I'd met with his wife Abby at a proto-Maoist meeting in Harvard Square, helped write a petition against the Cuba policy. It was signed by seventy academics in the Boston area—including Herbert Marcuse, David Riesman, and Frank Manuel—and ran in the *New York Times* in May 1961.

I watched the movement from the sidelines: the Committee met at Riesman's very elegant house or at the Friends meeting house off Longfellow Park, and I would sometimes go. I hung around with members of the Tocsin crowd, too, socially and professionally. I didn't take much to David's liberals—they were too high-minded. I was in those days, sort of, a man of the Left. But the Left was hysterical over Cuba and nuclear war. And I, ever the realist, didn't think the great powers were going to destroy themselves.

The hysteria on the Left seemed like sentimentality pervaded by ideology and informed by aesthetics. Cuba was a singular case—its capitalism so gross and excessive, its dictator Fulgencio Batista so fat and corrupt. And Fidel Castro was so galvanizing: his unlikely victory coming out of the Sierra Maestra, his guerillas swimming in the sea of the people, his machismo, his sexuality, his cigar. Castro in those days was like a movie star. When he came to speak in Cambridge in April 1959, right after he took power, the crowd at Harvard Stadium was overflowing.

I didn't go. Big political gatherings like that always felt to me like preludes to a pogrom, and showing up for what was, in essence, an anti-American cause felt like marching against the Jews. But I wasn't without sympathy for Castro or Cuba. I thought the hard-line Kennedy policy on Cuba probably radicalized Castro quicker than he would've radicalized otherwise. One evening in 1962, I debated this with a Kennedy proxy, a state legislator named Michael Dukakis, at the Community Church of Boston in front of a lot of Quakers and ex-Communist Jews. I won easily. Dukakis was a zero, which made him a perfect type for the Kennedys, who filled their inner circle with opportunists and imitators.

That was the other thing I liked about Castro: he was an adversary of the Kennedys, who I thought were phonies. Leftists thought Jack's very un-radical popularity drained Left radicalism of its potency and despised Bobby as a hatchet man for Joe McCarthy on his infamous senate committee. But I wasn't a leftist. I saw in the Kennedys the American establishment at its worst: corrupt and eager to play everything both ways, no matter how big the issue or how small.

Joseph P. Kennedy, the patriarch, caught the Irish American rise to wealth and influence in his fist and never unclenched it. He came up in a political family in Boston when the old-line Protestants held social prominence and politics was the Irish route up. He attended Harvard, where he lived in Winthrop House and was blackballed from the Porcellian Club—the most elite of the private Harvard clubs. He married the mayor's daughter, Rose Fitzgerald, and made money shorting stocks in the market in 1929, and then off real estate investments in the Great Depression. Everybody said he was also a bootlegger even though he never came close to being caught. FDR appointed him the first chairman of the Securities and Exchange Commission, reputedly saying "it takes a thief to catch a thief," and then as ambassador to the Court of St. James, an irony and an achievement for an Irishman. His policy as ambassador was that the United States could do business with Hitler. But this was not FDR's policy, and it effectively ended Kennedy's political career. So he poured his focus, and his influence, into his sons. Twenty years after Joe left England in disgrace, Jack was in the White House and Bobby was at the Department of Justice—and Joe was perceived by many as the satanic figure behind their rise.

While living in Massachusetts, I got a good view of the underside of the Kennedy mystique and how Jack used the various aspects of his persona to get votes. He was a good Catholic family man but also as sexy as Elvis, which distracted people from the fact that he would say anything to get elected. He won the presidency by charging that the Eisenhower administration wasn't anti-Communist enough, a ridiculous notion. The Kennedys wanted to help America. But really they wanted to help themselves. And they couldn't quite tell the difference.

The Kennedys were at their zenith when, in 1962, Massachusetts held a special election to fill the Senate seat vacated by John Kennedy when he became president. The tame governor had agreeably appointed John's Harvard roommate, Benjamin A. Smith II, to fill the position until his younger brother Teddy turned thirty and became eligible to run. Still, Teddy's win wasn't a sure thing: John McCormack, who had just become speaker of the House of Representatives at Sam Rayburn's death, had a nephew, Edward, running as a Democrat. He narrowly lost to Teddy in a vicious primary. The Republican candidate was George Lodge, the son of Henry Cabot Lodge, whom Jack had beaten in 1952 for the very same seat that Teddy was now contesting.

There was a fourth candidate in the general election, a long shot: H. Stuart Hughes, the grandson of Charles Evans Hughes, the chief justice of the Supreme Court from 1930 to 1941, and a Harvard professor whose platform was the antinuclear, pro-Cuba policy of the Committee of Correspondence. His independent campaign against Lodge and Kennedy was my first experience in partisan politics.

During the war, Stuart had worked in the OSS with Herbert; later he had been transformed by psychotherapy, which brought him close to Erik Erikson. Herbert and Erik together pushed him toward the new field of psychohistory. He had been a Henry Wallace enthusiast in 1948, and Cuba was a natural extension of Wallace's peace-with-the-Soviets view: he was one of the writers of the letter against American policy toward Cuba in the *Times*.

Academically, Stuart was serious, with a graceful prose style. Personally, he was stiff and a little odd. After a first marriage to a French society lady, he married a student. The behavioral theories of B. F. Skinner were a fad among overeducated people at the time and when they had a baby they raised it in a Skinner box. You didn't pick up the baby; the baby lived in the box. I don't think Stuart and his wife were that serious—they more than dabbled but were less than committed. My academic friends didn't think much of him: Michael Walzer supported him tepidly; Adam Ulam ridiculed him; Max Lerner was too pragmatic to care. Obviously Kennedy was going to win, so why bother?

My enthusiasm was not so much about Stuart as it was about the campaign: a fusion of the Left of the old Protestant elite, who wanted a better world and were willing to help financially, and their new allies on the intellectual Jewish Left. I had prodigious energy, a real hunger, and I was attentive, active, worked well with people. When I saw an opportunity I liked, I took it. If it didn't work out, I'd try the next. I became one of the top four or five people in Stuart's small campaign of ten, maybe twelve, people.

I was close with Jerry Grossman, who really ran the campaign. He was the president of Massachusetts Envelope Company and had worked on the Wallace campaign in 1948. I don't know where his politics were, exactly, but they were definitively Left. His sister Ruth and her husband, Dr. Victor Sidel, were top contributors and actually Communists. I was a connection to the brains and also to the street: my foot was in all the worlds and not quite in any of them.

At twenty-three I'd already spent time in civil rights activism, almost as an extension of my Brandeis education. In 1960, we had started an integration organization in Michael and Judy Walzer's kitchen, the Emergency Public Integration Committee, EPIC. I was captain of the picket line at the Woolworth's on Tremont Street, which was one of many formed around the country to support the sit-ins to desegregate lunch counters in the South.

The civil rights movement was a model for all my activisms to follow because it drew in all kinds, many of them politically minded Jews. There were lots of sentimentalists, types I recognized from the Bronx and Brandeis, who wanted a better world and thought their good intentions would make it happen. There were people with clear, inherited politics whom I also recognized—socialists like Michael and Communists still quiet about their allegiances because McCarthyism was only just waning. There was always a lot of bullshit, usually associated with the sentimentalists. As early as 1960, at an EPIC meeting for eighty or ninety people at a center in Roxbury, I was speaking and I uttered the phrase "You folks." There were sixty or seventy black people in the room and maybe eight or twelve white people, all Jews of course. I was immediately attacked, mostly by the Jews.

There was also a celebrity component, which was standard when it came to Left causes. Norman Mailer heard about EPIC's work and came to Brandeis to support us. The $200 speaking fee could only have sweetened the deal. He gave a speech about politics as existentialism, masculine rebellion against consumerism, and sexual liberation against technocracy—a synthesis of a lot of what was floating around the popular and intellectual culture courtesy of Allen Ginsberg, the beatniks, and Jean-Paul Sartre. The kids ate it up. But in the audience was Joseph Israel Cheskis, a professor of Romance languages whose brother had been the rector of Moscow State University until he was purged—actually murdered—by Stalin and who had a pretty clear view of the world for a leftist. Cheskis had been cynical about the Woolworths boycott: "When did the blacks picket for us? They will soon be picketing against us!" Halfway through Norman's speech, Cheskis got up, all five feet one of him, and muttered to his wife so everyone could hear: "Esther, this kissing, shitting, fucking, and sucking, it's an old business. Let's go!" She got up, and they left. Norman, for the first and only time I ever saw, was completely thrown.

Many of the people who collected around the civil rights movement also showed up for Stuart in his Senate campaign. But they were all white. Boston's black community was nowhere to be seen. Stuart was for civil rights, but he didn't have a black following. His main issues—world peace, nuclear disarmament, and a new politics of understanding and transparency—were too abstract to interest people who were fighting for their concrete rights.

The Communists came out of the woodwork, bolder now because, at least with the nuclear issue, they saw history coming back around their way. The Quakers were with us: they were the quintessential sentimentalists who could only see good in the Left because the Left talks about peace. The beatniks came because even though Stuart was square, his politics were hip. Joan Baez and Bob Dylan performed at Club 47 in Cambridge for the campaign. But truth to tell, Club 47 was tiny and only thirty, maybe forty, heard them sing.

Anyone could see Teddy was always going to win. But we figured we'd get 8 percent of the vote. Then, in the home stretch of the campaign, the *real* Cuban crisis happened, with ships and missiles—what we thought was the beginning of a nuclear war. Kennedy made Nikita Khrushchev back down while the world hid in bed for a week, Teddy's support surged, and he beat George Lodge by fourteen points while we got about 2 percent. "People were less ready than we thought," I told the *Harvard Crimson* in the aftermath.

Still, the election felt like the rising of something new in politics. For seven days in October of 1962, the world had been on the nuclear brink, and the fear on the Left of an out-of-control national security state had been justified by events in a way it hadn't been before. Personally, my involvement with the campaign brought me notice: I was a popular teacher and now I was a man on the political scene.

* * *

The winter after Hughes lost, I got a call from Jason Epstein, a young publisher active with the New York literary set. It was a "get to know you" sort of call, but it was clear that its purpose was to feel me out for the publisher's spot at a new journal that he, Elizabeth Hardwick, Barbara Epstein, and Robert Silvers were starting. A typographer's union strike had shut down every newspaper in New York for 117 days that winter and book reviewing had ground to a halt, which New York intellectuals found intolerable. Their solution was the *New York Review of Books*.

I knew this crowd through Max, who took me to parties in New York, and through Philip Rahv. His politics were like a cross between Max's and my father's, and he was always egging me on to "Punch 'em"—"'em" being everyone to his left, from the Communists to Irving Howe. Like me, he was a committed Yiddishist and Zionist, and when he died a decade or so later, he left his entire fortune— thanks to his rich wife who, poor woman, died in a fire—to the state of Israel.

Right then, because of *Partisan Review*, Philip was at the center of this world; everybody collected around him, Jews and goyim alike. He had Dwight Macdonald, Edmund Wilson, and Mary McCarthy (who'd been his lover but didn't share his politics), Lionel and Diana Trilling (who in this universe were almost gods), the sociologist Daniel Bell, and the young, zealous, literary Norman Podhoretz, who was running *Commentary*, a small Jewish magazine of ideas that punched above its weight. Both *Partisan Review* and *Commentary* were like the Grand Concourse and Brandeis, places where people went to fisticuffs over ideas. I felt an affinity there. I knew Elizabeth Hardwick through her husband, Robert Lowell, the great, tormented, aristocratic American poet who taught at Harvard off and on when he could and used to spend time in Cambridge. Lowell was friends with the poet Charles Reznikoff, Marie Syrkin's hidden husband, and spoke at his funeral.

But the real luminary of this group that I knew, who had been responsible for Jason Epstein sending out the feeler in the first place, was Norman Mailer. After Norman spoke at Brandeis, he, I, and a few others went out for pizza in Waltham, and we somehow hit it off. He invited me to New York to visit him, and that Christmas I ended up sitting with Norman and Adele Mailer in their apartment on Perry Street in the West Village.

Norman was legitimately crazy and a drinker and always in trouble—the subject of a hundred crazy stories, most of them true. He stabbed Adele in the shoulder at a cocktail party full of New York intellectuals, including me. Another time he bit off a piece of Rip Torn's ear. He was a brilliant self-promoter, and he used all his real crazy to burnish his legend. We saw a lot of each other, especially after I came to Harvard, where I'd organize outings for him. "Dear Marty," went a typical letter, in this instance thanking me for getting him tickets to the game:

> *The seats were superb, and thank you very much. Unfortunately it was the coldest day of the year and I decided I didn't love Harvard so much as the care and preservation of my balls, so I separated my ass from the cold stone slopes of Palmer Stadium at the half.*

Even in private, in a dashed-off note to a younger friend, Norman was still advertising for himself.

In real life, I liked him because he saw me so clearly. He knew I was gay; I don't remember how, since I wasn't so gay then. I didn't do it or talk about it much. And he saw some of my strengths for the *New York Review* job: I wasn't married, I was an intellectual entrepreneur, I put people together at Harvard, and I sponsored interesting things. He was trying to do me a favor, and I think he had the sense I might fit in well. And, because the feeler came through Norman, I took it seriously.

But the more I looked, the more I drew back. A big part was Jason Epstein, who'd called me in the first place: he was very flashy and loudly cosmopolitan. I thought: here was a lot of thunder but not much behind it—one of those artistic or literary "types" whose sense of politics was blurred, attitudinal, or nonexistent.

I was about to say "no" to the *New York Review* half-offer when it was withdrawn. I don't think they thought I was literary enough. But then something happened that winter of 1963 that made it clear to me that the *New York Review* people weren't for me in a deeper way.

Adolf Eichmann was the SS officer who administered the Holocaust in Eastern Europe. There was a lot of evidence that he'd committed terrible crimes. He escaped to Argentina after the war, where he lived under an assumed identity. But in 1960, on orders from Israeli Prime Minister David Ben-Gurion, the Israelis kidnapped him, brought him back to Jerusalem, and put him on trial in a glass box, like a virus. Public opinion in America, and in the American press, was in favor of the trial. But Hannah Arendt, reporting on the trial for the *New Yorker*, wrote a scholarly critique of Israel's actions that received enormous attention and that deposited a precisely timed detonating device in American and Jewish intellectual life.

Arendt's piece, "Eichmann in Jerusalem," was so potent because it located in Israel's kidnapping of Eichmann the fears of every universalist, from David Riesman to Arthur Sulzberger, who believed in a postwar world of individuals, not a Wilsonian one of peoples. Who, she argued, are these people of a state (Israel) where the crime didn't happen (it happened in Europe) to prosecute a noncitizen (Eichmann) for it? Were ethnicity and religion, the things the Enlightenment was trying to subdue, now going to trump a lawful liberal order? In articulating these fears, she was in effect forcing American Jews to take a stand for or against Israel's legitimacy: could it represent the Jews as a people?

Among the Jewish intellectuals who criticized Israel's actions, most were second-generation Americans. They were of the generation before mine, who, for the most part, had rejected their college-age Marxism in favor of liberalism and the universalist framework that underlay the postwar order—the same framework that had allowed them to rise in American society. The path upward was more assimilative and less ethnic in those days. And though they didn't oppose Israel outright, they didn't talk about it much or identify with it: there was no place for it, and the nationalism it represented, in their theory.

This all became clear to me when Irving Howe convened a meeting at the First Parish in Cambridge, a Unitarian Universalist church, to discuss "Eichmann in Jerusalem." The place was packed: a hundred and fifty people, crowded not in the chapel but in an adjoining lounge, either standing against the walls or sitting on the floor. Arendt was in absentia. (Maybe she wasn't even invited.) Irving convened the meeting like he was Cotton Mather. He, along with Phil Rahv and Alfred Kazin, were for Israel and against Arendt. Mary McCarthy, Robert Lowell, and Dwight Macdonald came to defend her.

Irving's side was clear where it stood. But they didn't know what attitude to take toward their comrade. It did seem like Arendt was on trial, so much so that Kazin stood up and said to Howe, "Hannah didn't commit any crimes." Clearly it pained Kazin to disagree with her. She was forcing him to confront an internal split—between his personal and intellectual commitments—that he wanted to avoid.

This was not my problem. I had come up later. My American generation, even its immigrants, didn't abide the pressure to assimilate. My childhood was populated by people who looked to the world of *peoples* from which they'd come, the model from which Woodrow Wilson tried to build after the First World War, as their creed, and who always thought that the "One World" and "Family of Man" slogans were bullshit.

My greatest scorn was reserved for Arendt's untroubled defenders, especially McCarthy, Lowell, and Macdonald, who I thought were coming from someplace less high-minded: they thought of themselves as the keepers of the American intellectual and literary flame. They'd been against Hitler and Stalin, but in some small way they feared the intellectual influence of the Jews. They were obsessed with Arendt's universalism, which seemed to erase her Jewishness while (I surmise) giving them an out on the Jewish question *because* she was a Jew.

As for Arendt, I suspected that by defending Eichmann she was in a way defending her lover, the philosopher Martin Heidegger, a Nazi party member. Ordinarily, a highly esteemed thinker who bedded down with a Nazi and carried on with him after the war might have been expelled from high-minded intellectual circles. But curiously, that was not the case here.

Already American Jews were nervous about Arendt because the attack first ran in the *New Yorker*, which sophisticated Americans read, and the book that followed became a bestseller. It was a crack in the American support for Israel, which had held sway for more than a decade. People took it seriously. And even then I knew, however unwillingly, that it mattered. After that, I couldn't see the *New York Review* crowd the same way. I realized I didn't want to be part of anything that allowed *that* in, even as a strain in a bigger whole.

I was more interested in politics that year, for it seemed like we were in the middle of an awakening. In August 1963, Martin Luther King led his March on Washington, and I was there in the crowd. I was twenty-four and what I remember most vividly from the march is not King but Josephine Baker. The legendary performer had quit Harlem for Paris; like James Baldwin, she felt American Negroes could be more themselves in France than in the United States. She told the 250,000 people gathered in front of her that this "salt-and-pepper" crowd was something new for her, for all of us.

I'd spent almost all summer in D.C., in part with Bayard Rustin, working to prepare for the march. I was happy to sharpen pencils, whatever anyone needed. I remember telling my mother what I was doing and she said, with ample irony, "Oh, it's a *shik'yingel*," which is Yiddish for "errand boy." I didn't care. I didn't want to miss any of it, this cosmic thing, as it was happening: a glittering, crystallizing moment of what I thought was possible of politics in America.

While it had support from northern leftists, sentimentalists, and brave, well-meaning liberals, civil rights was a southern movement of the black church, the black middle class, and white southerners who took their Christianity seriously, sometimes against their own interests. My hero was Rustin, an endlessly impressive man who, along with A. Philip Randolph, the great leader of the Brotherhood of Sleeping Car Porters, had been working to change the laws for twenty years. The March on Washington, long in the making and organizing, was an expression of their vision, their values. They weren't fighting for an image or against a system: they were fighting for themselves. They wanted barriers broken down for individuals, and they wouldn't pretend that the end would be us all singing songs together.

Back in Cambridge, the political climate was changing in a direction I didn't like. There was this new guy, Carl Oglesby, who'd been president of Students for a Democratic Society. SDS had begun on the University of Michigan campus in response to the nuclear scare and then mutated into a bigger, more revolutionary movement, a conscious and explicit break with the shibboleths of what was then the liberal center. I'd seen this divide at Brandeis, between Irving and Herbert, and then at Harvard, between David Riesman and Barrington Moore. But I hadn't seen anybody like Oglesby before.

He was intense, wiry, scary thin—he reminded me of a Picasso caricature. He didn't generate attitudes or beliefs—those were already in the air—but he was out in the streets crystallizing those attitudes and beliefs into an invented structure, an ideology. It was all about the system that had built postwar America and broken its citizens' souls, reducing people to unfulfilled desires and misdirected anger. The way to fight back was to express your way out of its norms, not just with polymorphous perversity but with political action. The theory was an explicit break with decades of comfortable, liberal, tolerant postwar muddling, and it was totalistic, bridging every divide and resolving every contradiction. It was, at once, totally theoretical and totally personal, totally determinist and totally empowering, totally communal and totally individualist; it fused old ascetics and young college kids, rich and radicalized; it drove the drifting and disaffected to action.

During the second half of the 1960s, as the US military commitment in Vietnam escalated, all the radical energy shifted to oppose the now full-blown war. Anti-Vietnam activism started to have national political import, and so did the divides among the activists. Unlike the side of the antiwar movement that just wanted the war to end, the Mobe, the National Mobilization Committee to End the War in Vietnam, wanted more than a cessation of hostilities—it wanted a change in society itself. This was the Oglesby wing—more a cult than a movement—and they were intent on fucking their way to freedom: on top of the usual hetero stuff, the leaders would instruct women to sleep with women, men with men. Norman Mailer was a touchstone for these people, a symbol of the machismo they found so attractive in Castro and the Vietcong. Of course, these fixations were delusional: certainly none of their idols would have wanted to be seen as icons for a group that encouraged gay sex. Herbert, whose books all the Mobe leaders had read or faked reading, dismissed them because he could see most of the people didn't care about theory, and their activism was mostly politics as theater: for example, Abbie Hoffman, still a hustler like he'd been at Brandeis, cut his teeth as an impresario there.

The Mobe's critique, or aspects of it, spoke to me. I respected Herbert intellectually. I liked Norman. Castro intrigued me. I hated the Kennedys and their satraps. Still, in 1969, I skipped the Mobe rally in Washington in favor of the more moderate Moratorium Day march from the Boston Commons, where for the first time I saw a large gay group with signs that said, "Bring Our Boys Home." I thought it was funny, but I didn't identify with it. Politically, at bottom, I was not gay. I was Jewish.

Really, when it came to politics, I was in conflict. I overlooked what I didn't like and didn't confront it. But the day was coming when I wouldn't—and couldn't—any longer.

CHAPTER FIVE

Converging Inheritances: Aristocrats and Arrivals

Anne Devereux Labouisse and I met in the early sixties at a political event in New York. At the time, she was married, more and more unhappily, to an Air Force doctor and raising two young children in a small apartment on upper First Avenue in Manhattan. First we were friends, then we were partners in politics, and finally, by 1967, we were partners in love and life.

She was dark and petite. She wore bohemian clothes—there was a blue jean skirt I remember especially not liking—and I remember us discovering elegant stores together: always in New York rather than Cambridge, and always more Madison Avenue than the Village. She had a sense of humor, and she laughed easily; she evoked sarcasm without a hint of bitterness. She's still that way.

Anne was different from anybody I'd met before. She was an artist, a painter, and she did impressionist renderings of the crumbling cliffs and disintegrating dunes of the Cape. I wasn't at all artistic. She was a psychologist by training, and I wasn't particularly inclined to psychology, thanks to my father. But Anne came from a place where she was forced to look inside. Her people weren't intellectuals or middle class—they were artists, internationalists, civil servants, humanitarians, art collectors, equestrians, and they were astoundingly, alienatingly rich.

In 1851, Anne's great-great-grandfather, Edward Cabot Clark, founded the Singer Sewing Machine Company with Isaac Merritt Singer. Singer was the inventor; Clark the lawyer. They manufactured a device that automated the manufacture of clothing: it ran on a foot pedal, and it could run a piece of thread through a bolt of cloth many times faster than the human hand. It was as consequential a machine as the McCormick reaper, and it sold millions and millions.

Clark used his profits to invest in New York real estate. He commissioned the Dakota, named because it seemed so far from Fifth Avenue and the rest of the city, and he owned four or five blocks north of Seventy-Second Street, from Central Park West clear to the Hudson River. It was farmland when he got it, and he sold it as lots for brownstones, twenty-five feet by a hundred, in what has to rank as one of the great real estate killings in New York City history. To those familiar with the geography of the place today, it is almost unimaginable that any one person could own all that. And indeed, the Clarks were wealthy almost beyond imagining.

Anne grew up in this family, feeling like she didn't deserve all that money. It felt like it all came from nowhere and kept raining down on her. As she got older, she realized that it also made her a target for unsavory people, and she responded by turning her money and attention to causes. You can trust a cause in ways you can't trust a person, and you can use a cause to direct the money raining down on you toward something more meaningful to your inner self. I was involved in many of the most exciting causes in Cambridge, and she and I kept meeting through them.

Anne was the first really serious relationship in my life. Sexually, it was a free time between women and men: we weren't loud about it, but we did a lot of it. There didn't seem to be much to fear because the rules between the sexes were clear: we were freer than our parents, but we still had their traditions to rely on. Today, people are even freer. But there are no traditions, so people don't know the rules, and I think there's less sex because people think more about it than we did. Eventually, we knew, we'd all settle down and make our lives. In the meantime, we were going to enjoy.

I had married once before, in 1962, to Linda Heller, the daughter of a Jewish citrus grower from Florida. We had met while working at *The Justice* at Brandeis. She was handsome, energetic, and politically active as a social democrat—the sort of dignified, intelligent person who didn't take herself too seriously.

But the marriage, which felt serious, wasn't. We were too young, and I'm not sure I was really committed. It lasted thirteen months, and it felt like thirteen days or maybe thirteen years. When it ended, I moved into Kirkland House at Harvard. That's where I was living when I started getting to know Anne.

In a way, it was a meeting of two people with similar political instincts but not similar political passions. And in a way, it was Protestant meets Jew. But mostly, it was two people who didn't add up but found each other anyway. We were fascinated by what made the other person tick. We liked each other, we were easy together, and we were also representations of something each of us had been looking for. For her, I was an escape. For me, she was an arrival.

❋　❋　❋

It was a complicated place that she was escaping from and I was arriving at. There was a lot to know about the family. Edward's son, Alfred Corning Clark, Anne's great-grandfather, was notable for having, in addition to his wife and child, a boyfriend—a Norwegian sculptor—whom he installed in a house next door to him on Riverside Drive. You can still see some of these mansions—depressing, dark, enormous—where the four Clark boys, Edward, Robert, Ambrose, and Stephen, grew up.

The next generation devoted themselves to charitable works and art collecting. Look at any picture frame in the Metropolitan Museum of Art: chances are it will bear the name of Stephen Clark, Anne's grandfather, who was chairman of the Met, a founder of the Museum of Modern Art, and the originator of the Baseball Hall of Fame, which he undertook not as a statement of taste but as a commercial for Cooperstown. Stephen took ethics seriously and taught them to Anne. When she was eight, he told her not to give money to the Red Cross because it had inspected the "model" concentration camp at Theresienstadt and given it a seal of approval in the eyes of the world.

Robert Sterling Clark was the black sheep. He was a drunk and a right winger. In 1933, he joined the Business Plot, a conspiracy to start a revolution against Roosevelt. Robert had a dictator all picked out, General Smedley Butler, who he'd served with in the Philippines. Butler turned state's evidence and testified about the rebellion in front of Congress. But strangely no one was ever prosecuted, least of all Robert, whose name adorns a fine art museum in Williamstown, Massachusetts, with a magnificent collection of works by the likes of John Singer Sargent, Winslow Homer, Pierre-Auguste Renoir, and Claude Monet.

Still, it didn't do the family reputation any good. Though the Clarks were as rich as the Fricks and maybe even the Rockefellers, they were never listed in the books of America's sixty or even four hundred families. There was the gay grandpa and a dissolute uncle who led a life of scandal. To make amends, Anne's mother, Elizabeth, was married to an aristocrat named Henry Labouisse.

The Labouisses were real aristocracy—their roots in America went all the way back to Jonathan Edwards, the Puritan theologian—and represented on their family tree were a host of signers of the Declaration of Independence, university presidents, soldiers on both sides of the Civil War, and other elite figures. Through her father, Anne was a direct descendant of all these people. The Labouisses lost a good deal of money supporting the wrong side in the Civil War, and by the days of Huey Long's southern populism, they were part of the bitter, sometimes crazy, opposition. Still, when Henry, who went by Harry, married Elizabeth, it was seen as an honor for the Clarks, who had the money but not the respectability. Harry was there to clear the air. And he knew it.

But then a tragedy: Elizabeth died of cancer when Anne was only six. To make things worse, Harry told Anne that God took her mother away because he needed her to help him in heaven. Imagine saying such a thing to a six-year-old! But Harry thought in those terms. He also thought God needed *him* here on earth. He was the inheritor of an Anglo-Presbyterian outlook that was very much about bettering the world, and he took the charge seriously. He was a real internationalist—a lead person at the State Department partially responsible for the Marshall Plan and later ambassador to Greece under Kennedy. He was a safe person to appoint because of his formal stature among the people who made up the upper ranks of the civil service. But Athens is not London, Paris, or Moscow, and it's certainly not Washington.

People like Harry had servants to raise the children while they did good in the world, and Anne, who became enraged with God after her father told her that He had taken away her mother, was lucky to find one who became a surrogate mother. Her name was Shippy, and she was the materfamilias of the entire family. I believe the fact that Anne is a very warm and likeable person is a result of Shippy's care. It made Anne independent, not frightened of her inheritance but wary of a lot that came with it and willing to rebel.

To Anne's people, I wasn't a complete surprise. I think Harry had had enough trouble with Anne that he wasn't amazed that she would home with a tempestuous Jewish left-winger. Not that he was especially thrilled about it. Certainly, at the beginning, I didn't know a lot of Anne's people, with one real exception.

Eve, Harry's second wife and Marie and Pierre Curie's daughter, was that exception, and she was a way into Harry's world for me. When Anne and I came to New York together, we would stay with the Labouisses at their apartment at One Sutton Place South. Since Harry was often away on his important work, Anne, Eve, and I developed a connection.

Living with Eve meant living with a "personage," someone part of a family that included not only Nobel Prize-winning parents but a Nobel Prize-winning child, Eve's sister, who shared the award with Eve's brother-in-law. Eve herself lived not an intellectual life but an adventurous one: she was a writer (she wrote a best-selling book about her mother), a pianist (she was a close friend of Arthur Rubinstein's), and also a journalist and fighter with the Free French during the Second World War. There's a picture of a French women's army unit marching and all of the women's skirts are below their knees. That is, every woman except for Eve—hers goes two inches above the knee.

In the meantime, Harry and I kept missing each other's cues. Once early on he asked me to lunch and listed the several clubs he belonged to as options. "Oh," I said—and this was not nice, but I didn't know that it was not nice—"you have a lot of clubs to choose from." And he said—and this was also not nice, but I don't think *he* knew it, either—"No, no, no, no, we'll go to the University Club," which was more academic and a social class below the rest. "You'll feel more comfortable there." Did Harry say "comfortable" to me because I was Jewish and intellectual—or pseudo-intellectual? I didn't pursue it. He was my father-in-law, but we lacked a common language. The Protestants, once you got to know them, were even stranger than they appeared from a distance. Once around this time, I met David Rockefeller at a dinner at the Morgan Library, and we talked for a while before he realized who I was, even though I had two of his children in my class at Harvard. "Oh, you're Anne Labouisse's husband," he said. "I'm great friends with her father. He's a great man."

I had more and more of these exchanges once I started going with Anne because the social centers of Cambridge opened up for us whether we wanted them to or not. The center of old-line society was Brattle Street, called Tory Row: most of Cambridge's Tories had lived there during the Revolutionary War and identified themselves by putting a stripe around the chimneys.

Perpendicular to Brattle was Fayerweather Street, where Adelaide Hooker Marquand lived. She was a descendent of Thomas Hooker, one of the founders of Connecticut, and because Anne was also a descendant of Thomas Hooker, Adelaide occasionally asked us to her house for Sunday tea. What I remember most about Adelaide was her funeral a few years later, where the minister said, "*And if perchance* there is an afterlife we commit the soul of Adelaide Hooker Marquand to thy care." The caveat was representative of the Protestant aristocracy many generations in: the beliefs were so spongy; it was only about the form.

Some of the more intellectual old-line Protestants I liked very much, like John Kenneth Galbraith, who was a giant of economics at 6'7" and got along very well with our Great Dane, Hamlet. Galbraith was a great man and apart—that's how he styled himself. Barrington Moore, another larger-than-life aristocrat, would come into a party, look around from a great height, and leave. I liked them better than the Jews who tried to fit in with them by not being quite so Jewish, like Anthony Lewis.

Lewis wrote for the *New York Times*, first as a Supreme Court reporter and then as a columnist, at a time when you really *did* want to know what the *Times* editorial page said every day. He was a Jew from New York, and he'd attended Harvard when they were taking Jews but only from German Jewish bastions like Horace Mann and Fieldston. He was very elegant, he wore a bow tie, and he seemed to speak for the moral establishment.

The young star of the social elites was John Kerry, who was not at all born into them. He was good looking, went to Yale, where he was in Skull and Bones, and married a beautiful daughter of a prominent diplomatic family. In 1970, at twenty-seven, he used the fame he had gained from starting Vietnam Veterans Against the War to run for a congressional seat on the Democratic ticket, but lost to Father Robert Drinan, the dean of Boston College Law School, whose antiwar chops were stronger. This was the first manifestation of John's ambition, which you could tell from the beginning was enormous: in every conversation he looked like he was scoping out just what to say to get you on board.

Lillian Hellman bestrode both the Protestant social and Jewish intellectual worlds like a plaster colossus. She'd taken a liking to me when we hung around Tocsin together, and once I met Anne, she tried to take us under her wing. Lillian adored Anne, in part because she was adorable, and in part because Lillian hailed from New Orleans and the Labouisses were New Orleans aristocrats, which Lillian never could be because she was Jewish. Poor Lillian. It was something she was always trying to overcome. People like Alfred Kazin hated her because she was a Communist and the lover of a Communist, the hardboiled fiction writer Dashiell Hammett. But she also was known to have Christmas with McGeorge Bundy's family. You couldn't do better for the operative representative of "American imperialism" than the architect of Johnson's policy in Vietnam. Lillian's views and associations were about subsuming contradictions in order to create a persona: a New York intellectual and radical, an aristocrat of the mien and the mind.

Inevitably, there was friction between us. We once spent a weekend at her place on Martha's Vineyard, and one night the talk turned to Israel. It went badly for her because she didn't know what she was talking about and I did. She looked at Anne, and she said, "I would appreciate it if you would leave the house with *this man* before breakfast."

* * *

By the time I met Anne, my father and I hardly spoke. Far from being impressed with my meteoric rise from the Grand Concourse to Harvard, he saw me and my successes with a jaundiced eye. He met Anne once early on, and he took me aside and said to me, "She's a shiksa, isn't she?" I didn't say anything because obviously she was a shiksa. It was the only thing he ever said to me about her. Then my mother got sick—it was cancer. My father wouldn't believe it, and he accused her of making up the cancer as an excuse to fuck the cancer doctor. This was, in an almost cliched way, an unconscious projection: he was the one always running around on her. But that was my father. I flew to New York each week to visit her until she died, and I said almost nothing to him. After she died, we didn't speak for three or four years: it was a relationship of avoidances. I could never fully relax with him because I never knew when he'd erupt. On the other hand, Anne stayed in touch with my father. I don't think she liked him, but she felt it was important to keep him in our lives.

But if my father wasn't in my life and my mother was gone, what I had inherited from them, my Jewishness, was only getting stronger. All the time I was walking through the world Anne had inherited, I was also walking through my own. Sometime in these years I was in Calcutta (now Kolkata), in transit to someplace else. It was the Sabbath, and I was a little lonely in this city of millions of people. But suddenly a little man came up to me and said, "Do you want to make Shabbos?" He must have spotted my big nose—he had one too—and I was delighted to accept his invitation, even though I was never very religious. So I went, and we talked. He had come to India in the thirties from Germany because the British didn't let Jews into Palestine. He invited me—and it was an honor—to say kiddush.

In these same years, my father had an apartment in Tel Aviv, and one day he was walking when a man about his age started talking to him in Yiddish. My father responded, and they sat down on a park bench. The man said, "Come home with me, my wife will give you a *glezel* tea and a *shtikl lekach*," a glass (not a cup!) of tea and a piece of cake. So my father went to the house, they showed him around, and he saw a picture on the wall of a group of girls and boys, a picture that was about twenty years old. And in that picture my father saw his sister. But of course it wasn't his sister because the ages didn't match. After the war he'd tried to find her, but he couldn't—he couldn't find anybody—and so he assumed that this was his sister's daughter. He asked the man and his wife if they knew her name, but they didn't.

So the man's wife said, "Let me call my daughter"—because she was in the group in the picture, too. They called and the daughter said, "The woman's name is Anja. I don't know her last name, but she lives in Kibbutz Sha'ar Ha'Golan," which was the kibbutz I had visited on my first trip to Israel. It was already a little bit late, but my father said, "I'm going," and he got in a taxi. When he arrived at the kibbutz, my father said to the guard, "I want to see Anja," and he told the story. The guard summoned her. But when she came, she was not his niece. The guard said, "Well, there's another Anja," and he called this Anja. That was my father's niece, who had left Levertov a month before the Second World War and come with a girlfriend to Palestine via Turkey.

This inheritance was the other line running through my life, the place where my father and I were one, and it put me on an eventual collision course with Harry.

Harry, like most high Protestants who became involved in the region, saw the Middle East through the prism of the Arabs, whom he felt a kind of historical duty and right to help. British and American Protestants had been trying to Christianize the Middle East by building institutions there for a hundred years. Frankly, this was pathetic: Christians were such a minority that they only had cache with a tiny segment of the elite. I saw the genesis of the attitude up close, when Anne and I visited the American Farm School, where Harry was chairman, in Thessaloniki, Greece. The city was very Jewish until many of them left for Palestine in the twenties and thirties to build the port of Haifa and before the rest (excluding a small group of survivors) were killed by Kurt Waldheim, then-Nazi officer and later UN secretary-general. Watching the school's commencement ceremony, I felt that the Farm School's curriculum kept the people down—teaching someone to farm, in the late twentieth century, even with the newest equipment, is not modernizing—and that it was meant to keep these people simple and Christian because Harry and his coterie thought they would be happier that way.

The newly established state of Israel did not fit that model. Israelis were scientists, not just agriculturalists. Israelis had their own state, and they didn't want colonial help. Israelis wanted to help their neighbors through commerce, trade, and invention, and they were willing to fight to do it. Israel wasn't just about advancing a cause; it was about a people saving itself. And that divergence between my view and Harry's was driven home early because Anne and I got married the week of June 5, 1967, the same week as the Six-Day War.

This wasn't our first wedding. We'd had a Jewish wedding the day before, I guess to try to fool my parents into thinking that Anne was Jewish, as if it fooled anybody at all. This was our real wedding, with the license. But Harry was late. We were all standing around waiting, Eve was uncharacteristically hysterical, and Anne didn't know what to do. Finally Harry showed up, and said, by way of apology, "I was stuck"—I remember him using the word "stuck"—"discussing aid for the Palestinians with David Rockefeller."

The Palestinians were the other thing about Harry. From 1954 to 1958, he had been director of the United Nations Relief and Works Agency for Palestinian Refugees (UNRWA): the people driven off the land in the 1948 war. I had no problem with the Palestinians, stateless pawns in the ambitions of the Arab states who had betrayed them and now held captive in refugee camps. But my people were the Jews, and they were fighting for their lives. About them, Harry never said a word, and this silence infused the relationship with not just distance but latent antagonism.

The Israeli military was confident in the run-up to the war. But for Jews outside of Zion it was terrifying. Immediately, there were marches, demonstrations, and a vigil at the UN; American Jews, many of them Holocaust survivors, were in the street for the first time, praying for America to help. On the second day of the war, I went to an emergency fundraising breakfast for United Jewish Appeal and gave the biggest gift I'd ever given at that time. I'd been in the stock market since my senior year at Brandeis because I had friends who gave me tips. I'd done pretty well, and I gave a third of what I had made, of what was then my fortune: $35,000.

Laurence Tisch, a self-made son of immigrants, was there, too. He gave two million, which I don't think dug nearly as deep into his fortune. I liked Larry and he liked me: we understood each other's loyalties. He was so different from Anne's wealthy friends, from my father-in-law—it was another universe of human being.

By June 10, the war was over, Israel had won, and Anne and I were married. But pretty soon Harry and I were continuing the war between ourselves.

CHAPTER SIX

Civil Wars, 1967-1968: Old Politics and New

In July 1967, a slaughtering ground opened up in a new country called Biafra. It was the first genocide experienced in real time by the world public. Every day, terrible pictures of starving children with swollen bellies and sticklike limbs could be seen on the front pages of American newspapers and, most significantly, on American television screens.

In creating the state of Nigeria, the British drew a border around various ethnic groups and religious sects who hated each other, trapping them in the same country without considering that, the minute they left, these people would immediately fly at each other's throats—which is exactly what happened when the country was liberated in 1960. The majority of Biafrans were from the Igbo tribe and were well educated, westernized, and Catholic. They had been colonial Nigeria's political and intellectual elite, favored by the British. They were also called "the Jews of Africa." Now they were being murdered by the new Muslim-dominated national government. When the Igbo tried to secede and create their own state, Biafra, on the eastern coastline of Nigeria, Nigerian militias attacked. They committed terrible atrocities, against the women especially, and cut off shipments of food and medicine. In 1966 alone, some thirty-thousand people were killed—and that number only grew.

Around this time, I met a Biafran in Hazens. He was wearing a green and yellow scarf, the colors of the new Biafran flag, and we began talking. What he said moved me. We got to be friends, and I started wearing that scarf. Already, Anne and I had helped start an organization called the American Committee to Keep Biafra Alive: we wanted the US and the UN to recognize Biafra. It's embarrassing to say, but in some way a mark of the time, that this was my first real engagement with Africa. But Anne and I were immediately committed, even if we didn't know a lot. We thought the rights and wrongs were so clear, and it seemed like there was something we could do.

When her father worked for the State Department, Anne had lived down the block from J. William Fulbright, now the chairman of the Senate Foreign Relations Committee. The family knew her well enough to send us a wedding present, but really we needed Harry's help to get in with Fulbright. He refused to do this. He was, or he said he was, a believer in a code that held it was wrong to open doors. But Anne called her friend Bosie, Fulbright's daughter, who said I should come to see her father.

I met Fulbright and his wife in the Senate dining room. He recommended that I order the Jackson bean soup. Then we got to business, and he asked, straight off: "Why are you so concerned with these pickaninnies?" This threw me off balance. I didn't know how to respond. It was a shocking thing to say, and I knew immediately he'd meant to say it. The conversation went nowhere from there, just as he'd intended.

Fulbright was the senator from Arkansas, where it took the national guard to integrate Little Rock High School just ten years before. Obviously, he did not love black people. His opposition to the Civil Rights Act of 1964 was self-evident; he was a signer of the Southern Manifesto along with every other senator from the South except Albert Gore Sr. In addition, he had his own political fortunes to consider: his constituents' sons were dying in Vietnam, their senator was the leading congressional opponent of the war, and it would look foolish to suggest replacing one war with another. He said almost as much in the letter he sent me after, protesting that "it still is not clear to me what you feel a Senator can do about a war of this kind, especially a Senator who has spent four years attempting to do something about our intervention in a civil war in Southeast Asia…."

I suspect that Fulbright was fairly clear-eyed about the short-term stakes: the relief of Biafra could not have been achieved without something like the Berlin airlift, and to do that in the face of Nigerian government opposition would have meant committing military resources that were already committed in Vietnam. But still, I was stunned. I didn't necessarily think we'd persuade him. But I didn't predict just how committed he would be to protecting what he saw as his immediate interests and how canny he would be about doing it. And most of the Washington powers-that-be held Fulbright's view. His great enemy over Vietnam, Lyndon Johnson, told State Department officials to: "Just get those n***** babies off my TV set." Yes, that's what he called them.

The anticolonialist, antiwestern leaders of Africa weren't going to break ranks with Nigeria over slaughtering ethnic minorities. And the international human rights community tried to avoid the issue; I could tell from my dealings with Harry. UNICEF made a great show of collecting goods for the Biafrans, but most of the supplies never reached Biafra. There was a small and insufficient Biafra airlift: many European countries participated along with the Catholic Church, and the Israelis sent trained aircrews and US planes in their possession. The Israeli public identified with the Biafrans, an encircled people, surrounded by oppressive regimes—new, very small, alone, and struggling to stay alive.

None of it—the pictures of starvation and death, the international outcry—made a difference. By 1970, Biafra had ceased to exist and well over a million Igbo, most of them children, were dead. It was the first time I saw how good works and good workers, the institutional internationalists and their charitable counterparts, operate under the framework of agreed-upon fictions. The biggest fiction was that the UN could uphold humanitarian values even with the USSR and China on the Security Council and a mandate to include all nations in the General Assembly, even those, like Nigeria, which were murdering their own citizens.

Anne and her father got into a huge fight about Biafra because, though he agonized and talked about obstacles to action, he essentially shrugged. He and his friends saw these organizations of theirs as stewardships, derivatives of British imperial policy whose byproduct were unfortunate but whose basic aim of bringing order to the chaos of nationalisms was sound. And this meant they would follow the institutional logic wherever it led. It was a sign we didn't quite see of coming shocks, as the excitement of political possibilities met the muscle of political realities.

In 1965, Herbert Marcuse reached mandatory retirement age at Brandeis and left to teach at the University of California at San Diego. He viewed with ambivalence his prominence as the intellectual progenitor of the activisms on the Left. But his ferocity was undiminished. He cut through debate like the sword through the Gordian knot: that was the function of his synthesis of Marx and Freud, to change the terms of the argument. By 1967, much of his synthesis seemed to correlate with what was happening in America. The establishment Democratic Party, which had essentially run America since 1933, was doubling down on the war in Vietnam just as inner cities, from Watts to Newark, were starting to burn; black progress from the civil rights movement was starting to stall; and college students were starting to move hard Left and suburban parents were starting to move Right. The party I had come up in could no longer govern the society it had helped create. In fact, its governance was worsening America's problems.

Anne and I were increasingly involved in Left causes: we bought a full-page ad in the *New York Times* with I. F. Stone's essay against the Gulf of Tonkin Resolution, and we supported *Ramparts*, a radical magazine in the Bay area that was run, nominally at least, by Bob Scheer. Bob was a Jewish socialist who'd come up a few years ahead of me in the Bronx. *Ramparts* was for a new generation of the Left: some readers of *Dissent*, Irving Howe's magazine, probably read *Ramparts*, but not many readers of *Ramparts* read *Dissent*. *Ramparts* offered a different version of socialism: less intellectual, more expressive, less hamstrung by concerns over decency, more distrustful of the liberal state, and less committed to the idea that a liberal center might be a necessity for a decent Left.

Besides Scheer, Warren Hinckle was the major figure at *Ramparts*, and he always defined for me what the magazine, if not its readers, were really about. He was fat with an eye patch that never got explained, and he liked to talk about people behind their backs. I can only imagine what he said about me. Like a lot of the swimmers in the increasingly heated waters of the hard Left, including parts of Mobe, Hinckle and his people at *Ramparts* were as much about gestures as they were about journalism: it was half politics and half theater.

The fact that the magazine had been anti-Vietnam from the start gave it the moral certitude and swagger to be vicious toward people with a more equivocal stance. In 1966, the magazine ran a cartoon savaging Max Lerner. He had been publicly in favor of the war as one of liberation, a humanitarian project, and now he was moving from support to skepticism—but not quickly enough to satisfy the editors. I thought this was a cheap shot because the attack conflated Max's stance (which I disagreed with) with the reasoning behind it (which I respected). I wrote *Ramparts* a letter stating that while "at this point in my life we disagree about a great deal," I knew that "few people agonize over their opinions with more honesty than [Max] does. Decency may not be one of the revolutionary virtues but without it we cannot possibly build a good society or, for that matter, have any notion of what a good society is."

Max wrote to thank me: "After my initial twinge of anger I have reached an indifference about them.... In my own mind I add that my positions have been most wrong when they are like those the editors are now taking, and most right when we differ so sharply."

But word reached me, from Bob Scheer, not disinterestedly, that there were storms in La Jolla, and so I wrote Herbert a letter saying I'd heard he had held off sending me a rebuke of my "rather tepid" defense of Max. I referenced E. M. Forster's comment that if he had to choose between his friend and his country he would rather choose his friend, and then I finished with a personal offering: "I should, however, have loved to receive your reproach. Because in my private moments I would probably admit that you were right, and mostly because I delight in hearing from you whenever I do."

Nine days later came the reply: "You asked for it, and I am enclosing the letter I intended to send to you but didn't send because I did not want to hurt you. The quotation from E. M. Forster which you cite in your letter did not apply. The problem as I see it is not the choice between a friend and political beliefs, but being able to have a friend who has the political beliefs Max Lerner has." He closed "cordially"—where I had said, as we always said to each other, "much love"—but the letter he enclosed was not really cordial.

> *While we are all, to a greater or lesser degree, accessories to the most hideous crimes against humanity, a journalist who professionally defends the policy perpetrating these crimes is, in my view, not only an accessory but an active participant. It is your business to call him your friend; it is your business to come out gratuitously to his defense...but it is my business to question the mentality of a man who can combine friendship and loyalty to two totally contradictory causes.*

Herbert had tried to control himself: he crossed out the original word "sincerity" and replaced it with "mentality." He didn't question my character, not quite, just the way I thought. But for him thinking was a zero-sum game. He had a strong theory, but he didn't make room for his own blind spots. He had seen Vietnam coming because he thought that the natural result of a quietly oppressive system was to send its own people out to die in the name of an ignoble cause. He would overlook the Soviets crushing Hungary because in that case the revolutionaries were the reactionaries. There was no room in this view for complications of values or petty concerns like friendship.

This was not even the most severe lesson I learned about the New Left in 1967. The National Conference on New Politics happened at the end of August. It was the worst thing I'd ever done, the worst organization I had ever been involved with, and the ultimate example of me being too vulnerable to people and causes on the Left. It was a pivotal moment for me. But it didn't start that way. It started with Martin Luther King Jr.

I'd met King at the March on Washington, but we exchanged nothing more than a handshake. Later, I got to know him better. Anne and I asked him over for dinner with ten or twelve other people and, since we were known for supporting causes, he came. I asked him and a top adviser, Andrew Young, for help on Biafra. "This is a very conflicted issue among blacks," Andy told me, a little defensively. But he went on to explain that since the fight was between Africans, black Americans didn't want to take sides against people they perceived as their own. So they were steering clear. I was surprised, but I understood: going against black leaders who spoke the language of anticolonialism, murderers or no, was too much of a distraction for the fragile movement King led. So I didn't blame him for that, and I didn't press him since obviously he didn't want to be drawn out.

King was fascinating to watch, the first political leader I knew who had to work to keep many different political groups from fighting each other. This was not an enviable position to be in: he had to dissatisfy all the groups to avoid dissatisfying any one of them. In the meantime, he was the face of a moral movement, and he was young, just ten years older than me. This made him a complex man, much more interesting than the civic hero he's been flattened into today.

Enemies were everywhere. J. Edgar Hoover had agents infiltrating the campaign and bugging King's rooms, in part because he knew King was close with the Communists who peopled the edges of all the reform movements and in part because Hoover saw civil rights as a threat to order. And Hoover was not even King's biggest enemy. The movement he was leading had provoked reaction that went to the heart of four hundred years of slavery and its aftereffects. He wasn't sure he'd survive. "I've been to the mountaintop…" he said in his last days.

The stresses on him told. King had women sent up to him most nights—this was an accepted, almost unspoken fact among people close to him. Hoover caught some sex on tape and used it to try and discredit King with politicians, the Nobel Prize Committee, and his wife Coretta. King also drank a lot. He was one of those preachers who, when he drank, spoke with greater vitality. The speeches themselves were thoughtful and variegated—he drew from scripture but also from scholars like C. Vann Woodward. He said once, with Woodward in the audience, that Woodward's book on Jim Crow was the "historical bible of the civil rights movement."

Even the leaders of the movement King led were divided. Bayard Rustin was a very brainy guy, an intellectual who liked the Jews and was vocal in his support for Israel. Julian Bond, who was important but adjacent to the top people, was a moderate and a decent man; I never heard him say anything demagogic. Andrew Young was trickier. Both his parents were Communists, and he'd come up in the ambit of the Highlander Folk School of Tennessee, a Communist front supported by two of Anne's spinster aunts, New Orleans aristocrats. Young was very charming and charismatic, and I liked him. But I was suspicious of him because of his Communist influences and because I knew that the presence of Communists in the movement was real. In fact, there was an ongoing fight for influence at the lower levels of the movement between the anti-Communists, led by Rustin, and the Communists and their comrades, represented not by Young, who kept his hands clean, but by Stanley Levison, who did not.

King stood above the fray. He'd come from black clerical royalty—he was deeply about the church and everybody understood it. But by 1967, he was in a more difficult place than he'd ever been. Of course black hardship hadn't disappeared with the passage of the Civil Rights Act. In the inner cities, things were getting worse. Activist momentum was shifting to the antiwar crowd, not churchgoers and middle-class professionals but college students and self-defined radicals. In any movement for a marginalized group, there will be people on the edges who define their entire politics by marginalization. But now the margins were coming closer to the movement's core.

The shift happened in the Student Nonviolent Coordinating Committee (SNCC), which had organized the sit-ins, Freedom Rides, and nonviolent marches of the early civil rights movement. John Lewis, beaten at the Pettus Bridge in Selma and already a hero in the movement at twenty-six, had been its leader before he left in 1966. Lewis was a moderate man, but he had stepped aside for

Stokely Carmichael, James Forman, and H. Rap Brown. These men were organizers, performers, and rejectionists who'd decided the American system's racism was so deep that the only way for blacks to reclaim their identities was to work outside it. They linked up naturally with people like the head of SDS, Carl Oglesby, whose synthesis of race and class struggle appealed to them.

King responded boldly. He was already leaning a little bit socialist in private, and he saw an opportunity to use his stature to co-opt the radicals and join different wings of activists together under the umbrella of practical democratic change. In April 1967, against the advice of many supporters, he staged a march to the United Nations against Vietnam and linked the civil rights and antiwar causes. It was an exciting moment: civil rights activists and anti-Vietnam activists weren't a majority of Democrats, but they were an emerging coalition not just of causes but of peoples.

A bunch of antiwar groups, with Anne and me among the main funders, planned a conference for the end of the summer to formalize the link between the causes. It would be called the National Conference for New Politics. Julian Bond would be convention co-chair, and King would be our keynote speaker. We hoped he would also be our presidential candidate if we decided to run an independent candidacy or a challenge in the Democratic primary in 1968, although no one had thought to ask him. Benjamin Spock, the famous pediatrician, would be our vice president, which would persuade the old Protestant elite to bless this new coalition.

I was twenty-seven years old, and there were realities I hadn't absorbed. For example, these groups and grouplets that were called "communities" were not really communities. They were a host of different groups with different and often competing interests, fighting over who gets to claim the mantle. The strongest group set the agenda. With civil rights, the movement's religious middle-class base was strong enough to preempt a challenge from the hard Left while taking in its concerns. The same was not true with Vietnam: it was a more radical social vision that mobilized the troops.

In midsummer, we hosted the planners of the conference at our rented place in Wellfleet. One night, after most people had gone back to their motels, I came downstairs to find blacks and whites together on my porch singing anti-Semitic songs about Jewish landlords overcharging and evicting black tenants in Harlem. Most of the whites singing were Jews, and I could see they were enjoying a kind of vicarious thrill, a subversive titillation, that went through them as they sang. I threw them off the porch, but I couldn't escape the issue: all that weekend I argued with James Forman, from SNCC, about whether Jewish landlords owed blacks reparations for rent abuses.

Forman was very close to Anne, and for a while he actually lived in a house she rented in Greenwich Village. I respected him for speaking for his people, but this was an issue that pricked me a little. My father's activities as a small-time landlord had given me a roof and sent me to college. He wasn't a bad guy as a landlord and always gave errant tenants, white or black, another week or month. It was true that Jews had had more opportunities in America than blacks. But we had struggled too, and now we wanted to break open the Establishment and help other people along. Forman didn't see things that way: the Six-Day War had given him proof that Jews belonged to the class of oppressor, like he'd suspected all along. SNCC sent out a "report" on the Six-Day War that read: "Zionists conquered the Arab hands and land through terror, force and massacres. This is the Gaza Strip, Palestine, not Dachau, Germany."

In the meantime, the practical organizational ground shifted underneath me. The gathering in Chicago was supposed to be a conference of the mainstream antiwar Left: the Committee for a Sane Nuclear Policy, SDS, the Free Speech Movement, Vietnam Summer, SNCC, and the Mississippi Freedom Democratic Party. But then, at a meeting in Atlanta after Wellfleet, which I made the mistake of not attending, the plan changed: it was decided to invite *all* the antiwar groups whether they were in the mainstream or not, and that was how the Maoist Progressive Labor Party and the Communist Party of the United States—people opposed, on principle, to American democracy—showed up in Chicago. This was the deciding factor for everything that would come.

The Palmer House is in Chicago's downtown Loop. First built in 1870, then rebuilt the following year after the Great Chicago

Fire, and then rebuilt again in the 1920s, it was intended to be the fanciest hotel in town. But in 1967, its enormous rooms and lobbies were more than a bit shabby. It was an odd setting for the alternate reality the conference became as the consequences of the guest list became clear. Right away, it divided into two groups: people committed in a vague way to a better world and democratic processes, and people who were certain the route to a better world went through revolution. The second group had arrived with a plan: about fifty of the more militant blacks split into their own caucus and commandeered a conference room, with the goal of provoking the convention into kicking them out so they could join an all-black revolutionary political convocation on the other side of town. Their excuse for leaving was that there wasn't enough black representation at our conference, even though Julian Bond was our co-chair and every effort had been made to ensure proportional representation on the different committees. The planning committee, members of group number one, were upset because they were terrified of losing black support.

The radical black caucus was aided and abetted by the radical white caucus, which formed the same day. Even though the radical black caucus wouldn't let them in, they shared their aim: to get the convention to vote itself out of existence in favor of local organizing and action on the street. Some of the white radicals' sympathizers were on the planning committee, and they helped shift the dialogue. By the time the conference started on Thursday night, the planning committee was at the throat of the steering committee, saying the whole organization needed to be reorganized before the conference started.

King, who might've focused things, was shouted at by the militants during his speech at the official Thursday night opening, and he left the next day. Julian Bond left too, followed by Andrew Young. That left H. Rap Brown, Stokely Carmichael, and Forman, and they threw their weight behind the radicals, who took control. The black caucus was now refusing to participate in the convention unless the committee submitted to its demands—including denunciations of Zionism as a colonial enterprise, condemnation of the US as a genocidal nation, and a rejection of systemic change in favor of revolution. On Saturday morning, the steering committee accepted the black caucus's demands, and Jim Forman went up to the microphone to announce himself the "dictator" of the convention. A few minutes later, the black caucus sent back another message: it now wanted 50 percent of the vote in the name of "equality and trust." The steering committee immediately agreed and made abolishing democratic politics the first official act of the New Politics Convention.

At this point everything went crazy. Black radical and white Communist toughs patrolled the halls, scaring the hotel guests. Sentimental Democrats performed rituals or confessionals: sweet John Maher talked revolution; nasty Bob Scheer talked about the anomie of the suburban middle class; and Arthur Waskow, not yet a Renewal rabbi and writer of titles like *The Worried Man's Guide to World Peace*, screamed, "After four hundred years of slavery, it is right that the whites should be castrated!"

I couldn't believe it—and yet I could. Since Wellfleet, I'd had an awful feeling that the anti-Semitism of the American Left was no different from that of the Communist parties in Eastern Europe, with the new element of race added to the mix. Here, decades later, was the American iteration of the Communist mistake, aided and abetted, again, by Jews rejecting their Jewish identity in the name of an ideology that persecuted Jews. I had helped set up the New Politics, and it clamped down on me and the things I cared about like a trap.

I felt like a fool. It was inevitable that a social-protest movement comprised of students, academics, and community activists would fall into factional disputes over competing particularisms. It didn't matter to these people, who gave zero thought to the realities of democratic politics, that their utopianism would have courted electoral backlash from the overwhelming majority in a country where most citizens were neither college students nor ethno-Marxist revolutionaries. That the convention turned into a dictatorship should not have come as a surprise. These were not people who cared about, or even understood, democracy.

I walked out twice, first when the steering committee debated the black caucus's ultimatum and then the next day when they endorsed it. I could have gone on walking out all day. Nobody cared whether I was there or not. I had no clout at all. I was supposed to be an activist and a benefactor, but I had compromised my point of view as an activist by allowing myself to be categorized as a moneybags. I was staying not at the Palmer House but at The Drake, a chic hotel at the other end of Michigan Avenue. I think I had done this to insulate myself from my fears about the conference. But it only served to reinforce my moneybags image. I had a feeling I might be shot as an enemy of the people.

Renata Adler, reporting for the *New Yorker*, stayed until the bitter end and came up with some bitter insights:

> *One of the reasons for the complete disintegration of the New Politics was the convention's persistent debasement of language.... The only way all these "revolutionaries" could find common ground...was by jettisoning meaning from vocabulary.... When words are used so cheaply, experience becomes surreal; acts are unhinged from consequences and all sense of personal responsibility is lost.*

Language debasement was the mechanism. But the outcome was anti-Semitism, an angle which, until Wellfleet, I had ruled out as my own paranoia. It completely stunned me. And I wondered why I hadn't gone to Atlanta. I felt stupid, like the Jewish Soviet poets and party members who were purged must have felt. (Of course a hefty number of them were executed, and I was not.) I remember Anne consoling me that night. She kept telling me this wasn't my fault. I felt she was being kind. A week later, Max sent me a letter:

> *My own feeling, for what it's worth, is that you should not regret having helped create something which a group with a racist and non-humanist outlook would be able to take over. There was always a chance that you could keep it a genuine organization for peace and for effective political action according to your own humanist lights....Let me repeat that I was proud of your stand, not only on the grounds of the anti-Israel plank, but on the grounds of humanism all down the line.*

He was being kind, too. But that was Max: humanism all down the line.

* * *

Then help came from an unexpected place. All that summer there had been rumblings of a Democratic primary challenge to Lyndon Johnson over Vietnam. The peace movement was desperately trying to enlist any senator who had uttered a peep against the war to run. The savior the kingmakers really desired was Bobby Kennedy. But, typically for a Kennedy, no one knew whether he was really against the war or still for it.

I first met Gene McCarthy, the senator from Minnesota, when a small group of Boston-area antiwar activists went to Washington to sound him out about a challenge. At fifty-one, he was still a young politician but he had older values even then. He'd grown up lower-middle class and Catholic and had even considered becoming a monk. Instead he did postgraduate work in economics and entered politics on the Democratic-Farmer-Labor Party ticket, a Midwestern tradition that went back to early century progressive attempts to bring big corporations under ordinary people's control.

In 1948, the year Gene ran for the House, he and Hubert Humphrey pushed for an expansive civil rights plank for the platform at the Democratic convention but lost to the Southerners who still dominated the party. Four years later, he opposed Joe McCarthy in a nationally televised debate and calmly and rationally took him apart. In the Senate, he served on Fulbright's Foreign Relations Committee and was adamantly against the Vietnam War, which he thought was something only an establishment completely removed from reality could think up. Eventually, at Anne's and my urging, he spoke up about Biafra, even though there weren't many votes in it for him. Personally, Gene reminded me of Bayard Rustin: the religiosity, the concern with decency, and the self-belief that comes from self-knowledge. His was my kind of leftism, if it even was leftism: ensuring freedom with an eye to the darkness of human nature. He didn't think politics could solve everything. But he thought they could make people's lives more manageable.

Gene was willing to run. But first he went to Bobby Kennedy and told him: "Bobby, if you're gonna run against Johnson, run." Then he upped the ante by saying publicly, "Senator Kennedy ought to do it, and if he did it I would support him." But Bobby wasn't sure the race was a winner, and he wouldn't commit. So McCarthy got serious. His announcement challenging Johnson, when he made it, was very low key. He said the war was immoral and wrong, and that it was eating away at the fabric of our country. He said it had to end. He was very clearly not an operator; he had a modest reputation he was risking for a Hail Mary pass. People saw this and they flocked to him.

The closest friend I met on the campaign was John Callahan, a professor of English at Lewis & Clark College in Portland. He'd been watching TV, and he saw this grey-haired man announce his run for president, his speech so uninflected and direct, and he thought: Yes. He became McCarthy's campaign director in Oregon, where he led a winning effort in the primary. It became a passion—more—an obsession. It did for a lot of people. Even today, when John and I meet, McCarthy is our first topic of conversation.

The campaign had the spirit I'd hoped for in the New Politics convention. But like any national electoral movement, the different interest groups acted as coolants on anything too crazy from any one of them. There was also a broader set of interest groups to begin with: there were committed leftists, but there were church people, union people, and farm interests in the mix, too. It looked like America.

There were young activists—Sam Brown the most prominent among them. He was the chief kid on the McCarthy campaign, and he reached out to Gene's young supporters. They were more hippie than Sam, but they agreed to go "Clean for Gene" so as not to detract from Gene's appeal with an older electorate. There were aspiring political mechanics who believed in ideals: John Podesta comes to mind, though I don't remember exactly what he did on the campaign. And there were believers who were troublemakers. Seymour Hersh was the press secretary for the campaign, and he was as he is now: his penetration leads him to the right places until his ideology steers him off course. He worked three or four weeks and then quit, telling viperish lies that McCarthy was racist and that was why the campaign didn't have enough blacks. In fact, Gene wasn't at all a racist: he was a straight-up integrationist. He didn't care whether you were Jewish or black or WASP or Catholic like him. He'd come up a poor boy, and he knew lots of different types of people—he judged them all as individuals.

We had celebrities: Paul Newman, who was a "flag liberal" with all the "right" beliefs, and Jane Fonda, who visited Anne once to talk about funding, getting out of her long, chauffeured car in her chic suit. Looking on, I thought, "Somebody like *this* is going to rally support from working Democrats?" This was four years before her famous trip to Hanoi, where she alienated even people who had liked her. Peter Yarrow came to sing for the campaign, where he met Gene's niece, Mary Beth. Eventually they married, and, eventually, unmarried.

Gene's financial backers met at the offices of Jerry Grossman's Massachusetts Envelope Company, just like in the Hughes campaign. There was Arnold Hiatt, a progressive Democrat who would soon be heading the Stride Rite shoe company, and, most important, Howard Stein, the chief executive of the Dreyfus mutual funds. It was a surprise for someone of his stature in the financial world, and without a political history, to make himself integral to a campaign. But he thought the war was terrible, and so he came on board. This was the core of the campaign, the people who got it off the ground. My job was much as it had been with Hughes but on a larger stage. I was a person who connected the different factions—moneymen, politicians, journalists, academics, and celebrities; democratic socialists, social democrats, and welfare liberals. I wasn't the only person doing it, but I was one of the most active, and I brought along people I respected. David Riesman wrote in the *New Republic* that, come November, Gene would stand a better chance against Nixon than Bobby Kennedy. Max Lerner wrote in the *Post* that "McCarthy behaves only like himself," and praised "[his] brand of liberalism, which is not that of the fanatical true believer, but a blend of reflective humanism tempered by the pragmatic."

To Gene, Vietnam was not just a moral wrong but a representation of the fissures of a country in transition: from city to suburb, road to highway, local to national, production to consumption, old to young. The point of the campaign was to yank us out of Vietnam and then start to address those changes. Really, Gene was part decent Left and part practical Right, a committed citizen who cared about strong communities and a free thinker who cared about civil liberties, with a moral view of foreign policy that drew on both schools of thought. He was too idiosyncratic, or purely practical, for political life, and we assumed he probably couldn't win. Still, at least he, we, were making a try.

Then came the New Hampshire primary in March. Gene lost, but it was closer than anyone expected: just six points—42 percent to 48. It was a psychic tidal wave: the press allowed us to believe we won and broadcast it that way because it hated Johnson so much. Still, everyone was stunned when LBJ took what would have been in ordinary times an ordinary win as a devastating defeat and withdrew. Suddenly, Gene's campaign, staffed and advised by a bunch of young amateurs like me, was the front runner for the Democratic presidential nomination.

Everyone expected Bobby Kennedy to jump in now that the coast was clear. It took him exactly four days. We knew some of our people might defect, particularly Richard Goodwin, who'd been a top Kennedy aide and then the chief speechwriter for Lyndon Johnson before he broke with the administration over Vietnam and joined up with McCarthy.

Goodwin was the archetypal Kennedy person, which is why I never liked or trusted him. He was very smart, but he always looked like he was thinking about what he was going to say when he wasn't talking. He was full of resentments. Like me, he hadn't been admitted to Harvard for college but unlike me he'd never shut up about it. He'd fallen hard for the Kennedys. Jews like him believed that the Kennedys would let them into the halls of power. But what they didn't see is how the family would use them along the way. It was on Goodwin's rhetoric, along with that of Ted Sorensen and Arthur Schlesinger, that the Kennedy political mythos rested. This was a version of Democratic politics that started and ended with the idea that a government run by experts in resourceful institutions could do anything—solve poverty, beat the Soviets, achieve black liberation, redeem humankind, save the world—and it attracted bright young people who never comprehended that the world, the real world, was a different place than they hoped it would be.

I was sure that the rhetoricians of this vision, like Goodwin, wanted to pass it to the next son, Bobby. And Bobby, besides working with Joseph McCarthy and then prosecuting the mob-affiliated union leaders who gave his brother the White House, seemed to me to have the worst of the Kennedy qualities: equivocation, angle playing, and vindictiveness. Joseph Kennedy once said, "Bobby's a hater, like me," and I think that's what Bobby really was.

It was a two-man race until April, when Hubert Humphrey, Johnson's vice president, announced his candidacy. Humphrey had Johnson's full support and didn't actually campaign. He worked the old Democratic machine to win delegates in states without primaries and where the party bosses controlled the works. So now we were encircled by two opponents with bigger political machines than our own. But we kept fighting, and we won Oregon against Kennedy.

I still had my teaching and my family but the campaign was my obsession all the same. It entered into every part of our lives. Our first child, Jesse, was born in May of 1968, and when he was two weeks old, Ben Spock held him in one hand—he had enormous hands, he was enormously tall—and passed him over to Gene McCarthy.

The California primary was the key race, and Bobby and Gene debated in Southern California. These were important debates, but Gene never wanted to practice for them, and I asked him why. He looked at me and said, "All of these issues have been with me all my life. They live with me. Why would I need to practice?" This was a version of his other refrain: "I believe in what I believe. I don't believe in what you tell me I should believe." It was Gene's greatest strength, a reason people admired him. But against Bobby it became a weakness.

The hot-button subject in the debate was integration. Gene wanted to integrate the whole society, whereas Kennedy wanted to put more money into the ghettos. In the debate, Bobby distorted Gene's stance, accusing him of wanting to move ten thousand blacks into Orange County. It was total bullshit, an utter lie, but Gene was blindsided: he couldn't believe the words had come out of Bobby's mouth.

Bobby damaged Gene not just by scaring liberals who said all the right things while worrying about property values, but by exposing Gene's flaw: he was so comfortable with himself that he wouldn't make little compromises. When you put that authenticity next to Bobby's willingness to sublimate himself to his goal, to play every angle, it crippled our chances. And then there were the hard demographic realities: inner-city politics was the Kennedy's playing field, and he had a lock on the votes of the Irish and the blacks. Gene covered academia, well-meaning liberals, Midwesterners, and agrarians—a less populous and more diffuse coalition. Still, I thought, if Gene won in California, there would be a chance. But on the night of the primary, June 4, even though Gene won New Jersey by five points, Bobby won the prize, California, by four. He gave his victory speech at the Ambassador Hotel in Los Angeles and walked out through the kitchen, where he met the assassin who shot him dead. The whole nation went into shock.

The assassin, Sirhan Sirhan, had a strange and troubling history: he was a Christian native of Mandate Palestine and a refugee from the 1948 war, where he'd seen his brother run over by a tank. He was a supporter of Bobby's until Bobby made a speech in favor of sending fighter jets to Israel; then Sirhan decided to kill him. So he was a nutcase, but a historically significant nutcase. Probably to avoid inflaming things more, the media didn't look seriously into the Palestinian angle, and the Zionists didn't protest because they were embarrassed by it themselves. As a result, an important event got rinsed of an essential part of its meaning.

All that we learned later. In the moment, all we knew was that everything was just fucked when Bobby died. Gene was shocked—he'd known the country was in turmoil—but nobody expected this. He thought he might've fanned some flame that led to Bobby's death and had a kind of breakdown. He left the campaign and went back to Minnesota, probably to atone. On June 11, not even campaigning, Gene won Illinois. What was left of the campaign was a lot of states that would be determined at the convention, where Humphrey had a meaningful but not insurmountable advantage. But Gene had retired from the action—he wasn't in the game any longer, and none of us could coax him back out of his shell. Even if Gene had stayed actively in the race, it is by no means sure he could have won against Humphrey and the Establishment.

I saw that reality later in the summer, a year almost to the day after the New Politics debacle, when the Democratic establishment anointed Hubert Humphrey at the party convention in Chicago. A lot of Gene's people were there, but we had no function because the decision had been made that it was Humphrey. We came as a ritual, out of loyalty to Gene, and it was clear we didn't belong. We didn't feel any solidarity with Humphrey, who we saw as an old-school sellout who never showed us a welcoming gesture, nor of course with Richard Daley, who set the police on the protestors at the convention on his behalf. But we didn't belong with the radicals either. Some of the protestors and rioters used the McCarthy headquarters as a refuge from the beatings the police were meting out, and they laughed at us even as we gave them water because in their eyes we were playing along with the system. We were caught between the street radicals and the liberal delegates, the very groups Gene's campaign had been trying to bridge.

Gene endorsed Humphrey in a very Gene way: "To be clear, this endorsement doesn't mean I'm trying to get back in the good graces of the Democrats. And to prove it, I pledge I won't run as a Democrat in 1972!" He was a very complicated, take-me-as-I-am person. It was cussedness, a stick at the Establishment; it didn't help anybody, but it was Gene.

In November, Humphrey lost the presidential election by one hundred thousand votes to Richard Nixon, who took three decisive states—Ohio, Illinois, and California. Nixon was the red baiter, the liar, the monster. The Left was in agony. He outperformed Humphrey in suburbs, northern cities, and the South. I don't think the votes from the antiwar Left hurt Nixon—the people who voted solely on the war issue were relatively small in number. Except for Uncle Benny, I didn't know anybody who was voting for Nixon, and the fact that my only experience with a Nixon voter was an old man I'd known since childhood was a real blind spot—of mine, of the campaign, and of the antiwar Left in general.

Civil rights and Vietnam, between them, had broken up the Democratic coalition I'd come up in and that had somehow held northern liberals, white southerners, and blacks together in some kind of dynamic tension. The 1968 election would realign American politics for a generation and more. What had looked to us like a new political era of promise was the last gasp of an older one.

* * *

Already in April, there had been a presentiment of the letdown to come. On April 4, just as Gene's campaign started to face head-winds, Martin Luther King, who, for all the past eight months' dis-illusionments, was still my symbol of what the Democrats could be, was shot dead by an assassin in Memphis. I'd known him as much as one can know a person who had already become both prophet and hero. In October of the last year, right after the New Politics de-bacle, I'd asked him over to our house when he was in Cambridge, offering "honest and tough and friendly dialogue." When the talk turned to Israel, he said, "When people criticize Zionists, they mean Jews. You're talking anti-Semitism." He wasn't anti-Semitic or an-ti-Zionist. But he was trying to lead a movement more and more in thrall to those impulses. Could he have pulled it through? I'm not sure. At the very least, he was the only leader capable of reconciling the radicalism of the New Left with the moderating forces that gave the movement popular legitimacy, chiefly black and white religious institutions. In King, the movement had not only an emancipa-tor but a compromiser, and the debacle at the convention in 1967 showed that it needed both.

The loss of King brought anger as well as sadness. I was asked by Harvard's president, Nathan Pusey, to give a speech to calm the campus. It was generous of Pusey to ask because he didn't like me, though we never got into words, and at faculty meetings I'd been a thorn in his side, if only a rhetorical one. But he was an old-fash-ioned liberal type who probably voted Republican and didn't think he could credibly eulogize Martin Luther King. So he asked me, a popular teacher and a credible voice on the political scene, to do it for him.

Harvard, like a lot of campuses that spring, was tense. It wasn't just the black radicals: the moderate black integrationist hero had been murdered, and it felt like a crystallizing moment. My speech was an official function of the university held in Memorial Church, and as such was organized by whites. The black students stayed away and made their own. Tom Williamson, the opposite of radical, wrote me a pained letter asking me why I wanted to give the speech in the first place. "I believe it is dangerously cathartic for blacks and whites to join hands in mourning and then go home to their separate communities," he wrote. "It seems tragically evident to me that we need new standards for defining responsibility to the black community.... Blacks can and will define new norms outside the lecture halls, the dining rooms and the churches of liberal America."

CHAPTER SEVEN

Inflection Points, 1968-1974:
Avoiding Apocalypse

Early in November, Herbert wrote, with many honeyed words and rhetorical flourishes before he got to the point: "I read that you are going to grace with your presence, one of the most repulsive gatherings of kept intellectuals: the Quatsch symposium in Princeton on the so-called future of this country...Apologize and don't go—tell them why..."

As usual when it came to Herbert, I compromised: I decided to go but as a dissenter, bearded and dressed like a lumberjack in a crowd of clean-shaven academics in suits. My session was called "Beyond the Proletariat," and pretty quickly it became me versus Daniel Bell.

Bell was still at Columbia where, that spring, SDS affiliated students had more or less taken over the whole campus. "If there is a problem for intellectuals," he said, "it would seem to me a double one, which is part of the role of a university in a postindustrial society. It's how you humanize a technocracy and how you tame the apocalypse. Having seen some of my students attain the apocalypse, I would submit that it is much easier to humanize a technocracy."

I admit, this was compelling stuff. But I was there for an argument, and I responded with a jab:

> *Without trying to teach Daniel Bell his Marxism—*
> *apparently he went through greater rigors of Marxist*

*training than I—it would seem to me that when intel-
lectuals make intellectuals [and the university] the
linchpin[s] of the future, we might at least contem-
plate...cui bono, who gains by the arrangements.*

He came right back at me:

*Mr. Peretz has discovered something called economic
power like a political virgin who has seen a primal
scene for the first time and said, "My god, what's
going on there?" The problems of America would be
much easier...if it were only a question of concen-
trated economic power. ...[But] since World War
Two...this country has become in a curious way for
the first time a national society...[where] groups of
individuals assert rights as groups, which...creates a
series of specific social strains and adds to the danger
of violence. I know I'm complicating the picture here.
I'm doing it deliberately.*

I didn't know it then, but Dan—who for years after would kid
me about the Princeton event: "Marty, stop crowding me!"—had
laid out the framework that would dominate my thinking over the
next half-decade: humanize the technocracy or attain the apocalypse. Avoiding the apocalypse would soon become my priority.

Back at Harvard, the class that had come in with Vietnam was
about to graduate, and the university around them had changed
more over five years of war than it had in the twenty-five before.
The children of the gentry weren't just dissolute: they were disillusioned with the order that had brought them to Harvard and
was sending them out to die in Southeast Asia. Jamie Kilbreth, by
now fully radicalized, tried for conscientious objector status, and
I wrote him a letter to help. The leftists—including those taking
Social Studies—were unbound and emboldened, like any group
that sees events matching its theories. The campus was in an uproar.
When Defense Secretary Robert McNamara came to campus, eight
hundred people, led by SDS, surrounded his car and rocked it back
and forth. The Reserve Officers' Training Corps had been uncon-

troversial a decade before; now students said ROTC rhymed with "Nazi" and should be banned from campus. The laissez-faire social attitudes—flouting the rules about jackets and ties at dinner by not wearing shirts—had become angry gestures: men wore ties made of toilet paper.

Stranger things were happening, too. One such odd phenomenon was Henry Murray, a very popular Harvard teacher in the Social Relations Department who was mixed up not just in psychological experiments but in the drug scene. He'd been brought up by wealthy, strict parents in Manhattan, in the West Fifties—the Rockefeller neighborhood. He was a big influence on Abraham Maslow at Brandeis, and he introduced Timothy Leary to psychedelics at Harvard at around the same time that he tested some of his psychological ideas on a mathematics graduate student named Ted Kaczynski. He was the eminence of a congeries of people in Harvard's permissive old order who were thinking things and doing things that were not just radical but psychologically and socially corrosive: for me, he was the last sign of the overripeness of the Protestant inheritance.

In the spring of 1969, Anne was pregnant with our second child, Evgenia. I was now the head tutor of Social Studies, where much of the trouble gestated. I didn't have a direct line to the real radicals, but I'd been warned by a few students that the radical Marxist groups on campus—the biggest one was the Maoist wing of SDS—were going to try something along the lines of what students had done at Columbia.

The rumors were correct. In early April, three hundred Harvard students took over University Hall. They rushed into the administrative offices and dragged F. Skiddy von Stade, the dean of freshman, across the hall and down the stairs. They roughed up Archie Epps, the one black administrator. This was not peaceful protest, and some of the people joining the violent crowd were my students: Jamie Kilbreth and Michael Kazin. Their stated purpose was ending university sponsorship of the ROTC: "a life-and-death issue for the people of the world whose lands are occupied by US troops, whose social revolutions are fought viciously by the US military." The real reason for it was four years of frustration and fear fed by advanced social theory. It was Marcuse and Oglesby in action, and none but the real radicals were prepared for it.

Nathan Pusey, then sixty-two years old and in his sixteenth year as Harvard president, was an old-fashioned and not even particularly distinguished college bureaucrat. He saw his responsibility as a question of law and order, of not allowing the university to be shut down by force—and, of course, preserving "the life of the mind." So he called in the cops. The Cambridge police were blue-collar, working class: their brothers, sons, friends, and neighbors were actually serving in Vietnam, not getting college deferments while play-acting revolution and spouting slogans. The first night of the occupation, they came and broke through the line of students in front. These were moderate antiwar kids, like Chuck Schumer, who had gathered in the yard when they heard the police were coming and linked arms, at least symbolically, to protect their classmates inside. Then they took a battering ram to the main doors. Arrests were made. There were injuries.

The raid was a turning point. Most of the students and faculty hadn't supported the University Hall takeover. Even the sympathizers outside University Hall hadn't been all in; they had been performing a caring gesture toward fellow students. But when Harvard brought in the force of the state, even if the state was only Cambridge, it felt like a betrayal. The next day students, over a thousand of them, streamed into Memorial Hall. I was asked to speak by somebody on the faculty, and my first words when I got up were, "Brothers and sisters..." Immediately I was hooted down. Nobody was brother and sister now.

Classes got cancelled for the term. Teachers who wanted to teach couldn't do it inside for fear of offending the radicals. Students spat on President Pusey as he was crossing the lawn, something he didn't deserve, even if he had made a big mistake in calling the cops. He'd always been a liberal, and he had a deservedly good reputation for fighting McCarthyism in the academy. Many of the older faculty stood with Pusey; they thought that if you were willing to break the law in order to dissent, you should be willing to be punished. Michael Walzer and I thought that, too. But on the other hand, we didn't want our students to get kicked out of Harvard. We formed what we rather pompously called the Social Democratic Rescue Committee, which tried to help students avoid expulsion by coaching them on how to answer some of the questions they might get.

Some kids were so conflicted about what they'd done. One was Jamie Kilbreth, who was kicked out of the university while he was indicted by a grand jury for attacking a dean. I always felt bad about what had happened to him. The main radicals, like Michael Kazin, the ones who drove the action, were terribly self-righteous, and the worst of them didn't suffer. Even as Kilbreth was prosecuted, Kazin was allowed to graduate. I can only imagine what his father, Alfred, said to him.

Each spring we'd have a dinner for the Social Studies seniors, and I'll always remember that year's gathering. We had it in the Holyoke Center penthouse across the street from Harvard Yard, the one with the hanging Rothkos. Richard Rockefeller and his cousins were there, and one of the cousins got up and made a radical speech. Then Richard got up and said—I paraphrase but this was the import—"We are very ungrateful. And some of you may say that I have a lot more to be grateful about. And that's true. But it's not true that we all shouldn't be grateful. We should. We should all be grateful to Harvard and to our society which allows us in a limited measure to choose a way of life."

Graduation Day, in June, did not feature anything nearly as inspiring as Richard's speech. It was a theater of the absurd. One of the speakers read a quote about law and order and then "revealed" it was from Hitler. That was one of the more coherent speeches; the rest were ranting. When Nathan Pusey got up, most of the students turned their backs on him. I felt bad for him, this plangent figure of a receding order.

Al Gore did not turn his back. He never made faux-dramatic gestures or conceded to fashion. Unlike the leftist theorists who had the luxury of idealism, he was in a special bind: his family connections meant he could escape active duty if he wanted, but Senator Gore was coming up for a difficult reelection the next year and his support for civil rights and his opposition to Vietnam had alienated him from his constituents. Al thought if he didn't serve, it might cost his father his seat. By graduation, he had decided on the army, and later, when he came back to visit campus wearing his military uniform, he was hooted and jeered at by a few of the students.

That September, David Riesman wrote me about his "fears... [that] people might well out of frustration destroy what has seemed to me the admirable sobriety and dedication of the [anti-Vietnam idea] by becoming its camp followers...I'm sure you've been haunted by this." I'd been haunted since Palmer House. But I also didn't agree with James Q. Wilson, Sam Huntington, and a few other slightly older intellectuals of the Right, who were now saying that if this new style of politics was what postwar tolerance and progress had produced, it was time to get very skeptical of the postwar liberal order itself.

I didn't agree with them because of my faith in my students, a new and widening strand of the American elite. Midwesterners, Irish, and Jews, they had grown up middle class in a peaceful and prosperous America and were thankful to the system for letting them into an elite university. They had few qualms or anxieties about whether they deserved it. But they were eager to prove their worth. They weren't in love with theory and they believed in incremental improvement for everybody. But now they were seeing violence interrupt their classes and their routines in their very first year away from home. I'm not sure any of the incoming class of 1968 or 1969 had a proper finals period until the spring of 1973.

A few of these students weren't too concerned. Chuck Schumer kept on going as if nothing had happened, moving quickly from Harvard to Harvard Law and then while there running for the state assembly. Somehow he figured out that he could simultaneously go to law school and campaign, and then serve. Believe it or not, he was an innocent. I think he wanted to go someplace, and he'd do whatever he had to. But he never calculated; he always acted on instinct. There's not much that can bother a person like that. But most of the students *were* concerned, and I thought my task at Harvard was to help them through it.

Of the students entering my sophomore seminar in the fall of 1969, I became closest to Jamie Gorelick. Her parents were left-wingers and she grew up in Great Neck, where she had joined the Girl Scouts. So her background was a mix of radical and mainstream. Jamie had been as unnerved by the University Hall takeover as me: she didn't like violence, and she found the rhetoric about the working class coming from middle-class and sometimes upper-class students fake. She was the right person temperamentally and by background to help me with a seminar I was putting together on McCarthy and McCarthyism. She read the transcripts of the hearings McCarthy conducted and the biographies of the people involved, and we made the course up together.

I used the course as a lesson in making room for different realities in a bifurcated place and time. I thought we should be able to condemn McCarthy for politicizing the culture and ruining lives, while acknowledging that his extremism didn't negate the threat of Communism in America. This was a personal commitment as much as an intellectual one: every time I heard about the evil of McCarthyism, I thought of Herbert Marcuse and that evening at his house with Stalin's Servants.

We had guest speakers. Lillian Hellman and Alger Hiss came and spoke about their experiences. Roy Cohn also talked about history, the same history, but differently of course—history that was only two decades old. The students in the course and others in those years were the type of people I could help find their place at Harvard in a strange time. One was a somewhat awkward and sweet, sweet kid from Fall River, Massachusetts, a declining mill town. I saw this brilliance in him—I don't know what it was exactly. But E. J. Dionne, a Catholic Democrat from the lower-middle classes, turned out to be one of the most thoughtful and provocative people in the class. He is now a columnist for the *Washington Post* and a professor of public policy at Georgetown.

Another smart boy, a doctor's son from suburban Detroit, came to the course from a distance. Even at eighteen or nineteen, Mike Kinsley was a skeptic—he originally hadn't wanted to take the course because he didn't want to get mixed up with me. Certain professors develop coteries, I was one, and Mike didn't trust that. But the course was meant to draw you in: the thesis was provocative, and the guests were living historic figures.

Also there was Nicholas Lemann, a boy from New Orleans who was brought up in what he calls a "super-Reform" synagogue. My notes from his interview for my seminar, scrawled across the page, read, "Conscious of New Orleans, a sensual city, basic for someone like him....journalism, Crimson – enthusiastic, but not as much as he hoped...[he has] subtler qualities."

In the fall of 1971, I interviewed a prospective student for the seminar. He was interested in history and was thinking of the law. My notes were, "very attractive person, success-oriented, self-conscious. Diamond in rough." This was Lloyd Blankfein. I wait-listed him for the seminar, and when somebody dropped, I let him in. I rejected Walter Isaacson, too, which he always, always reminds me of when we meet. None of these students needed much help; they just needed, in a confusing time, in a convulsed university, a hand. I don't know if I saw it this way at the time, but I had bought into the framework that Dan Bell had laid out at Princeton in 1968: this was my way of helping to humanize the technocracy.

✳ ✳ ✳

I hadn't taken my finger off the political pulse. I hoped Gene McCarthy would run in 1972, despite what he'd said about never running as a Democrat again. In 1971, he left the Senate and began to write books and poetry and ran two peculiar independent campaigns for president: he became more of a truth teller than a man of influence.

After 1969, the Kennedys were out of the picture, too, when after a party, Teddy Kennedy drove his car off the Dike Bridge in Chappaquiddick on Martha's Vineyard and a young staffer, Mary Jo Kopechne, drowned. Anne and I were having a party in Truro the next night, and first to arrive were Diana and Lionel Trilling. The first thing Lionel said was "He won't be president anymore." Diana responded, "You don't know the Kennedys." Sandra Goodwin and Marion Schlesinger came, and everybody knew why Richard and Arthur weren't there: their husbands were at Kennedy headquarters at Hyannisport, on the phone to lawyers, trying to clean up Teddy's mess.

By this point I knew Richard pretty well. But I didn't try to get him to tell me about Chappaquiddick; he and I were always at odds because he knew I was wise to him. A few years later, Richard was in the Bahamas with his new girlfriend, the historian Doris Kearns, and his almost ex-wife Sandra could not be found at the mental institution where she was supposed to be staying. Richard called me asking for help, but I had a class, so Anne, a bit spooked, went over to Sandra's apartment with a friend to make a search. They looked around the apartment and Sandra wasn't there. Anne recalled that they had not looked in the closets, so they looked in one, and then another, and in the next one they found Sandra, sitting perfectly still because she was dead. For a few years after, Anne couldn't check into a hotel without asking me to check the closets first.

I got back from class, and we called Richard. We told him the news and suddenly, about three exchanges in, he declared, "But you'll charter a plane to take me back, won't you?" This was the point at which Anne got off the phone. I said there were lots of commercial flights from the Bahamas to Boston and that he should take one.

On Friday afternoon, at Levine Chapel in Brookline, we had to wait thirty minutes, then an hour, because Richard wouldn't let the rabbi start until Teddy came. Finally, the rabbi, with the sun going down on the Sabbath, insisted on starting. Teddy pulled up just as we were leaving—the planes from Washington had been delayed, or the Senate had been in session. Even though it was Sandra who had died, the funeral was all about Teddy. The experience became a signpost for me: a reminder of the detritus that the Kennedy satraps, with their self-importance and irresponsibility, left in their wake.

Another more significant piece of Kennedy detritus was the leading candidate for the 1972 Democratic nomination, George McGovern. In 1971, having heard him speak, I wrote to David Riesman:

> *He tells you too much, leaving you with no sense of mystery and no notion that he puzzles about anything. One of our colleagues suggested that he was rather like an exhibitionist, stripping off every layer of protection—and every layer seems to be surface. The litany of evil overwhelms me. I shudder to think what the accumulated grievance must look like to other Americans.*

McGovern was a senator from South Dakota, a delegate to Henry Wallace's Progressive Convention in 1948 and an early opponent of the Vietnam War. He was one of the "maybe" contenders for the 1968 Democratic presidential nomination who kept dithering and then threw his hat in the ring two weeks before the Chicago convention in the name of "the goals for which Robert Kennedy gave his life." He collected Kennedy-supporting delegates behind him and then threw them to Humphrey, which was seen by anti-Vietnam activists as a betrayal. So he was a good fit for the Kennedys: half idealist, half opportunist, and most comfortable using whatever political shibboleths of the moment helped him paper over contradictions. The Democratic Party picked him because, his endorsement of Humphrey aside, he had a strong record on Vietnam. And, as the war kept dragging on, the peaceniks had begun to capture the inner workings of the party—even as the rank-and-file union men who were the party's backbone had views on the war that were almost diametrically opposed.

I knew this from talking to union leaders while working for McCarthy. I met Paul Schrade, Bill Dodds, and the head of the AFL-CIO, Lane Kirkland, who was married to an Israeli, a fact which may have at least partially explained his passion for Israel. Talking to them, I could see that almost none of the obsessions of McGovern's antiwar followers resonated with the Democratic base. Many of these workers were connected in some way to the defense industry and opposing Vietnam meant in effect opposing their jobs.

Even in 1970 I'd been writing David Riesman about the gap:

> *I, of course, agree with you about protecting the jobs of the people in defense plants. Too many of the economists, at least the young ones, are now so intent on proving that nothing good can happen under the present social system that it is difficult to get them to help with formulating the relevant notions from the perspectives of both peace-concerned individuals and justifiably insecure workers.*

I was corresponding with Al Gore and getting a similar reaction back from him: the Republicans were corrupt; left Democrats were out of touch with reality. Al hadn't been shipped out to Vietnam until December of 1971, a year after his father, Albert, lost his Senate race—a delay that Al saw as the hidden hand of Richard Nixon, who wanted to deny Albert sympathy votes if Al was injured. When Al got to Vietnam, he saw that a lot of South Vietnamese wanted no part of the Vietcong and came back to America caught between Nixon, who he saw as corrupted by power, and the Left, who he saw as corrupted by ideology. He went to Vanderbilt University Divinity School on a Rockefeller Foundation Scholarship. I didn't blame him. I was ten years older and in the same place. "Just think," he wrote. "Your former student is now a proper monk."

Still, I signed onto McGovern's campaign as chairman of his foreign policy committee for the Middle East—which might have met once or not at all. Anne and I gave an enormous amount of money to his campaign because he opposed Vietnam. But I never entertained the fantasy that McGovern would win. I wanted to keep the Left with Israel even as it opposed Vietnam. But McGovern wasn't the answer to that question. Really, I was stuck with my various and contradictory opinions.

Like all campaigns, McGovern's needed money, and it was a seedbed for a new generation of Jewish Democrats, people of my generation who had made a success of themselves in the market and wanted to support social democratic politics. Arnie Hiatt, from McCarthy's campaign, actually thought McGovern might win. During the campaign, I became close to Mort Zuckerman, a real estate developer who went on to own *U.S. News & World Report* and *The Atlantic*, among other publications, and Max Palevsky, a pioneer in computer science who sold his company to Xerox in 1969 for $920 million. Max wanted to be thought of as a man on the Left—that was what the sophisticated people did.

Celebrities came out. Gloria Steinem, who was Mort Zuckerman's girlfriend for a while, tepidly endorsed McGovern as "the best white male candidate." Warren Beatty came out for McGovern, too. He was actually a serious intellectual for Hollywood, but he was caught between his concern for the issues of the day and his friend Lillian Hellman's nostalgia for the old Communist dream. Certainly, she did him no favors advising him on a script he was writing, *Comrades*, about the American Communist John Reed, which would later be called *Reds*. I read it too, and I pushed Warren to cut some of the Lillian Hellman-isms I saw.

But there was always real politics as well. The Friday night before the election, the telephone rang and it was a man I'd never heard of from Delaware named Joe Biden who was running for the Senate against a Republican named J. Caleb Boggs. He told us the race was tight and asked if we could help; he could still win it. We sent him $5,000 or maybe $10,000, either of which would have been a lot of money in those days. On Tuesday night, he won by 3,162 votes. "Dear Joe," I wrote right before the election,

> *I was so glad to meet you yesterday, sensing a rapport and affinity I had only once before felt with anyone in politics…My wife and I hope we will be able to get to know you well.*

We didn't get to know him well, but Joe Biden was the one good thing to come out of that election. McGovern lost in a landslide, winning only Massachusetts. Later in the Nixon presidency, there was a bumper sticker that said, "Don't blame me, I'm from Massachusetts."

I was one of those Massachusetts voters who went for Nixon. It was my first Republican vote and at the time I didn't even tell my wife. Maybe I reassured myself that McGovern would in no case be elected, and that he would win Massachusetts, so my vote wouldn't matter. And this was a true prediction. I certainly didn't vote for Nixon because I wanted him—not in a million years. But had McGovern won, I was convinced it would've been a disaster for the country—maybe for the world. I knew that too much of what he believed was what the Left did: that threats to democracy abroad were nonexistent, that the only war was the one here at home. And to be perfectly frank, my vote for Nixon was a vote for Israel, which I was sure McGovern had in his sights.

* * *

In January of 1973, the defeated tatters of the McGovern campaign and the antiwar movement gathered in D.C. to protest Nixon's second inauguration. The Philadelphia Orchestra was scheduled to play, and at least two of the musicians refused in advance on account of Vietnam. I heard about that and had an idea: there should be a separate concert for people opposed to the war. I was still, always, trying to find my own way of doing things.

So I called Leonard Bernstein and said, "Why don't you conduct the *Missa in tempore belli* by Haydn, and I'll get the National Cathedral and you'll get the rest?" I'd known Lenny after we met at Brandeis and my friend Robert Renfield had taken me to a backer's audition for *West Side Story* at his mother's apartment where I spent the evening trying to flirt with Rita Moreno. I liked Lenny. He was open about being a Yiddish Jew and as openly gay as anyone I'd met. When I called him with my idea he said, immediately, "Fine, let's do it." We hired the members of the National Symphony Orchestra as individuals because the orchestra wouldn't allow us to use its name.

There were protests at the inauguration. But this was something more dignified, a Mass against the war. We called it a Concert for Peace. It drew a crowd of twelve thousand: the cathedral was packed with Quakers, Communists, liberals, socialists, intellectuals, rich people, and students—a standing-room-only crowd with more outside in the freezing rain. Lenny gave an absolutely magnificent performance; he made the place tremble. There's a record of it that I think you can still listen to today.

It was a nice gesture, but clearly our symbol had come to nothing. Nixon was president, the war would continue. That night, looking out at the church and the church grounds in the blackness and the rain, I saw a procession of innocents, a pageant of the easily feeling and easily led, people who hid from reality behind the constructs of desperate belief, a crowd that nobody, in a year, would remember had been there.

At the same time that I was moving away from the Left's politics, I was also starting to feel alienated from the intellectual forces in this crowd: they seemed to me removed from reality.

Susan Sontag was an example. I'd met her at Brandeis, when she was still married to Philip Rieff. Martin Buber, the great Jewish theologian and mystic, old as Moses, had come to speak and actually picked her out of a crowd. "Young lady," he'd said, "come sit here next to me." There was an intellectual frisson to her, an excitement. Even in the days when she hadn't actually done anything, she was known to be brilliant. Now we knew each other, in a wave-across-the-room sort of way.

When she first got sick with cancer, Roger Straus—an heir to the Guggenheim fortune who founded Farrar, Straus and Giroux and prided himself on losing money on really good literature: Isaac Bashevis Singer, Joseph Brodsky, Robert Lowell, Aleksandr Solzhenitsyn—called me to ask if I'd help with Susan's cancer treatments. After a little discussion, Anne and I said yes, even though we felt strange giving money to someone we didn't really know who had very rich friends. If I tell myself the entire truth, I might have been pleased to be asked: it felt like I was being let into the cultured inner sanctum. We sent her $25,000 and then we used some more money from a fund set up by Anne's grandmother to help impoverished sick artists. Grandmother Clark would've turned over in her grave if she knew her money was being used to help a Jewish lesbian.

Straus thanked us. But Sontag never did. Not long after this, she was a visiting professor at Harvard for a year, and one night she came to our house for dinner. When I was a graduate student, I was in an old bookstore and saw a little paperback copy of John Stuart Mill and inside was written "Susan Sontag." I bought it, and that night, years later, as a welcome to Harvard, I presented it to her. She was cold in response, and I felt put down. But she wasn't through with us yet. She said to Anne as she left: "You are a very good homemaker." The contempt for normal things, normal life, good manners, common decency—it startled me.

All through 1972 and 1973, as I was moving away from the Left instinctually and politically, I was talking to two friends in the Nixon White House who made me see his administration as something less than devilish—and maybe more responsible than the people who were my nominal allies.

The first was Daniel Patrick Moynihan, whom I'd met in the late sixties when, after being Lyndon Johnson's policy adviser, he had come to Cambridge. Because everybody wanted him but nobody wanted all of him, he taught in multiple departments. He had one of the beautiful houses off the square that Harvard gives to the eminent at a discounted rent, and we used to have brunch with his family some Sundays. On these mornings, Pat would wear a smoking jacket and velvet shoes with an insignia: it represented nothing really, he just liked the feeling of being a British aristocrat. You couldn't blame a guy who'd grown up over a bar in Hell's Kitchen for wearing velvet shoes; it wasn't like he was a snob. He was Irish, as Irish as I was Jewish, and we embraced each other as fellow children of immigrants. He and Nat Glazer had coauthored a groundbreaking book, *Beyond the Melting Pot*, which argued that the whole idea of America as an assimilating country wasn't realistic to Americans as they actually lived: people mixed, but Jews stayed Jews, Irish Irish, Italians Italian, blacks black—and then the next group of ethnicities did the same thing.

Pat's obsession was poverty. During the Great Depression, his father had deserted his mother, leaving her and Pat to make their own way. That experience drove his policy interests. In the Johnson White House, he had led a study on inner-city poverty. What he found was that the decline of the black family not only tracked with declining socioeconomic conditions, but it also exacerbated them. The memorandum Pat prepared for Johnson said that, and it became his albatross. It leaked to the press and got inflated by Left radicals to essentially read "Moynihan Blames Black Family!" It's always offended me that radicals didn't see Moynihan's passion for the poor.

In early 1969, Pat left Harvard to go back to government, working on urban affairs in the Nixon White House. There he joined another friend, or sort-of friend, of mine, Henry Kissinger.

I knew Kissinger a little from Harvard. I'd sat in his class, and it was an experience. When he spoke, he never stopped for a minute; sometimes he had notes but mostly it was off the top of his head. This was, is, a brilliant man. He lived in Belmont, the next town over, and he used to come to our house to pick up his son David, who was in Anne's daughter Lisa's class. The kids got to be friends, so we got to be sort of friends. Of course, he was a strange friend to have, in context of what my other friends believed. But I cared less and less what they believed, and I liked Kissinger, I have to say it.

I saw his flaws: he must've known what Nixon was about, which was power, and he was willing to overlook what Nixon was about for what he thought was the greater good of his foreign policy, which everyone has to admit changed the world. With Nixon, and Henry, we got out of Vietnam and made peace with China, and if one in four people in Cambodia had to die to achieve this end, then that was what it took to be the American Metternich. (Yes, one in four Cambodians really did die—it's a shocking statistic.) Henry was a refugee, which meant he'd never taken order for granted. If he became Metternich, it was because he didn't feel he had a choice. What was the alternative, to play the Red Cross game against the Communists? We had all seen where that led. I have a letter of mine to Henry from 1971 in which I say, "With regard to the Vietnam question at the moment, I have been appalled at the ease with which yesterday's hawks and this morning's equivocators have embraced the simple withdrawal formula. Their new position is the gimmicky mirror image of the panaceas for victory which engaged them for almost a decade." This was not something I would've written two years before.

In October of 1973, I had occasion to not regret my vote for Richard Nixon when the Arabs launched a surprise attack on Israel, the second in just over six years. This was probably the most precarious single moment in Israel's existence. Golda Meir, who was prime minister, knew about the invasion beforehand, but she didn't move first because she feared that Washington wouldn't support her if she did. By now Russia explicitly supported the Arabs, which meant that the United States would be risking a superpower confrontation. Golda's necessary restraint put Israel at a military disadvantage: suddenly the Syrians were beating the Israel Defense Forces (IDF), and it looked to Jews watching in America like they might take Tel Aviv.

I was on the Cape when the war started. I don't know how I found out, maybe someone called me. I immediately called Simcha Dinitz, Israel's ambassador to America. "What's going on?" I asked, and he said, "What's going on is too important for me to be talking to you now." That's when I knew we were in trouble.

I'd met Simcha through Golda, to whom I'd been introduced by Marie Syrkin. Golda and I liked each other right off, and I started visiting her whenever I came to Israel. Why did Golda pay attention to me? I have no idea. I wasn't a material asset. Golda was warm and also iron: her politics weren't at all dovish; she thought violence could be a moral necessity and to absolve yourself of responsibility for it was a deeply immoral act. In this way, she was very like Henry. Simcha was Golda's right hand, his loyalty so beyond question he could even disagree with her in public. Once, in a meeting with me and Michael Walzer, she called Menachem Begin a fascist, and Simcha immediately said, "No, he's not!" And they began to have a little spat, but in Hebrew, so neither Michael nor I could follow.

When Golda became prime minister, Simcha became ambassador in Washington, which was resented in Israel because he wasn't a career diplomat. He was also resented in America, at least by Democrats, because he had a relationship with Henry Kissinger, who they saw as a rank imperialist. But being close to Henry meant that Simcha had an immediate route to American policymaking because America's foreign policy right then was Kissinger and Nixon.

I'd call Simcha every morning, at six or seven, and he'd have spoken to Henry already. My calls were purposeless. But at thirty-four, I was the nervous grandfather of Israel, and I trusted Simcha never to tell me something that wasn't true. On the second day, all he said was: "Everything is at stake." He urged me to do whatever I could, and I did a little. Michael Walzer and I ran an advertisement in the *Times* asking for aid to Israel. I paid, and Michael got the signatures, an impressive list of names. Then Michael and I, joined by Sam Huntington, a respected hawk, and others on the Harvard faculty, went directly to Henry at the State Department (at that point he was both secretary of state and national security advisor), all of us urging him to send Israel arms quick. There, in his office, Henry ribbed me about my work for the Hughes campaign, saying "Marty, I thought you were a disarmer."

Aside from the brave the young men fighting the war, Henry Kissinger was the most important asset Israel had. His heart might not palpitate for Israel like mine did, but he never stopped hearing what people like me had to say. And while he was hearing us, he was scouting the tricky White House terrain, where he was up against a president and a national security apparatus who, for different reasons, were suspicious of the Zionist project.

At bottom, Kissinger was playing a game, not with the other foreign policy professionals, Anglo-Protestant types who looked down on Zionism, but with Richard Nixon and with Richard Nixon's feelings toward Jews. Kissinger knew that Nixon's was a kind of vulgar anti-Semitism. But he also knew that Nixon didn't have anything particular against Israel. Kissinger used that knowledge to make his case.

Nine days after the war started, Nixon made his choice: America sent Israel supplies to replenish what the Syrians had destroyed. Then, one day, on our morning call, Simcha told me that, no matter what the newspapers said, he had "incontrovertible evidence" that "the tide had turned." Leonard Cohen was traveling to the front to perform for IDF troops. If they'd been losing, they would never have let him in.

By the end of October, twenty days after the first attack, we had won. Simcha saved us; Golda saved us; Henry saved us; Nixon saved us. If McGovern had been in the White House, he would have been guided by some combination of the moral abstractions of activists and the institutional equivocations of the State Department crowd. And he, they, would have let Israel drown.

✳ ✳ ✳

In February of 1974, a man named Horace Kallen died. I never knew him. But his legacy was of deep interest to me. He had been among the progressive philosophers at Cornell and Wisconsin in the teens and twenties and had coined the term "cultural pluralism." This meant that culture and cultural variety were important, not just an outgrowth of economics or politics.

In 1914, Kallen joined with John Dewey, Randolph Bourne, Herbert Croly, and Walter Lippmann to start a new magazine, the *New Republic*. Dewey, Croly, and Lippmann were more managerial types, interested in shaping policies of the new administrative state. Bourne was a man of the earthy, intellectual Left, opposed to the First World War but in love with his idea of America. As an undergraduate at Columbia, he fought to raise the pay of the college scrubwomen against the awful Nicholas Murray Butler. Kallen was the real pluralist of the group. He thought a lot like I. L. Peretz did. He was also a Jew, a Zionist who thought that the state of Israel should be a Jewish state to protect a threatened people and who advocated for American universities to take in Jewish academics to help them escape Europe.

From the beginning, it was a fighting magazine. When Louis Brandeis was nominated to the Supreme Court in 1914, the entire Boston establishment came out against him because he was a liberal and because he was a Jew. In the first year of its publication. The *New Republic* editors did a feature on the Boston establishment turning against Brandeis, called "The Motive of Class Consciousness," that included a chart of thirty-five prominent Bostonians who had sent an anti-Brandeis petition to President Wilson.

"All these men," went the editorial, then in galleys,

> *Worked together and married into each other's families, had the same stocks and investments, went to the same board meetings, and belonged to the same clubs. The social pattern of these gentlemen amounted to nothing less than a class psychology.*

The owner in that first iteration of the *New Republic*, Willard Straight, had been born to American missionaries in the Far East, attended Cornell, served in a variety of diplomatic positions, joined J. P. Morgan, and married somebody richer than him—although he was already quite rich. The fact that he wasn't completely a part of the Establishment made him insecure about crossing it. At the last minute, he refused to allow the editorial and feature to appear. But Louis Brandeis was appointed to the Supreme Court anyway and he, the first Jew to be appointed to the court, also became the leading American Zionist, arguing, just as Kallen did, that Zionism was for Jews an intrinsic element in their being Americans.

After Straight died, his wife Dorothy Payne Whitney supported the *New Republic*, passing it on to her son Michael. Michael, who was publisher from 1945 to 1953, was a Communist and a spy for Stalin, one of the "Cambridge Five" who leaked classified British intelligence to the Soviets. Straight's *New Republic* hired Henry Wallace as editor right before his 1948 presidential campaign.

In 1953, Michael Straight sold the magazine to Gilbert Harrison, who repositioned it on the non-Communist Left. He was a man who was for whatever the good people on the intellectual Left were for: he was for civil rights; he was for Vietnam very, very early on and then he turned against it; he refused to endorse Humphrey in 1968 and endorsed Gene instead.

By 1974, that line of Herbert's—"It is my business to question the mentality of a man who can combine friendship and loyalty to two totally contradictory causes"—was sticking in my mind. He was right, as far as it went. But he was also a little inhumane, and if the last six years had shown me anything, it was that Herbert's inhumanity was not for me. I wanted "humanism all down the line," like Max had said. I decided to chuck the theory, take the choices, the causes, and the people how and when they came.

Into this moment came Horace Kallen's magazine—tired, in the red, and ready for a buyer. Anne saw the opportunity before anyone, and she liked it. I liked it, too. We talked about it, we thought it over, and we decided.

I met Harrison for the first time at Gene McCarthy's, and I don't think that was an accident. I think Gene saw a path for me through the *New Republic*. I think he knew I wouldn't end up in organized politics, but that, as an intellectual entrepreneur, I could push politics from the sides. In March, we bought this little magazine for $380,000, and I made my way, for really the first time, to Washington, D.C.

CHAPTER EIGHT

Washington, D.C.: Upstarts

When I bought the *New Republic*, it was a respectable Washington thing: a flagship magazine of the then-governing classes that, after sixty years, had gone to seed but was still occasionally worth reading. The readership was probably fifty thousand, maybe a little more. The demographic was the genteel liberal who believed in "justice and peace." The writers were stalwarts of welfare-state liberalism and social democratic values. The mainstays were Andrew Kopkind, who'd written for *Ramparts*, *The Nation*, and the *New York Review*, and Walter Pincus, an acolyte and former employee of J. William Fulbright. The magazine occupied an old Victorian house on Nineteenth St. NW, a little ways from Dupont Circle and painted grey as befitted a convalescent home for tired Stevensonians. The editorial meetings were dull affairs: contributors would say what they were writing, and there would be almost no exchange of impressions or viewpoints. I think that Gil Harrison was comfortable that way.

The capital city around them was still a bit of an aristocratic backwater: redolent of older administrations, a place of experts and businessmen plus some rich people from Cambridge or New York there to do good. Its certified intellectuals were Arthur Schlesinger Jr. and John Kenneth Galbraith. Anthony Lewis fit in well there with Harrison and his writers, many of whom were friends of my father-in-law.

I was not worried about fitting in, and I certainly didn't intend to be silent or diplomatic. My first act was to fire the old guard or provoke them into quitting. The new sheriff soon trained his sights on UNESCO, the United Nations Educational, Scientific and Cultural Organization, the usually uncontroversial protector of historic and natural sites worldwide. They had passed a resolution condemning Israel's excavation of ancient Jewish sites in Jerusalem as shunting aside the city's Arab heritage. The Arab states controlled the board and they were denying Israel a place in UNESCO on the garbled logic that membership was allotted by region, and they didn't want Israel to count as part of their region. It was the kind of thing Harrison would have ignored in the name of politesse or stability. The old guard saw the floodgates opening, they pushed back, and pretty soon they were out. Harrison decamped to his mansion and Walter Pincus decamped to the *Washington Post*, the publication favored by established Washington. Like the exhausted Protestants at Harvard, they didn't push back much against their defenestration.

The people who noticed were not from the liberal establishment but from the hard Left. Alexander Cockburn, a Stalinist scion of a Scottish noble family, wrote a column in the *Village Voice* titled "Incubus of The New Republic": I was "practically the official spokesman for Simcha Dinitiz." I was "totally paranoid and [reacted] hysterically to criticism." I was "frightful." It was a kind of reflexive lashing from the Left, what *Ramparts* would have published if it had lived long enough to see itself marginalized.

Secure in the knowledge that I was pissing off the right people, I focused on building a new *New Republic*: an argumentative magazine that could not fail to be noticed, a magazine from the Left but not of it, intellectual but not academic, a publication of ideas that was also where the action was. I started looking for people who could help me make the magazine what I wanted it to be. I got three from Harvard and one from an advertisement: Mike Kinsley, Rick Hertzberg, Leon Wieseltier, and Charles Krauthammer.

Each of these men represented a part of me, a different manifestation of my personality. I saw in them the competing value centers of the next generation. They all liked my plan for the magazine: poke the polite rationalist establishment in the eye, argue for the old Left belief in political action to better society, champion the humanist concern with the health of the culture, contest policies from first principles, and argue for why Zionism mattered.

Mike Kinsley, who had kept his distance from me in the McCarthy course, ran into me in Rome while out with his classmate Wendell Willkie II, grandson of the Republican candidate for president in 1940. Mike had just read that his old professor had bought the *New Republic,* and here I was having coffee with my wife in the Piazza Navona. "Marty," he said. "I know exactly what you should do with it." Because I hadn't finished my coffee I said, "Send me a memo," and instead of being brushed off, he wrote a very good one. So when there was an opening, I brought him in to the magazine.

Mike was an unattached man, a practical thinker allergic to grand schemes. He was part of the first middle-class suburban cohort to get into Harvard, only to find that nobody in that ruling citadel knew what they were doing. The Establishment was overreaching with Vietnam, the Left was responding insanely. It made him see everything clinically, and it made him hate the hypocrisy of moralists, of the well-intentioned who saw things through a gauzy haze. Washington in the late seventies was a good place for a person like that.

Rick Hertzberg was the last thing in the world from a skeptic. Soon after he left Harvard, Rick enlisted in the navy, a strange move for a man with pacifist inclinations. Unsurprisingly, he ended up applying for conscientious objector status, which was rejected. After he was finally discharged, he tried old-school journalism at the *New Yorker* and then went to D.C and wrote speeches for Jimmy Carter for three years, crafting old-fashioned social spending rhetoric with bearded dudes who smoked pot. I always liked Rick, and we spent a fair amount of time together socially in Washington when Carter was president. Before the administration ended, we were talking about him coming to work at the *New Republic.*

We knew it might be a tough thing between us because I thought the Carter administration was a cul-de-sac for the Democrats. I remember Anne and I going to the Democratic National Convention in 1976, where Carter was anointed, and it seemed so clear to me that the Democratic platform was nothing and so was the nominee and his people in general—do-gooders who thought good intentions were enough. This view was borne out by the fiasco of the hostage rescue mission in Iran. Mike and I ran a cover with the downed helicopter on it that read "A Jimmy Carter Classic" and we endorsed for president that year the third-party centrist, John Anderson, the closest thing to a liberal still standing.

Despite our political differences, Rick and I were good friends, and we figured we'd work the rest out if he came on as editor. He took over from Mike in January 1981 and stayed until 1985, when Mike came back. But the whole time, even as he was working at *Harper's*, Mike kept writing for us.

The other refugee from the Carter administration was Charles Krauthammer, who'd been chief speechwriter for Walter Mondale. Charles grew up in New York and then Montreal; his father was a Yiddish Jew, an Orthodox Jew, who'd come to America to escape the Soviets and become an avid New Dealer. Charles had gone to McGill University, where he flirted with Left activism for about fifteen minutes, and then to Oxford for political philosophy. But then, because his father wanted him to, he went to medical school. When he had to decide what type of medicine to practice, he chose psychiatry as a compromise between medicine, which he hated, and ideas, which he loved. But pretty quickly he realized he wasn't especially interested in the interior lives of other people. So he was stuck.

About this time, he saw an ad Mike put in the magazine: "The *New Republic* seeks managing editor. Apply here." Charles applied, and Mike and I went out to lunch with him. But when we got to the Italian restaurant where Mike had made a reservation, we found that it was down a flight of steps. That wasn't going to work because of a fact neither of us had known until the moment we met Charles: he was paralyzed from the neck down. We looked at the steps; he looked at the steps. We were horrified, but he said, perfectly calmly, "Ooops. I can't go down." So we went to The Palm, the celebrity steakhouse in the lobby of the building across from our offices, and hit it off.

When we met him, Charles had been in a wheelchair since 1972, when he had taken an ill-considered dive into a near empty Harvard pool that had left him paralyzed. After this happened, he gave no sign of quitting: he doubled down on medical school, finishing his studies from his hospital bed. What really depressed him, he told me, wasn't being trapped in a wheelchair, but trapped in the profession of psychology, confined to the sidelines, not participating in the fights that mattered.

Mike and I hired him as a senior writer, and he immediately made himself a hit: an old-fashioned Democrat losing patience with a party in sway to the Left. Charles started working for us part-time, and his writing got him noticed by Walter Mondale. Speechwriting for Mondale helped Charles get away from the sidelines, but he was too independent, too spiky, to be a speechwriting type. Right after Election Day 1980, I called and offered him a full-time job. His first day, and Rick's, was the day Ronald Reagan was sworn in as president. The *New Republic* gave Charles the space for the freedom of motion he craved, and he knew it immediately.

Then there was Leon. We met in 1979, when he was twenty-seven, a wunderkind at the elite Harvard Society of Fellows, whose brilliant members have included George Homans, B. F. Skinner, and Noam Chomsky, along with political intellectuals like McGeorge Bundy and Arthur Schlesinger.

Leon was writing for the *New York Review of Books*, and he'd just written an article on Hannah Arendt that was so critical of her that Bob Silvers wouldn't publish it. Arendt had died and Mary McCarthy, who was Arendt's friend and now a presiding deity at the *Review*, wouldn't have any heresy about her published in its pages. So Leon called me up, and we took to each other right away. We published the piece, and after a few years, he was writing regularly for the magazine. In 1983, I eased out our literary editor Jack Beatty and gave Leon the position.

Beatty had taken over as literary editor from my old friend Roger Rosenblatt, who had added an elegant literary stripe before he moved on to writing essays for *Time*—more lucrative, I imagine. Beatty was non-elite, a rough product of South Boston with a townie accent that seemed to say: here are my working-class bona fides, so what do you know about anything? This attitude, constantly maintained, ensured that he was never intimidated by the elite writers he worked with. Much as I admired him, there was absolutely no rapport between us.

Leon was the furthest thing from Beatty that you can imagine. He immediately he struck me as a genius. My view has not changed through the years. But he also has the liabilities of a genius: he knows he's a genius, and so he's not prone to see wisdom in other people. He'd come from Holocaust survivors in Brooklyn, where he'd attended an intensely Zionist Orthodox yeshiva. He'd been part of a group of Jewish thugs led by Meir Kahane, the ultra-Right Jewish rabbi who went out looking for street fights with anti-Jewish thugs. He told me he got in the gang not so much because he was tough but because he was tall. He was still wearing a kippah when, in 1971, he went to Columbia and met the *Partisan Review* crowd. Lionel Trilling took him under his wing: he and Diana couldn't figure out how someone who could read George Eliot could also be Orthodox. "What's a smart young man such as yourself doing with that on your head?" Lionel would say. Eventually, Leon took off the kippah, for many reasons I think. He was always a believer: it was just unclear what he believed in. I'm not sure anyone knows Leon's actual view of religion. No doubt, at bottom, it is a very constructed, very philosophical, very dense one.

When Leon went to Oxford to study philosophy, Lionel recommended him to Isaiah Berlin, who became his other mentor. Trilling and Berlin were *the* postwar intellectuals, monuments to something bigger than themselves, representatives of all the battered wisdom about idealism that Jews had come to after two wars, the Holocaust, and the founding of a new state. In politics, they were anti-Communist and anti-McCarthy. But really they were humanists. What most frightened them were totalities because they'd seen in Europe what totalities could do to human beings. Before anything, they wanted to protect the private life of individuals from overarching political theories. They wanted culture to have its own space apart from politics, and they thought the best guarantor for that cultural autonomy was the liberal welfare state.

At the magazine, Leon gave culture its own space, related to politics but not defined by it, something Left and Right journals of the time never did. He brought something else, too: the outlook of his elders but the lifestyle of his juniors; the urge, since he'd thrown off the kippah, to use his intellect to get ahead in the world in a worldly way. He liked drugs and sex; he had fabulous girlfriends. He liked the undercover gay scene, too. He wasn't gay, but he liked gay people a lot. He cultivated a personal style that was so flourishing, so over the top, it was almost performatively gay.

Together we were upstarts—young and pluralist, Jewish and intellectual, not afraid to provoke. But we also came with the imprimatur of the best institutions: Harvard, Columbia, and Oxford. We weren't like anything old Washington had ever seen. We were not on anybody's invitation list in those days. What we had was their attention. And we used it.

Those people thought they had me pegged as a smart-ass pushy Jew. But they didn't expect the heft, the sheer braininess. They didn't expect the intellectual commitment. We had in our hearts the worst atrocity in recorded history, and it affected our thinking, our approach, to the issues of the day. We were something altogether new. There had never been such a widely read magazine of Jewish journalists before.

Mike and Rick, who served as the actual editors, didn't care much about the Jewish stuff. But Charles and Leon, who identified, were the authoritative voices in the pages. So, though this was never my conscious plan, the *New Republic* was a break for identifying Jews and Zionists in Washington.

But this was in the background. What was upfront was politics, the politics of a Democratic party in transition. The Carter administration had not been able to figure out where it or its party fit in America. This had been the Democrats' problem since Hubert Humphrey: the party's base was the unions and the white working class, and the economy was changing; America was deindustrializing, becoming more and more a consumer economy. It was, increasingly, a party of the environmental and social concerns of a mobile middle class, underpinned by big financial contributors. But here, too, nothing was fixed. Republicans in 1980, on the other hand, knew exactly who they were: procapitalist, pro-American, and anti-Communist. Like a lot of things that hadn't had time to get corrupted, or really tested, by reality, the new Right was a movement of clear principles and its increasing success became a useful foil in our efforts to establish a new Democratic middle ground.

* * *

Our ambitious project attracted many talented and original thinkers. The first was Bernard-Henri Lévy. BHL came from wealth,
and like most smart and well-to-do French boys and girls, went to
École normale supérieure, where he studied with Jacques Derrida,
the leading deconstructionist thinker of the time. Then he worked
as a war correspondent for *Combat*, the magazine Albert Camus
had founded during the French-Algerian Wars, and followed this
inclination to India and eventually Bangladesh, answering André
Malraux's call to help the Bangladeshis fight for their freedom. He
wrote his first book, *Bangladesh: Nationalism in the Revolution*, and
then he spent time there working for some ministries, helping them
form their government. A few years later, the country plunged into
a series of coups and countercoups so the result of the revolution
was mixed. I imagine that this was a lesson, up close and on the
ground, for BHL—not only of the power of nationalism, which
most of the intellectual West had discarded, but of the unpredict-
ability of any revolutionary movement.

Eventually, he came back to France and wrote *Barbarism with a
Human Face*, attacking the intellectual dominance of Marxism and
arguing that the reason Marxism never created freedom was inbuilt
in the philosophy: its determinism, and its putting of systems and
positions over people and individuality, made people less important
than outcomes. It couldn't be reasoned with because it didn't believe
in reason—reason was just a scrim for power. And if you tried
to reason with it, you were accepting its terms. It could only be
rejected. This was a bold thing to write in France in 1977—and
BHL wasn't yet thirty. Of course, I loved it. I wanted him to write
for us—and he did. He was my answer to the lure of the European
Left, the Marxists or Marxist apologists like Herbert Marcuse who
still dominated the leftist imagination. BHL was also a little bit of
a showboat, you couldn't deny that. He was easy for some people to
hate. But he didn't care. And I didn't either.

My other connection with Communism's reality came through
Yugoslavia, through the enormous personage of Vladimir Dedijer,
a major figure in the Communist world. He was one of the parti-

sans who joined with Josip Broz Tito to fight the Nazi occupiers. When he broke with Tito, he became a figure in the non-Communist world as well, embraced by Eleanor Roosevelt and other people of international stature. When I knew him, he was living, grandly, in exile, as a comrade of Jean-Paul Sartre, even though they were willing to let him back in Yugoslavia.

I met Vlado through H. Stuart Hughes, who'd known him from the OSS during the war. He was immensely charming. But he was unreliable; he had fantasies. Vlado lived in Cambridge for a while, and one night he called to tell us he'd just been shot at. I suggested he call the police, but he said no. "Who shot at you?" I asked. Well, the Yugoslav government, of course. Or maybe the CIA. I don't think there was any shot. I think really it was that we hadn't called him in a couple of weeks. He was a liar, but he lied mostly to himself. In family life, he was impossible: the personality traits that circumstance had forged in him made him awful as a father, and two of his sons killed themselves.

Anne, her kids, and I were "there" for the suicide of his son Boro, who was then in his twenties. My brother, Gerry, was hiking with Boro in the mountains near the Slovenian town of Bohinj, where Vlado and his family had a summer home. Anne and I were elsewhere on the mountain but nearby. Suddenly we heard Gerry screaming that Boro had jumped. When we met up he said, "This was deliberate." An ambulance came, but it carried a dead man away. Vlado immediately "decided" that the political police had pushed him. But there were no political police. We had all seen the argumentative prelude between father and son. Vlado's life had been rocked enough by brute forces to rationalize this fantasizing, no matter what it did to those around him. Some of it, how much I can't be sure, was because of the awful system he was forced to exist within, to define himself against.

My anti-Communism was out of step with the times because the Communists in general, and the Soviets specifically, got a lot of cover from the Left and also from the genteel Establishment, which was, like it was on every hard issue, for some kind of détente. I could never understand this: it seemed like a bizarre affectation because in my mind, always, were the ethnic minorities crushed beneath totalizing Soviet dogma, and us doing nothing to rescue them. I wouldn't be quiet about it.

Communism was much in the news in 1981. Ronald Reagan, who brought his party into power on a hard anti-Soviet position, had reignited all the political flash points that had been dormant since the Kennedys. First and foremost was the issue of nuclear weapons, which again brought out the moralists on both sides. With Reagan in office, nuclear freeze became a cause célèbre of the Left. But like Kennedy, Reagan (and Kissinger) took seriously the nuclear threat, and in 1983 he announced a plan for a missile defense shield called Star Wars.

There were howls against it from the Left as an escalation of the nuclear arms race. But I was in a different place than I had been with Stuart Hughes twenty years before. By now it was clear to me that the Left thought the only threat was America's nuclear weapons; they were completely blind to the intentions of the Soviet Union. The only responsible people, for all of their irresponsibility in proposing this very unrealistic defense expenditure, were the Reaganites. I didn't want to support them, either. So we took a two-prong strategy. Charles went on the attack against the nuclear freeze, which took care of the Left. And Leon followed up with a book-length piece that was a dazzling freestyle performance. It criticized both the Star Wars proponents and the nuclear freeze proponents as idealists: totalizing thinkers who were looking for a single answer to a complex question. He argued that deterrence—maintaining nuclear weapons—was necessary because it submitted to the reality of a world of opposing states. But arms reduction was also demanded to lower the chances and opportunities of using nuclear weapons because it submitted to the reality that someday deterrence might not work. The argument wasn't a contradiction: it was holding two positions in tension. It showed we weren't typical leftists, not sentimental or doctrinaire, and that we could outthink the Right.

That same year, there was another flashback to the Kennedy era: a conflict in Latin America that divided Right and Left. The story and the competing principles were much the same as in Cuba twenty years before, only the location had changed to Nicaragua. The Sandinistas, who took their name from the hero of the resistance to the US occupation of Nicaragua fifty years before, had overthrown Anastasio Somoza, like Batista a corrupt right-winger, and were running the country. Daniel Ortega was the president and his brother Humberto ran the army. Like the Castro brothers, the Ortegas were unapologetic Marxists who purged the moderates from their party and ruled by decree.

In late 1983, an independent scholar named Bob Leiken, a friend of mine from his days as a Harvard undergraduate (when his tutor was the sub rosa fascist Paul de Man), sent me reports on crimes being committed under the Communist Nicaraguan regime that were being whitewashed and suppressed in the Left press. It looked to me like Nicaragua was not just a repeat of Cuba but a mirror image of the Soviet bloc. The facts came from a source I trusted: Bob was a labor community organizer, a strong anti-Communist, and an adventurous man intellectually.

The Nicaragua issue was as explosive as nukes. People at *The Nation*, the Left's magazine for longer than the *New Republic* had existed, was once again denouncing American imperialism in Latin America. To them, the Sandinistas were latter-day Castros, heroic resisters of America's imperial designs.

Reagan's people took the opposite stance: they'd come in determined to support anti-Communists, and they'd been funneling money to the Contras. The man in charge of policy toward the Contras was Elliott Abrams, a right-wing State Department official and the son-in-law of Norman Podhoretz, who, like his father-in-law, tended to the doctrinaire. Norman, who had moved from being zealous and literary and Left to zealous and political and Right, supported the policy of the government in the pages of *Commentary*. The *Public Interest*—founded by Dan Bell and his old City College comrade, Irving Kristol—did too.

Norman had made over *Commentary* in the image of his new politics. The magazine was dogmatic, and it's not a coincidence that Norman was a migrant from the doctrinaire Left: his approach hadn't changed, he'd just found a new catechism. As for the *Public Interest*, which was really the inventive intellectual organ of the New Right, Irving had his friends Nat, Dan, and occasionally Pat Moynihan to offer skepticism toward Democratic shibboleths in foreign and domestic policy.

These were clear political and intellectual battle lines with recognizable players—*The Nation* and the *New York Review* versus *Commentary* and the *Public Interest*, Left versus Right. The *New Republic* waded in every so often in favor of the Reagan administration and this was one of those times. We ran Leiken's piece as "Sins of the Sandinistas" and it hit immediately. It went to members of Congress and the White House, which loved it. The Left went crazy, and so did a lot of people in our own office, who were worried that my zeal for anti-Communism would put us in bed with right-wing authoritarian types.

What was going on in Nicaragua wasn't completely clear. The Contras were old Somocistas, the ancient régime, who were fighting for their old place in society against the Sandinistas who had displaced them. Both sides claimed authority, and from the point of view of an ordinary Nicaraguan, no doubt, the main difference between them was rhetoric, not reality. But even though I didn't support authoritarians, I hated totalitarians more. Authoritarians will leave people alone as long as they conform on the outside; totalitarians won't—they'll tell you what you have to think. I didn't like the Contras, but they weren't totalitarians; the Sandinistas were Soviet puppets, which meant they had totalitarian instincts.

A war started in our office over Nicaragua, in the editorial meetings and in our pages. In 1985, Jeff Morley—one of Rick's hires, whose conspiratorial, anti-American politics I absolutely despised, but, like other people I despised, I tolerated—ran a long interview with a former Contra who trashed the rebels as CIA dupes. Seven months later, Charles, backed by me and Leon, wrote a full editorial endorsing the Reagan administration's position on the Contras: we weren't sending ground troops; it wasn't another Vietnam. But we were helping people who were fighting for their freedom to make a stand. This was Bernard-Henri Lévy's stance too. Around this time, he gathered a group of intellectuals from France, England, Spain, and Luxembourg to sign an open letter that he placed in *Le Monde* against the Sandinistas and for the Contras.

Back in Washington, Mike wrote an unsigned column calling our editorial "preposterous." The next week, Jeff Morley wrote another critique of the editorial. The week after we ran a follow-up editorial that answered the criticisms. The next week Mike and I wrote dueling pieces. The follow-up to that included a letter to the editor authored by Rick and signed by a bunch of contributing editors, Michael Walzer among them, that objected to the pro-Contra position. A couple of months later, Elliott Abrams wrote me:

> *Your editorials on Central America must shock your readers, for they are totally contradicted by numerous articles on the subject printed in the* New Republic. *I do not subscribe to* The Nation *because I cannot abide this kind of journalism. While you are permitting it in your pages, and indeed promoting it in cover stories, please delete my name from your subscriber list.*

Some people don't understand the function of vigorous debate in a democracy. But this was not my problem. At the same time, I was having a lively exchange of views with my former students, Michael Kazin and Todd Gitlin, on a piece they had written about the *New Republic*'s support of the Contras. Here was their stance in a private letter sent to me by Kazin:

> *As for your comment on certain Contras, our point was that it sounded precisely like the "Ho Chi Minh, live like him" stuff we (or at least I) used to mouth twenty years back. While I'm no admirer of Ortega and his crew, I fail to understand how a guerilla army organized by the likes of Casey, Abrams and North will bring real democracy to Nicaragua.*

The contradictions existed—but in a way that was the point, even if it made us enemies on both sides. It was the cost of doing business when you ran a magazine whose subscribers and contributors came from the Establishment and the Left. And our business was argument at the level of philosophies, of worldviews, of conflicts that couldn't be elided and couldn't be reduced.

And through all the noise of argument, we had a bottom line: we thought totalisms were the worst thing there was, and we thought sustaining a society of multiplicity meant taking a firm line against totalisms, wherever, whenever, and in whatever guise they existed.

It was a very Jewish philosophical line to take. Jewish thought throughout the ages was oppositional, discordant, argumentative, and intricate—you came to solutions by arguing with yourself.

People couldn't predict what we'd say each week, and the magazine's reputation was "eminent" enough that whatever side we came down on could use us for support. Congresspeople read us, senators read us, the White House read us. "Even the liberal *New Republic*…" was a catchphrase for Republicans ginning up support for anti-Communist policies. I was happy with that because it served a double purpose: it helped advance the policies, and it made anti-Communism something my side of the argument, the Democrats, had to take seriously again.

* * *

Domestically, we took the same course. I never lost my midcentury liberalism; I just tried to adapt it. This put me in between three extremes.

The ideological Right, the Reaganites and Podhoretzes, were standing on the midcentury successes of liberal government (interstate highways, the G.I. Bill, Social Security) even as they wanted to curtail the state that made it possible. Liberals clung to the Kennedy legacy, upheld in public by supporting players like Goodwin and Schlesinger, believers in the government as the unifying force in an increasingly fractured American society. It was the mirror image of the Reaganite faith in capitalism, a vision that rinsed any pluralism or complexity out of the state-market synthesis that made America work. And the Left, shut out of any power, gnashed its teeth and doubled down on its distrust of America. We weren't like that: we let the new ideological arguments in as long as they didn't reject the faith entirely. But we held the midcentury faith—with adaptations that were meant to push our party, the Democrats, back towards political relevance and coherence.

One way we did this was to compromise on economics: Republicans were winning that argument and thoughtful Democrats were beginning to wonder if in order for the welfare state to be sustained, it was going to have to be smaller. Instead, we focused on the issues that Democrats increasingly talked about, especially as the makeup of the party started to change from old-line unionists or anti-Vietnam leftists to college-educated, white-collar professionals. Those issues were social—about the way free individuals, individuals of David Riesman's America, identified. But we didn't take the easy route on these issues: we pushed against the grain.

The obvious social issue was race, which had shifted away from an economic argument and toward questions of individuation: how were black Americans represented in America's culture, society, economy, and politics? We, like the midcentury liberal Democratic Party, were for racial equality but wary of racial preference. The idea of government, the market, or culture defining people by their membership in racial groups seemed exactly like what the civil rights movement had been created to transcend.

Our stance had two prongs. The first was cultural: to represent black artists because of their brilliance and not their blackness. One of the most controversial pieces Leon ran in the back of the book was Stanley Crouch's attack on Miles Davis. It was immensely controversial. Though many had gone after Davis since his embrace of jazz fusion in the late 1960s, no previous critic had dared to say anything as sacrilegious as: "Beyond the terrible performances and the terrible recordings, Davis has also become the most remarkable licker of monied boots in the music business." You wouldn't find something like that at any other place that boasted a liberal and left-wing audience: a critique of one black artist's and intellectual's work by another, not deferring to political or social niceties. And Stanley, despite his cutting words, was not a contrarian for the sake of contrariness: he wrote from a position of deep respect—for jazz, for Davis.

The second prong was social, and it hinged on the major social issue when it came to race, and so the major racial issue in America: affirmative action. We published Glenn Loury, already a young superstar partly owing to a piece he published in the *New Republic* in 1984, at the age of thirty-one, called "A New American Dilemma." It was a reexamination of *The American Dilemma*, a 1944 book by the Nobel Prize winner Gunnar Myrdal, which argued that race was the fundamental fissure running through the ideals of the American republic. Now, forty years later, after a civil rights revolution, Loury was defining a new American dilemma over race:

Today the civil rights debate is dominated by the issue of affirmative action, in which the question is whether the history of racism warrant special—not simply equal—treatment for blacks.... The bottom stratum of the black community has compelling problems which can no longer be blamed solely on white racism, and which force us to confront fundamental failures in black society. The social disorganization among poor blacks, the lagging academic performance of black students, the disturbingly high rate of black-on-black crime, and the alarming increase in early unwed pregnancies among blacks now looms as the primary obstacles to progress.... If the new American dilemma is not dealt with soon, we may face the possibility of a permanent split in our political system along racial lines.

For someone like Glenn, then and now, there were very few places to be his own intellectual force, and he was grateful for "the brilliance of the writing in the magazine, the uniquely sensible and sensitive political perspectives regularly to be found in your pages, and my own stake in the journal's reputation..." I was grateful to him, too, for helping us flag a problem, the underclass of the inner cities, which politicians were distorting to get votes.

The distortions were on both sides. Republicans had been hostile to affirmative action and the post-civil rights policies that funneled government dollars to the inner cities. The Left-liberal response in *The Nation*, or certain faculty lounges, to any question about the efficacy of Democratic policies was to say it was an attack on black America. Glenn wasn't afraid to criticize the Reagan administration for, say, their early stance on a compromise extension of the Voting Rights Act. But he also pushed them to continue conservative policies he thought did some good: "enterprise zones, a sub-minimum wage for the hard-to-employ, ownership possibilities for responsible public housing tenants." In the context of political realities, this was a brave thing to write.

Eventually I found another cause I was willing to push for—or really to allow the *New Republic* writers to push for, and to back them when they did. It was so thoroughly ignored by the Right, by the Establishment, and by most parts of the Left that Washington didn't yet define it as a political issue. And it was personal to me. It was the issue that would become gay rights, and its most obvious manifestation was AIDS.

It was unfathomable—so many people were dying and sick, cut off from their families—and it seemed like there was no way out. The sick were dying horrible deaths, and more people were getting infected every year. The hysteria was everywhere. According to the media, anybody who'd ever kissed a gay guy had AIDS. My son Jesse was then in high school, and he came home one day literally shaking: a professor on the Harvard medical faculty, John Mack, had spoken at a school assembly and had warned the boys and girls against kissing. Kissing, he said, could be a gateway to AIDS. On the spot, I called my friend at Harvard Medical School, Jerry Groopman, who would become a leading AIDS researcher. I told him what John Mack had said, and he said, "Bullshit."

The Republicans didn't care about AIDS: they were irritated by it, they dismissed it, and they thought it was gay people's fault. The polemicists among them, like William Buckley, worried that gayness, if it was "out," would feminize the culture. At the height of the epidemic, in the *New York Times*, he called for anyone who tested positive to be tattooed on the buttock as a public health measure. But we had at our magazine a man of the Right who was just as witty, intelligent, and pugnacious as Buckley, yet bucked the trend. I'd met him when he was a graduate student at Harvard, and he'd interned for us before coming on full time. His name was Andrew Sullivan. He was an Irish Catholic Thatcher supporter and an Oxford graduate; and he was gay.

Henry Fairlie was our resident Tory writer. He thought some of the New Right's reforms were too socially radical to be really conservative, while the Kennedy Democrats were focused on the "exaltation of the power of the state." Henry was a sharp, eloquent writer and a raging drunk. He'd burned through everything in his life and was sleeping on a couch in our offices, working on an electric typewriter while chain-smoking his way to the grave. He treated Andrew like a long-lost son and heir. He was also a robust heterosexual, and when Andrew came out of the closet, Henry was so disappointed that he wrote Andrew a letter of actual dismay.

Leon and Andrew became friends, too. They both had studied with political philosophical giants from Oxford—Andrew did his dissertation on Michael Oakeshott, Isaiah Berlin's conservative intellectual rival—and they both saw, and respected, each other's approach to their respective religions. Leon was a devout but not exactly rigorously observant Jew. Andrew was a committed Catholic who gave himself freedom to sin as he chose. Andrew also liked Mike Kinsley because they were both witty but deadly serious, and he got along with Rick, whom he'd first met at the Kennedy School during Rick's sabbatical from the magazine. Andrew, who was just in the process of coming out but was dating a woman, asked Rick for advice, which Rick, a certified expert on women, was glad to give.

Intellectually, Andrew, like Fairlie, was a manifestation of a current of British influence at the magazine. It was a kind of skeptical conservatism inherited from Edmund Burke that was very much about organic evolution; the view from a country that hadn't been successfully invaded in a thousand years. Mike had the style: the unassailable dryness, the willingness to cut through inflated ideologies. Henry had the philosophy. Andrew, more philosophical than Mike and hipper than Henry, was their inheritor.

Andrew was also very involved in New York's and Washington's undercover gay scene. He had good friends who'd gotten sick and died as he ministered to them. In 1986, at his urging, we put a pink triangle against a black background on our cover. We knew it went to virtually every member of Congress, even Jesse Helms, the arch-conservative Dixiecrat Republican senator from North Carolina who was a notorious homophobe. A while later, Mike and Andrew were having some discussion about gay relationships and Andrew said, "Why don't we just have the right to marry? It's the obvious institution to get us mainstream." Mike immediately said, "Write that. It'll piss off all the right people, on the Right and the Left."

An article like this was a risk for Andrew, and a risk for me. If you wrote about homosexuality, it was automatically assumed that you must be gay, or were somehow connected to gays, which was partly why nobody wrote about it. A lot of people suspected, among my friends and even in the gutter press, that I was gay: Gore Vidal told the *Washington Post* that I was the uncrowned queen of

Israel, and nobody minded that it was a lowball comment because at the *Post* they thought of me as an antagonist. Around the same time, Henry Fairlie told *Vanity Fair* that the *New Republic* was like a Greek gymnasium. Fairlie said it because it was funny—he didn't mind if it wasn't accurate. So an article supporting gay marriage would bring attention to the *New Republic* and might bring attention to me personally in a way I didn't want: it might bring the rumors in the gutter press into the mainstream.

The other risk was that the piece might fall flat. There wasn't a clear audience for a pro-gay marriage argument. The Right didn't want to hear about gays—it wanted to send them to conversion therapy. The Left thought marriage was a bourgeois institution, a throwback. But Mike kept prodding Andrew. He kept saying, "Write this. You won't have the balls to in ten years' time." I said go ahead and Andrew did, and we put it on the cover. There was a huge fuss. It was the first cover story on the subject ever to appear in the "mainstream" American media, and it prodded the idea into Washington.

I didn't identify as part of the gay rights movement. I hadn't thought much about the subject after the first time I'd seen gay rights protestors on the Commons. Still, I wanted gays to be out in the culture, literally and otherwise. And I wanted to publish Andrew's article because it was the kind of move that meant something—introducing to the national debate an issue that hadn't occurred to anybody and making it something the Establishment couldn't ignore. Thirty years later, gay marriage is legal in all fifty states under a 2015 Supreme Court decision. I'm proud of the small part we played.

CHAPTER NINE

Washington, D.C.: Recruiters

As the years went by, we settled into a rhythm of provocation: the staff expanded, the editors hired people who agreed with their views or who shared their style, and the arguments between the editors became choruses of tonal dissonance that somehow held together, like something out of Schoenberg. We made room for anyone who wasn't a dogmatist, especially after Rick decided to make the *New Republic* officially "a journal of opinion," which meant that we could put forward a clear editorial stance and also dissents: you would see different opinions and not be confused about where the magazine stood.

Mike and I brought in Mort Kondracke and Fred Barnes, center-rightists with a line to the Reagan White House. Rick loved Sidney Blumenthal, who I hadn't seen since the New Politics Convention, and promoted him to cover politics. Rick also brought in Bob Kuttner, from the Left, on economics, and of course Jeff Morley of the Contra arguments, who was haughty in his skepticism about America's foreign policy and thought he had a map to the future. Thirty-five years later, the future is here, and it's not the way it looked on his map. Charles didn't recruit people, but he brought in a readership increasingly from the Right—readers like him: former Democrats who were tired of the New Left and had lost faith in liberal social programs.

I brought in Paul Berman, who would have been nobody's choice but mine: a socialist, a Jew, and ten years younger than me. He was a regular writer for marginal but intellectually cutting publications like the *New Leader*. It was the English language hangout for the Russian Menshevik exiles from the Soviet Union and their American acolytes that, unlike *The Nation* and the earlier *New Republic*, knew the truth about Soviet Russia. Paul grew up on this brand of socialism, and his hero was Emma Goldman, despite her disdain for her fellow Jews. He was never afraid that a decent leftism didn't match up with reality; he thought it should, and he had an exuberance about his writing, a realness, that I think came from not being trained in a PhD program.

Leon was recruiting for the back of the book. In a break with book review custom, he didn't outsource pieces on the developing world or black America to Anglo writers with expertise: he went directly to the source. He had the best people in the field at a time when their voices were starting to break through, and he gave them a platform: Mario Vargas Llosa, Octavio Paz, Derek Walcott, Skip Gates, Stanley Crouch, John McWhorter, Caryl Phillips, Wynton Marsalis, Albert Murray, Glenn Loury, Juan Williams, Shiva Naipaul, Amartya Sen, Amitav Ghosh, Anita Desai, Ahmed Rashid. Beat that, *New York Review*; beat that, *New Yorker*.

I was sometimes an editor and sometimes a publisher. I didn't really run the magazine, not when it got going. First of all, I still lived in Cambridge. I was teaching half the time and another quarter I was spending in New York. A big misunderstanding everybody has about running a magazine is that the person in charge gets to be a tyrant. I had veto power on a couple of subjects, but besides that it was always a negotiation. Finally, most importantly, I had a method: I believed in getting talented people, putting them into play and letting things ride. It always seemed like a risk worth taking.

Early on, I'd sold Harrison's Victorian house for a profit and moved us into a place almost across the street: a new six-story glass building built in the real estate boom that opened up the city around the time Reagan arrived. I decided I didn't want hierarchy, so the interns sat together on one side of a pit in the hallway; on the other side of the pit were the business offices, run by a splendid woman named Joan Stapleton. I was in the front around the corner, Mike and then Rick were at the bend, Leon was on the opposite side along with Charles, and nearby were Fred Barnes, Mort Kondracke, and eventually Andrew. "The Avenue of the Righteous Gentiles" is what Leon called that stretch. Laura Obolensky, my assistant, was a Russian aristocrat from an ancient family that got out before Lenin. She would work next door to me, but when I wasn't in the office, I'd sometimes call her in the middle of the week from Cambridge with a "What's up?" just to talk and drive her mad.

Every week had a fixed rhythm. We'd crawl to deadline on Wednesday evening and Thursday there would be the magazine, which meant we got the payoff right away. It made the intense conflicts seem to matter even more because they all had such immediate outcomes. The editors and I clashed over all sorts of things in the run-up to publication: Mike said a piece, written by a friend of the woman I'd sat next to at a dinner party a couple weeks before that, was terrible but I wanted him to run it. Or it was a report from Arnaud de Borchgrave, a right-wing adventurer and raconteur who'd write foreign stories that I found intriguing and Rick found preposterous. Or John Callahan, who each time an anniversary of Gene McCarthy's campaign rolled around wanted to write something to remind the Democrats. No one at the magazine except Leon much cared for McCarthy anymore. But I did. I knew he was important, and I made sure John's piece went in.

Sometimes I won our fights, sometimes one or another editor did. But the basic principle was: "My bullshit goes in, so does yours." Then we'd close the magazine and go downstairs to The Palm. Rick's and Charles's first day, on Reagan's inauguration, I took everybody out, and Henry Fairlie got drunk, pounded the table, and insulted us all. That was a pretty normal day.

And the energy in the office bristled through the pages—it got us attention and made people want to read us and to write for us, too. Politics aside, we got real writers and reporters: Michael Lewis, Ann Hulbert, Dorothy Wickenden, Tim Noah. David Samuels gained attention with a cover story on rap music that's still lauded and controversial. Lewis, who's absolutely huge now and certainly no less a stylist, had originally written to Mike Kinsley when he was about to graduate from Princeton asking to do a piece, and eventually Mike commissioned from him a piece called "When Bad Things Happen to Rich People." From there he got the contract to write his first book, *Liar's Poker*.

We were famous. This was the first time that journalists were regularly on TV. National media had come to Washington, D.C. at about the same time as the Reaganites and the real estate boom, and naturally I encouraged my people to go on TV: it was free advertising. They parlayed the notoriety from these appearances into shockingly lucrative speaking gigs, and Mike commissioned Jake Weisberg, an intern, to do a piece on the gigs, even though Mike was one of the guys getting the gigs. Two of the four people on *The McLaughlin Group*, the first real Washington talk show, were Mort Kondracke and Mike Kinsley. So we weren't afraid of the blowback, even against ourselves, which was a great feeling to have.

Our readers were almost constantly angry at us for something. Charles suggested that we should have an intern choose the most vitriolic cancellation letter, publish it, and then cancel the subscription without a refund. But more readers came than left because we were so hot, and they could trust us to be in the thick of whatever was happening. We even looked good, which was one of the things Rick gave the magazine: he made it glossy, interesting, and contemporary while retaining the old-fashioned layout and serif body type to satisfy the older subscribers. When it came to magazine operations, I farmed it out to other people to buy paper, pay the rent, and negotiate with printers. I did get involved in the selling of ads, but that merely meant speaking to people who were already my friends: I'd call Larry Tisch and say, "Hey Larry, do you want to buy an ad?"

We never made money: this was an accepted fact. The two years or so we were in the black, I threw a party to celebrate, and it put us back in the red. Occasionally I'd keep a lookout for a silent partner who might offset some of the losses. At one point I hired Richard Holbrooke—who was then working at Lehman Brothers after serving as assistant secretary of state for East Asian and Pacific affairs under Jimmy Carter—to act as an intermediary between the magazine and potential partners. Through Holbrooke, I found myself talking to the Canadian press magnate Conrad Black, long before he went to prison but when he was already a name. It was odd and ironic that a committed liberal like Holbrooke would try to set me up with a conservative like Black. But he did. Black was very nice, very intelligent, very right wing, and of course it was out of the question: our readership would have gone crazy. I would have gone crazy. I liked to push my readers from the Right, but I wasn't an ideologue. There's a point to which you can push people to think beyond their beliefs, and this was that point.

But pushing was what we did at the magazine, and it created a fascinating environment, especially for the interns. We practiced, in those years, a kind of friendly nepotism. We found brilliant people and made them members of our extended community, helping them on their careers so that they eventually might help run and analyze United States commerce, culture, and government: it was our way, like Dan Bell had said, of humanizing the technocracy. These interns would sit in the editorial meetings, arguing along with the rest of us—young people, a few of whom I'd taken from Harvard, who now got to be in a different seminar, one with an effect on national policy.

They were remarkable people. Emily Yoffe, fresh from Wellesley, was an early hire. Years later, she reminded me that I stopped by her desk one day and told her that I liked her work, that she came at things from an "acute angle." Larry Grafstein, a Harvard student who'd taken my class twice, and who was going into law and business, kept coming back to the *New Republic*—in 1982, 1983, and 1984—because he told me that nowhere else could you find a place where people were this happy and civil even as they fought and impressed each other. He told me it made him better—it made everybody better—and it made him excited to come to work at a place this earthy, intellectual, and extreme. And he used our craziness to his advantage: he made connections among future journalists that were rare for a person who had his eye on a career in finance. For example, one of his co-interns was Bart Gellman, and another was Amity Shlaes, who was there in the summer of 1983 and now is an intellectual star known for her conservative reinterpretations of the New Deal. Another one of those years, Larry interned with Jason DeParle, who went on to make himself the most authoritative and sensitive interpreter of migration in America.

Later there were others: James Bennet, whose name readers of yesterday's *New York Times* will know, Dana Milbank, and Antony Blinken, whose name is much in the news these days as secretary of state. Tony is a careful man, a little too careful for me. But maybe a secretary of state should be. I met him at Harvard, where he was bright and easy to get on with—which is not true of everyone you meet at Harvard. He worked at the *New Republic* for a year after graduating. "Blinken is an immensely talented writer with what is at once a fast and deep intelligence," I wrote in a recommendation letter for him. "At the *New Republic* Blinken's record would be extraordinary even if he were an older journalist. But for someone so young what he accomplished was, as I watched it, simply exhilarating." My letter didn't help at 02138, and he went to Columbia Law School instead.

All that arguing took its toll on the main players. Leon and Charles quit speaking to each other over a fight they had about Israeli Prime Minister Yitzhak Shamir calling the Palestinians "grasshoppers." Charles said Shamir was quoting from the Bible, Leon said it didn't matter, and they both wrote pieces against each other. The whole place was on eggshells. Charles and Rick got into a giant fight about the nuclear freeze. Charles came close to saying it was a Soviet plot, or at least that the freeze people were fellow travelers, and Rick never forgave him. It turned nasty and petty. One day when Rick was out of the office, a technician came to set up some new computers, and Charles had him set the unchangeable password for the master hard drive to "Kemp," after Jack Kemp, the conservative congressman who was just then making his name. Rick never forgot that, either.

Mike constantly wanted to fire Leon because he thought Leon ran his section like a fiefdom and ignored popular culture—which was true. But why would you mess with success? Rick and I would argue constantly. But then we'd let it pass and go back to work. We liked each other too much for any hate to seep in. As for Leon, he was intellectually aggressive, and he understood me completely, which sometimes made me uncomfortable. But living with discomforts was one of my strengths. I had the most interesting group of friends and most of them were much smarter than me. I never really minded if some discomfort was the cost.

Bruised egos are the price you pay for good argument, and it all bears such immediate fruit. I'd walk down the hall, and I'd hear Mike and Charles arguing some point, always intensely but without anger, getting down to the root of where they differed: an opposing philosophy of human nature, a different idea of what the state is for.

But the contentious atmosphere we fostered in the office could put off outsiders. Here is Saul Bellow, irate at Leon, writing to me:

> In reviewing my last novel Leon said that I was a misogynist, a racist, a sexist, a colonialist, a reactionary, and he charged me with disliking our country and just about everything else he could think of short of downright treason. He was not satisfied with attacking my book which he had a Constitutional right to do. He went on to identify me with every bad thing he could think of. Well, that is journalism at a point where it borders on show biz....I don't know quite how to describe Leon's case, whether he needs a psychiatrist or a demonologist. As horrors go, this one is relatively low on the scale. (This is one of the odd things about our century of horrors—wars and genocides have made everything else look trivial.) Yet Leon is the literary editor of The New Republic, and there are rules of conduct to observe. You don't tear a man's reputation to tatters because you don't like his novel.

Mostly, it was a bright time. Our people entered the Washington firmament. After "Nuclear War, Nuclear Peace," which was eventually published as a book and got a favorable review from McGeorge Bundy in the *New York Times*, Leon became a man about town. Washington didn't have that many deep intellectuals, and Leon was a star. He met people, and he charmed them—in Washington and outside of it, men and women alike. We'd be in a staff meeting, and Shirley MacLaine would be on the phone for Leon. He'd rush out of the room, and the place would explode in laughter.

Mike eventually ended up on *Crossfire*—the first of the truly big, argumentatively political TV shows, where he played the liberal to Pat Buchanan's conservative. Once we were on a trip to Saudi Arabia and we ended up in Dhahran, which was an encampment for employees of Aramco, like a suburb in Southern California only in Saudi Arabia. They had American TV, and *Crossfire* was on every night, so everyone knew Mike. We got invited to a big dinner at someone's house and Mike was a movie star: the kids literally jumped all over him.

Charles left the magazine in 1987 to write for the *Washington Post*, where he won a Pulitzer. He was a perfect choice for them: he knew what he believed, he was articulate, droll, and fierce about it, and he had an audience.

Rick left on less good terms, and he didn't stay in Washington. He went to teach at the Kennedy School at Harvard. He'd spent five years holding a Left-liberal line at the magazine. It was, between Charles and Leon and Mike and me, an uphill battle. But then, a few years later, Rick came back. Everybody came back eventually.

When the incredibly talented Mort Kondracke left his full-time post as an editor and writer with us to work at the *Washington Post*, he sent me a letter of thanks, calling me "an alchemist of talent at TNR. You don't produce pure gold from the ingredients you find and mix, but a very precious metal."

❋   ❋   ❋

The magazine community extended outside the offices. After a stint as a lawyer at the Department of Energy during the Carter administration, Jamie Gorelick was now working for a law firm again, and she would come by for editorial meetings or to hear a speaker I brought in to address the staff. Tom Williamson would sometimes stop by. He'd also become a lawyer and worked for the Department of Energy under Carter, and he had then gone back into private practice at Covington and Burling. They were the brilliant, young civil servants whom I knew would someday staff the upper echelons of a Democratic administration.

Then there were the politicians.

In 1976, Pat Moynihan had won a US Senate seat from New York in a tough race, especially the primary. His Democratic opponents were Paul O'Dwyer, who was the brother of Mayor William O'Dwyer, and was certainly a Communist or at least a fellow traveler; Ramsey Clark, who was already a left-winger, certifiably nuts; and Abe Hirschfeld, who would later run unsuccessfully for every position from New York state comptroller to Manhattan borough president. Plus, of course, the adored, broad-rimmed, hat-wearing Bella Abzug, the congresswoman from the Upper West Side, who thought her Zionism made up for her fellow traveling.

Pat had made the fight against poverty the center of his political life, and it's ironic that lefties like Bella would go after such a palpably progressive politician. But they did, and they were self-righteous about it. I went in support of Pat to some debate at the Commodore or Biltmore Hotel. I lingered before I went in, and Bella Abzug was climbing the stairs breathlessly. As soon as she saw me, she started shouting, "Fuck YOU! Fuck YOU! Fuck YOU!" She still lost, and Pat came to Washington for four terms as a senator. He would drop in on the editorial meetings sometimes. He was the rare real intellectual in Washington politics and a moralist in international politics and domestic affairs. His arrival for me was another sign of a cultivated, responsible liberal center coming back from low ebb.

In 1988, Nita Lowey, who used to be Nita Melnikoff when she, Emily Cohen, and I made a group together on the Grand Concourse, entered the Democratic primary for US representative in New York's 17th Congressional District in Westchester. Her opponent was a man named Hamilton Fish V, who was Republican political royalty: his grandfather, Hamilton Fish III, was a Republican congressman from Dutchess County who opposed involvement in the Second World War until after Pearl Harbor. Ham V had executed the old Protestant aristocratic move Left, but Ham III wasn't having it. He publicly called his grandson a Communist and came out against him. Ham V was a tall, imposing scion of the aristocracy: he thought it would all come to him. But it didn't, courtesy of a Jewish girl from the Grand Concourse, on whose behalf I was doing all I could.

Finally, there was Al Gore, at the crest of a new wave of Democrats who were starting to respond to a changing political reality. The party still controlled Congress, as it had for generations. But it was the Reaganites who had momentum: they had tapped into the mobile, consumer tendencies of voters who exhibited little solidarity. A cohort of mostly new arrivals on the Hill were positioning themselves as alternatives to either Tip O'Neill's fading Democratic Party of wards and unions or George McGovern's reflexive Left politics that didn't make as much sense now that we were out of Vietnam. They were willing to listen to Republican critiques of the welfare state: they would say that Communism was worse than capitalism, that they were not hostile to the increasingly powerful corporate sector, and that they were against high taxes. They increasingly came from high-earning professional coteries who cared about social issues. They weren't necessarily following our lead at the *New Republic*. But we were pulling these Democrats on ideas, and they were increasingly pulling the party on politics.

They were called the New Democrats. One was Gary Hart, whose challenge to Walter Mondale at the 1984 convention exploded after he was photographed in the arms of a woman who was not his wife. Another was John Kerry, though you couldn't really tell if he was a New Democrat because he would say different things to different people. Another was Joe Biden, who was settling into his Senate seat as a relative moderate, an old-fashioned, back-slapping, working-class pol who wasn't perceived as hostile to suburbia or capitalism. And there was Al, who had left law school early to run for a seat in Congress, been elected to the House seat in 1976 that his father held twenty years earlier, and arrived in the Senate in 1984. He came into the Senate in the same class as John Kerry, but because Kerry succeeded Paul Tsongas, a New Democrat battling cancer, and Tsongas resigned a day early, John was considered more senior than Al and got a spot on the Foreign Relations Committee. He and Al disliked each other, I think intensely, though I'm sure each of them would deny it.

Al and I saw each other often but not regularly in Washington: he was a new congressman, I was a new publisher, and we were both busy. He passed my stuff around in Congress; I strategized with him over issues he could make his own. I was beginning to see Al as a plausible, more than plausible, standard bearer—a leader to take on the mantle of the Democratic Party as a kind of counter-Kennedy. He'd been raised a Washington prince. But unlike Jack or Bobby, nobody ever thought of him as the anointed one.

Al was more like Gene McCarthy than anyone I'd ever met. His politics were centered on managing transitions in American life: he used his intellectual training to understand the concepts behind them and his practical, expert imagination to start proposing solutions. He'd been focused on the environment since the 1970s, when he entered the House of Representatives, and he held the very first hearings on climate change. Al's religion had taught him reverence for nature. What modernity did to nature, in his view, was the most potent expression of what modernity did to the self: it split us, and alienated us from ourselves. Al's advocacy was bolstered by new science that he had trouble getting his old-line Democratic colleagues interested in. Once some of them actually fell asleep during his presentation.

He also started to write legislation supporting the internet, which had begun as a project of the Advanced Research Projects Agency, an arm of the Pentagon. The ARPANET was a robust network of computers, created to preserve data connections in the event of the Cold War getting hot. Al listened to the scientists who created the network, and he imagined its potential, maybe its inevitability, when it came to the society at large.

I wanted to be helpful to Al, to find ways to lengthen his exposure as well as to fill in the area where he was less of an expert: foreign affairs, the area that Democrats had ceded to the Republicans ten or even fifteen years before. In 1987, right before he turned forty, Al started positioning himself to run for the Democratic nomination for president in 1988 as a forward-seeing Democrat domestically and a tough one abroad.

* * *

The *New Republic* celebrated its seventieth anniversary in 1984 with a big party at the National Portrait Gallery. Al spoke, and so did Henry Kissinger. Gene McCarthy was there, and Bill Bradley. Irving Kristol was there, and so was Barney Frank, who'd succeeded Robert Drinan in Congress. Renata Adler came, and Mort Zuckerman. Robert Drinan himself came and complained to the *Post* about how I'd undercut the magazine's Left-liberal heritage. And Christopher Hitchens was there to write about the party. He made it a habit to taunt me whenever he could. He hadn't been invited, so he came disguised as a waiter and, yes, he went on to taunt me in print. Hitchens was probably there stalking Kissinger, who he didn't think should be invited to nice parties.

I could tell we had breached the wall when the *Washington Post* publisher Katharine Graham came to our party. She was the Washington media eminence, and her paper had been anti-*New Republic* since I came in. We were a threat to the genteel Washington the paper presided over. But then, in the early eighties, we arranged a syndication deal on some of our columns—that's what brought Charles his following, writing for the *New Republic* but having those pieces also run in the *Post*—and after ten years, we'd become something of an institution in Washington ourselves. So when Kay came, it meant something literal and symbolic. She was signaling that now I, we, belonged.

But in other, unspoken, ways she signified the ways I never would. Kay was a lot like my father-in-law, and not only in her indirect way of speaking and acting. Her world was for the very high and the very low; she didn't have sympathy, or room, for people in the middle, people without place, and this extended to the Jews, even though she was part-Jewish herself. Katharine's father, Eugene, who had the money that had bought the *Post*, was Jewish but married to a German Lutheran and not really involved in Jewish communal life, outside of getting some relatives out of Nazi Europe via his connection to Franklin Roosevelt. Katharine's best friend, Meg Greenwald, who was also a friend of my old girlfriend Susie Black and the editor of the *Washington Post's* editorial page, was honest about that with me once, over lunch. She told me, "We German Jews don't like Zionism. It doesn't appeal to us. It intrudes on our Americanism." And I appreciated the honesty. But I also knew that this was a sticking point for me and for them.

The *New Republic* was a pro-Israel magazine—this was known to everybody in Washington, the staffers, the readers, the politicians, and the critics. They thought it was my obsession, and they were right about that. Zionism was the one thing I absolutely would not compromise on, the one way I unilaterally exercised my ownership prerogative. When it came to Israel, I answered to no one but myself. I knew what I was talking about.

Family portrait, mid 1940s (Credit: Gus Wittmayer Studio).

Marching to Shabbos dinner at Camp Boiberik, early 1950s. The historian Yosef Yerushalmi, then a camp counselor, is in front of me.

With Max Lerner, 1957 (Credit: Henry Grossman).

With Herbert Marcuse and H. Stuart Hughes and his wife Judith.

Soon before his suicide, Vlado Dedijer's son Boro (left) sharing a smoke with my brother, Gerry (right), 1966. (Credit: Anne Peretz).

On my honeymoon, 1967 (Credit: Anne Peretz).

With Ed Zwick at a beach in Truro, 1970s (Credit: Anne Peretz).

Introducing Roger and Ginny Rosenblatt to Golda Meir at an event celebrating the addition of her portrait to the National Portrait Gallery, 1976.

Alongside Golda, Bella Abzug, and Henry Kissinger at the same event, 1976.

Walking to the Jerusalem Cinematheque with Warren Beatty, 1984.

Meeting with Vice President Dan Quayle (second from left) at the White House along-side the *New Republic* staff, including Mort Kondracke, Ann Hulbert, Mickey Kaus, Rick Hertzberg, and Leon Wieseltier, 1989 (Credit: Official White House Photo).

With Fran Lebowitz and Andrew Sullivan, early 1990s.

Deep in conversation with Henry Kissinger (Credit: David Karp).

With Anne and Al Gore, 2000 (Credit: Official White House Photo).

In disagreement with Teddy Kollek in Jerusalem.

On better terms, 2000 (Credit: P. Hausner).

With Jim Cramer.

With Henry Rosovsky and Skip Gates.

With Anne and Yo-Yo Ma.

Fouad Ajami (Credit: Anne Mandelbaum).

Charles Krauthammer and his son Daniel (Credit: Anne Mandelbaum).

Rick Hertzberg (Credit: Anne Mandelbaum).

Leon Wieseltier (Credit: Anne Mandelbaum).

Anne.

My son Jesse (Credit: Anne Peretz).

My daughter Evgenia (Credit: Anne Peretz).

CHAPTER TEN

Israel and its Enemies: Peoples and Parodies

There were lots of realities people in Washington, D.C. did not understand about Israel and about Jews. Some of these they found out about in the *New Republic*. Others were too deeply embedded in our culture for people to understand unless they wanted to, and most people didn't want to. Even many Washington Jews were Jewish without knowing a thing about the Jews. There was something quaint about this ignorance: the less they knew, the less they thought there was to know.

There is a lot to know.

The Jews have a long history: this is year 5783 in the Jewish calendar. Each year at Passover, we celebrate our deliverance from Egypt and God's promise of the Holy Land to our people, in 1446 BC. For nearly two thousand years since we rebelled against the Romans and were expelled from the Holy Land, we have recited the phrase: "Next year in Jerusalem." Though the rise of nationalisms in the nineteenth century set the political stage for our claim to Israel, our claim, like the claims of other peoples who were also nations, went back to the times before states existed.

But our claim was unique because of the expulsion and the diaspora that grew from it. These meant that, unlike the other late nineteenth-century nationalisms, Zionism was not geographically bound. It was a worldwide movement, involving not only the Jews of Vienna, Prague, Vilna, Paris, and New York, but Moroccans, Persians, and Iraqis. (In fact, Zionists were accused of bombing Jewish cafés in Baghdad as a trick to accelerate the exodus, and this may be true.) After Israel's founding, Jews began to arrive by the thousands. But since they came in 1948 instead of 1938, the world's Jewish population had already been reduced by a third.

Their new neighbors weren't very glad to see them. But they had problems of their own. The borders the Allied Powers drew on the carcass of the Ottoman Empire at the Versailles conference were parodies of the Wilsonian ideal. Peoples who'd lived for generations in the same place found themselves either stateless or in states that weren't consonant with their identities. Different peoples with long histories of mutual animosities were jammed into the same countries, designed to be warred over. This was particularly true in Iraq where Sunni, Shia, and Kurds lived under the unsteady minority leadership of King Faisal of the Sunni Hashemites. Faisal's brother, Abdullah, ruled the new country of Transjordan to the southwest. The Arabian peninsula, with its vast reserves of oil, was ruled by the family of Ibn Saud, a desert tribe now installed by the British as rulers of what would be called Saudi Arabia. The French ruled Syria, a multiethnic protectorate that shared an uneasy border with Iraq and Lebanon. Lebanon was a largely Christian state created to protect the Christian Maronites along with unwilling Muslim and Druze. Eventually, after the Second World War, when Britain and France left the rulers of these places to look after themselves, they turned to the idea of Arab nationalism to control this hodgepodge, merging it with anticolonial, sometimes Marxist, ideas to give them Western enemies to rail against.

There was also Palestine, under British control and an especially difficult case that affected all of the others.

During the First World War, the British tried to foment a revolt in the Ottoman Empire with a two-pronged strategy targeting Muslims and Jews. They wrote to the Hussein family of the Hashemite clan, the descendants of the prophets to whom the British later gave Iraq and Transjordan, promising them not just Mecca but also Jerusalem if they revolted against the Turks. Lord Arthur Balfour, a conservative Christian Zionist who believed the foundation of a Jewish state was written into the Bible, sent a letter (after much negotiation) to the 2nd Baron Rothschild almost promising the Jews a state in exchange, implicitly, for support for the war effort. The Jews were already in Palestine in significant numbers, and a cadre of Jewish entrepreneurs working through the Jewish Agency had been buying land from the Palestinian effendi, the landowners, including many of the members of the Arab Higher Committee, which had been formed to represent the Palestinian people. After the Balfour Declaration, more Jews paid higher prices for more land.

This was the situation in the Holy Land that the British inherited from themselves in 1918: Palestine had been promised to both the Hashemites and the Jews. It was then cut up to create Transjordan to satisfy the Hashemites and the remainder was split between Jews who had bought land and local Arabs who were themselves very much divided—by Christianity or Sunni Islam, by social class, and by particular loyalties to neighboring Arab states. By the 1930s, the Palestinian effendi who had sold Jews their land supported Arab revolts against the growing Jewish population. So did the grand mufti of Jerusalem, Hajj Amin al-Husseini, who had founded the Arab Higher Committee and who spent much of the war in Berlin as an ally of Hitler.

After the war, when it was clear that the British eventually would have to leave their colonial projects behind, the new United Nations proposed a partition whereby the Jews would take slightly more land with a large Palestinian Arab minority. But much of this—the whole Negev—was desert, while the Palestinian state would be almost without Jews. The Zionists said "yes" to the deal, taking whatever they could get, but the Palestinian leadership and the Arab states wouldn't accept it. When the British left on May 14, 1948, without a deal in place, they left a power vacuum. David Ben-Gurion declared the Jewish state that same day, and five Arab states immediately attacked it.

Everyone watched to see what the United States would do. The Zionist movement in the US had sympathizers in both parties. But the foreign policy establishment, personified by George Marshall, didn't want to alienate the Arabs by siding with the Jews because they might be important allies against the Soviets. Eventually Marshall was overruled by Truman, who came from Missouri farmers and who had been a Shabbos goy for his devout Jewish neighbors. He recognized the Jewish state within a quarter hour of its declaration of independence. Still, Truman's recognition did not include US military support, and so the Jews were on their own.

The Zionists were already buying arms on the black market and volunteer fighters came from all over the world with arms of their own. The Zionist militias had been in training for more than a decade. There were two groups: the Haganah, who favored pragmatic territorial compromise, and the more militant and radically ultra-Zionist Irgun, who wanted both sides of the river for Israel. Ben-Gurion brought the Irgun to heel by sinking the *Altalena*, a ship bringing them munitions, in the Tel Aviv harbor.

Most of the Jews who commanded this army weren't exactly military people but more like astonishingly cultivated amateurs. The army they commanded was informal—the men had uniforms, or they didn't—but this made the Israelis actually more punctilious about how they acted when they fought. There is a Hebrew concept called *tohar haneshek*, which in clumsier English means "purity of arms" or "morality of arms," where fighters imposed strict limits on themselves to avoid unnecessary bloodshed.

On the Arab side, the fighting was disorganized, with each state seeking territorial gain without reference to the others, which impeded the overall effort. Looking back, partisans of the Arabs or the Jews try to impose a narrative on the events of 1948, but mostly there was confusion. There was searing heroism: at Kibbutz Yad Mordechai, a few Holocaust survivors held off a portion of the Egyptian army while the Israelis regrouped. At the same time, there were forced marches of Palestinian Arabs out of Israeli territory, defenseless civilians machine gunned outside Lydda, and the whole village of Deir Yassin razed to the ground. There is a great historical struggle over what happened, how much killing, who instigated it, with serious people on both sides of the argument, and much propaganda. There were also Palestinian Arab villages like Abu Ghosh whose inhabitants fought alongside the Zionists. I later knew the son of the village head, Subhi Abu-Ghosh, and his village was, by then, a prosperous Muslim-Christian town outside Jerusalem in Israel.

The Palestinian Arabs who fought against the Israelis went to refugee camps in places like Ramallah. Some who remained became Israeli citizens while others were dispersed into neighboring Arab states. The Egyptians lost, but they did keep the Gaza Strip. And, after two thousand years, the Jews had their state. The reality of winning meant they were coming home to a crazy region of unstable states ruled over by petty dictators desperate to project national unity and keep their people from civil war. It helped them to have an external enemy to focus upon. Varieties of Marxian and Arabist nationalism got taken up by Gamal Abdel Nasser in Egypt and by the fast-rotating heads of Syria and Iraq: they used the ideas as fictions to bolster their control, as ways to distract from colonially created problems at home and to project a sham unity abroad. Israel was the obvious target for this projection: they were not Arab, not Marxist, not Islamic, and settled by people from and allied with states of the Christian West. And this was before the most potent anti-Israeli nationalism, Palestinian nationalism, came into play.

I was one of the few people of influence in Washington, D.C. who understood these realities, though not because of any special brilliance. My upbringing and experiences meant that I understood the realities of tribes, nations, and peoples. Washington's strategic philosophy was that of the international institutionalists like Harry Labouisse who saw themselves administering a world of individuals. To the standard American politician, Republican or Democrat, the tribal and national complications made very little sense: whatever peoples' origins, they were Americans now. It wasn't like that in Israel, an embattled new democracy where individuals were rooted in a tribe, a people, a culture, and a nation but were always aware of the need to protect what they had made for themselves. I wanted to help other influential people in America understand the Israeli situation.

My primary point of connection was Teddy Kollek. He had started his Zionist political career as a demonstrator in Vienna and rose quickly as an aide to Chaim Weizmann, finally becoming mayor of Jerusalem in 1965. This was maybe the last job an ambitious Israeli would want: the city couldn't even seem to pick up the trash, let alone manage tensions between the Jews in West Jerusalem and Arabs in the eastern part of the city, which the Jordanians controlled. During the Six-Day War in 1967, Teddy's third year on the job, Israel took control of Jordanian Jerusalem and its restive population. But Teddy wasn't deterred. He had a vision of what Jerusalem should look like: the reality of his childhood home of interwar Vienna with its daring mosaic of cultures, minus the fascism.

The first thing he did was to get good uniforms for the sanitation workers so they would have some esprit de corps and pick up the trash; then he gave the Arab leaders special social services, which calmed some of the most immediate tensions. The real challenge, at least for the Jews, was the Haredi and other ultra-Orthodox groups, divided among themselves into sects and sectlets but still a powerful force utterly opposed to urbanity or cosmopolitanism. They put up a nasty fight to stop movies from being shown in Jerusalem on Friday nights, throwing punches and screaming "Nazis" at the police.

Teddy outflanked the Haredi by getting international Jews invested in the city's success. With their support, he built the Jerusalem Theater and the Israel Museum; he funded the Jerusalem Zoo through the Tisch family; and he founded the Jerusalem Foundation. He also issued a more direct answer to the Haredi and their puritanism: he helped Lia van Leer, a Bessarabian émigré from what is now Moldova, found the pathbreaking Jerusalem Cinematheque, which, after a while, showed movies on Friday nights.

I would do anything for Teddy—and for Israel. Michael Walzer and I were actual tour guides of Israel on behalf of Yigal Allon, the hero from the war of independence who was now foreign minister under Yitzhak Rabin's Labor government. Allon had been impressed by our ad effort during the Yom Kippur War, and he wanted to use us to attract important Americans to Israel. The groups we brought would be roughly half Jew and half non-Jew—academics and people who were influential intellectually, politically, professionally, or all three. We would be hosted by the Israeli government, and we would see people in the government: the prime minister, the foreign minister, all the way down the political and social ladders.

I started fundraising in the States for the Jerusalem Foundation. I went on a speaking tour to raise money for parks, concert halls, athletic fields, extracurricular school programs, and theatres. My first stop was in Miami, where I was picked up by a rabbi in a gold Cadillac convertible who drove me to his congregation on the beach. "This audience is very rich, but there are some people who are also very tight," he said. I needn't have worried. "Sandra Friedman, your husband is already dead three years, and you haven't parted with a dime," he said. "Table 17, what are you, shy? None of you is shy. One of you get up and *give me* fifty-thousand dollars."

In Chicago, a delegation of us went to see the Crown family, one of the two richest Jewish families in Chicago. After we left them, we went to see the Pritzkers, the other richest Jewish family, and I recognized behind us the Crown driver who had driven us to the first meeting: he was tailing us because Lester Crown suspected we were going to meet Abe Pritzker. Abe and I became friendly, and a few years later he called me up and asked me to look after his grandson, who was attending boarding school in Massachusetts, by taking him out for lunch every month or so. And I did. JB was a shy boy but smart and eager to learn, and later when he worked in Washington, he would come to *New Republic* editorial meetings. Now he is the governor of Illinois, and there is much talk of his candidacy for president.

Then I spoke in Las Vegas. This was before Sheldon Adelson and the other modern finance moguls legalized and smoothed out the place's edges. It was a small event, and as my host made the pitch, he took out a gun and put it on a table. That's all. And when he had raised the money, he said, "And now give again." And they did.

The last stop on the tour, San Francisco, was this strange moment of clarity because it showed just how much the Jewish approach to Israel had changed after 1967 and 1973 and how the existential threat to the Jewish state had made some American Jewish assimilationists find loyalties they didn't know they had. Walter Haas, ex-chairman of Levi Strauss, was my host. He came from a family of German Jews, people whom I associated with trying to keep Yiddish immigrants out of the cities they called home. So I thought I knew what to expect. And yet, fifteen minutes into our ride, he said, "Golda Meir is coming to San Francisco, and we are very excited," which was a jarring adjective because he never seemed like he could be excited about anything; he was too much of an aristocrat. I asked him why he was so excited, and he said, "Because in 1946 or 1947, when she came to raise money for arms for Jewish Palestine, I refused her and others refused her and she has not been back to San Francisco since. Now we have a chance to make it right."

* * *

After I bought the *New Republic*, James Jesus Angleton, the famous chief of counterintelligence for the CIA, asked me to come to lunch at the Army and Navy Club in Washington. It was completely out of the blue, and I was a little nervous. When we sat down he said, "I'm not gonna waste any time. I'm gonna tell you that you have a Soviet spy on your staff."

Teddy Kollek had put him on to me. Before Israel was a state, Teddy had been a Zionist operative in America, doing an occasional favor for his hosts, and at a party in 1948 or 1949 at the British embassy in Washington, he ran into his old American friend James—they'd both been on the borders of spying and diplomacy during the war. They shook hands, and just then Teddy also saw a man whom he knew from a long time back, in Vienna. "There is a Communist agent," he told Angleton quietly. "We fought, Zionists versus Communists, on the streets of Vienna. Don't tell me he isn't." The man was Kim Philby, Michael Straight's comrade. That's part of what started Angleton on the quest that he was pursuing twenty-five years later with me at the Navy Club.

I didn't know this until later. All I knew at the time was that the chief of counterintelligence for the CIA was telling me I had a Soviet spy on staff. "Who?" I asked. "Tad Szulc." Now Tad Szulc was a very distinguished journalist, and my first retort was, "He was either thrown out of Czechoslovakia by the Soviets or left in a huff." Angleton said, "You're so naïve…he was thrown out because they had no *need* for him anymore in Czechoslovakia. Anyway he's now working for Cuba, and you have to fire him." I said, "I can't. I have no evidence, just your word. But I'll watch his stuff." And then I paused for a few seconds and finally said, "Why do you trust me?

I have sort of a radical history." And after another few moments' pause and without elaboration, he said, "Because you're a Zionist."

Angleton was close to Simcha Dinitz, and he used to come to dinner in Washington, D.C. when Simcha was ambassador. I would bring dessert and Angleton would bring orchids, which he raised, and sometimes he'd bring a big fish because he fished, too. His worldview was dark, dark, dark—one where everything was fated because the Communists had infiltrated too many places. But he saw Israel as a mirror of America: a democratic beacon pressed by Communists and authoritarians, a false step or two away from a fall. He was a bit paranoid, I suppose. But was he wrong?

* * *

From the beginning of my ownership, everyone knew the *New Republic* would take a different approach to Zionism. The year I bought it, Harry Labouisse, who could see it coming, set up a meeting between me and Walter Lippmann, one of the magazine's original founders. Lippmann was an intimate friend of his and very, very old—by the end of the year he'd be dead. So it was a ceremony to go and talk to him at his apartment on Park Avenue. We said hello, sat down, and I immediately knew it was a setup: the one thing Lippman wanted to talk about was Israel. He wanted me to make sure that Gilbert Harrison, who was Jewish and still editing the magazine, would carry on maintaining the distance he'd kept as owner between the magazine and the Jewish state. This was, on its face, absurd: Gilbert Harrison was about as Jewish as Harry Truman, except he liked Israel much less. And besides, he was on his way out.

I made the changes in the *New Republic*'s policy toward Israel by the year's end, and they didn't just amount to easing Harrison out. From now on, Israel wasn't going to be a marginal issue in Washington, a tribal problem a million miles away. Suddenly Washington's main weekly magazine of politics and ideas was going to run articles about Israel that were more than afterthoughts.

We weren't afraid to hold the past to account. The *New Republic* published pieces critical of the Roosevelt administration's handling of the Jewish question during the war, and John McCloy, Harry's old friend who'd been head of the World Bank and before that assistant secretary of state during the Second World War, got upset. He got to me through Howard Stein, chairman of the Dreyfus funds—we both were board members—and Howard arranged for us to meet. We argued over whether FDR should have done more to help the Jews. McCloy was old and frail, a very stiff man, the product of a different era, and I knew that. But I wouldn't apologize for pointing out what he and his compatriots had gotten wrong.

I also got more aggressive on Jewish issues with people I looked up to for non-Jewish reasons. I called out David Riesman in a letter for what I saw as his blind spots about Israel. It was the same lacuna I'd seen in *The Lonely Crowd*: he never took ethnicity or tribe into account, least of all in himself.

He replied in kind, civilly but attached to his views: "I do not believe that Jews are 'a chosen people' but believe in decent human standards that have developed in the great religious traditions at their best, including the Judeo-Christian tradition." We assured each other of our continuing high regard for the other. But, again, I didn't regret calling him to account.

I wasn't operating in a vacuum: American Jewish sentiment was shifting, and the bigger geopolitics of the era cooperated as well to bring Israel, American Jews, and Americans closer together. By 1980, America was looking at a different map of the Middle East than it had before. The kingdom of Iraq had collapsed in 1958 and was replaced by a "republic," which lasted until 1979, when it was taken over by the murderous dictator Saddam Hussein. Ayatollah Khomeini had taken over in Iran, deposing the brutal shah and replacing him with an even more brutal regime. Egypt had moved away from its pan-Arabism and made a formal pragmatic peace with Israel. Meanwhile, Saudi Arabia had become the financial arbiter of the petroleum world. Israel was our most reliable ally in the region. This changed the domestic political calculus. When Al ran for president in 1988, he ran as an unambivalent supporter of the Jewish people and the Jewish state, the first Democratic candidate to do that in twenty years.

✳   ✳   ✳

There was a new factor in American-Israeli relations: Palestinian nationalism came to public attention in 1967 after the Six-Day War and over the next fifteen years it slowly began to affect the American perception of Israel, widening the natural divide between Americans who were free from danger and Israelis who increasingly lived under terrorist threat.

After the Six-Day War, Israel found itself responsible for the Palestinian refugees in the territories it had captured in the West Bank and Gaza, which Jordan and Egypt refused to take back. For the sake of their own security, the Israelis had to occupy the territories they had taken in the war, becoming responsible for supplying electric and water utilities to a population in more or less open revolt against them. Yigal Allon tried to solve the problem by proposing to give the Palestinians their own state, or a state shared with the Jordanians in the West Bank, in exchange for Israel annexing much of the Jordan Valley and East Jerusalem. But the king of Jordan rejected it out of hand. So the status quo stayed—and festered. It became not just a local breeding ground for militants but increasingly a siren song for the discontented in the West—an international cause.

Sirhan Sirhan, in 1968, was the first sign of what was to come. But the terror really registered with me in the summer of 1972. Anne and I were at the house we rented in Wellfleet, and the phone rang; it was Elena Levin, a neighbor and the wife of Harry Levin, the eminent Harvard literary scholar and Paul de Man's tutor, a man who never really identified as a Jew. She said, "A terrible thing has happened at the Olympics. The Palestinians are killing the Jews!" We didn't have a TV, so they asked us to come over and watch as the Munich massacre, committed by the Palestinian liberation group Black September, unfolded. And Harry, who didn't identify as a Jew, was shaking. He'd never imagined in all his years a threat like this. Neither had I. The second spectacle came a few years later, when the PFLP, the Popular Front for the Liberation of Palestine, a Marxist-Leninist group, hijacked an Air France flight out of Tel Aviv scheduled to Paris. The passengers were taken hostage and flown to Entebbe, Uganda. Israel responded with a daring rescue mission by night, led by Ehud Barak, that freed the hostages. There was one Israeli death: a soldier named Yonatan Netanyahu.

Yasser Arafat, the leader of the Palestinian Liberation Organization, the PLO, the most dominant Palestinian militant group, was not directly involved in either attack. But he had ties to both groups, and his militancy went back to the founding of Israel. Born in Egypt to Palestinian parents and educated at university there, he had gone on to fight with the Palestinian militias during the 1948 war. He had founded the PLO in 1964—even before Israel was in the West Bank, Gaza, or East Jerusalem. The PLO claimed to be the sole representative of the Palestinian people and stated as its aim the armed liberation of Palestine. In 1970, they started the Black September uprising to overthrow King Hussein of Jordan, where many Palestinians also lived. The PLO fought a nine-day war against the Jordanian army and lost. After that, Arafat bent his efforts solely on Israel, which was a hard target militarily but an easier target when it came to money, media, and arms.

Arafat knew the Arab autocrats wouldn't actually help his people. But he could count on their support against Israel: it was the perfect way for leaders to distract attention from their own failings. He also found sympathizers in America and Europe: aristocrats, leftists, or establishment types who didn't like the idea of Jews with a state and an army of their own. Naturally, he found support at the UN, the project of the rational institutionalists, which was now dominated by undemocratic leaders of post-colonial states—there were so many of them and they all had a vote in the General Assembly.

As a mountebank in international affairs, Arafat had few peers. He was accepted as the representative of the Palestinian people, even as he waved a gun in a speech to the UN General Assembly in 1974, painting himself as a moderate who could keep the radicals under control. Palestinian society, both before and after 1948, was a complex interweaving of tribes, bosses, mayors, little militias, and clans who were very much divided along these lines. None of them had elected Arafat and many of these Palestinians didn't trust him and didn't want him representing them. Unfortunately, they had little choice in the matter. Once I met Muhammad Ali

Ja'abari, who'd been the mayor of Hebron since 1948 and had his own militia. "The Israelis are worse than the Jordanians," he said, "the Jordanians were worse than the British, the British were worse than the Turks. But God forbid if Arafat comes to rule us." But people like Ja'abari were stuck with Arafat because the world recognized him as a responsible spokesperson for the Palestinian cause.

The new Palestinian nationalism had its effects on Israel. In 1977, partly in response to Arafat's new prominence and a wave of terrorist attacks on Israelis, there was a changing of Israel's political guard. Labor, which had been in power since the state's foundation, was out. The Right, Likud, took control under Golda's old nemesis Begin, commander of the Irgun in the days before the state and the unchallenged leader of the Revisionist position, which wanted all of the Holy Land on both sides of the Jordan.

Labor, the Labor I had known, was in its twilight. Golda lived a few years after she retired and every time I came to Israel, she had me bring her five cartons of Chesterfield cigarettes, which she hid from her staff, doctors, and family. I think she had other people doing the same because after she died in 1978, I went to her tiny house in Tel Aviv, and I asked her secretary, "What did Golda do with all of her Chesterfields?" "First of all," she said, "she smoked them. But second...follow me." She took me to the bedroom and showed me a closet full of Chesterfields. Full. And she also asked, "Would you like some?"

Yigal Allon lived a little more than a year after Golda died. He was still a member of Kibbutz Ginosar on the western side of the Kinneret, the Sea of Galilee, and every time I went to see him, he was sitting by his machine. I don't know what the fuck it made, but it was an old-fashioned industrial thing. I think Allon was consciously putting himself out of the new time. Old Labor's time—ascetic yet respectful of culture, learned yet fierce, willing to fight but with a preference for pragmatism, commercial but not capitalist—had passed.

Begin and Moshe Dayan, who led the vanguard that replaced it, were strange men. Dayan, who had been a Labor man and then moved to one of the smaller parties in the Knesset, had taken a bullet through his binoculars and wore an eyepatch. His relationship with this eyepatch was both understated and symbolic: he never mentioned it but anytime he walked into the room, people were intimidated. Begin in public was dull and pedantic; in private he was irascible. Once in his presence, I innocently referred to the occupied territories as "occupied," and he blew up. We never met again. Begin was dismissive of us, and he had his reasons. He was bent on facing an enemy, and he thought Americans, even American Jews with influential magazines, safe across several seas and oceans, were incapable of understanding that.

In some ways, he wasn't wrong. I remember a dinner around this time with Norman Mailer that pretty much made his point for him. We'd invited Simcha and his wife, Vivian, to visit at our house on the Cape. Simcha, as ambassador, was always trying to make new Zionists. I invited Norman because he was very political, he was Jewish, and a lot of his writing had to do with Jews and strength, Jews and sex, Jews and power, and mostly Jews as men. But he had never been to Israel. Somebody—I think it was Frederick Wiseman's wife, Zipporah, or "Chippy," who had been to Israel lots of times—asked Norman why he'd never been to Israel and he answered, "I will go to Israel if they can produce another Entebbe."

I was stunned by Norman's answer, and not only because another Entebbe assumes another hijacking. Simcha responded with a scalding lecture on how Israel has an Entebbe every day. He asked him if he read the news—why, thirty-seven people had just died in a bus attack.

It was a telling moment. Norman hadn't meant the joke offensively. In fact, Entebbe had all of Norman's favorite themes: manliness, Jewish manliness, Jewish power. But these were all abstractions to him. It's the difference between people in a state under constant, immediate threat and an American who gets to summer on the Cape.

The Palestinian problem wouldn't go away because it was the result of so many fractures that wracked the region. The case in point was Lebanon, a leftover colonial "arrangement," or misarrangement. It was a weak state bordered by hostile powers, dominated by Syria, and riven by sectarian competition. Sunni and Shia Muslims coexisted, although the largely rural Shia resented the Sunni urban elites who had worked with the Maronite Christians to carve up the country between them. The Druze, the Kurds, and the

Greek Orthodox also had a place in the country. The political order was predetermined by these realities—the president was mandated by the constitution to be a Maronite Christian, the prime minister to be a Sunni, and the speaker of the legislature to be Shia.

This was a fragile, easily disrupted ecosystem: there had been no census for over a generation, lest fresh figures disrupt the formula for denominational representation. When the PLO, backed by the Syrians, came looking for shelter in the mid-1970s, after the failure of Black September, the delicate balance was immediately upset. The PLO essentially became a roving nation—really, a gang that claimed to be a nation, making trouble wherever it went. It took control of the south of Lebanon, and the central government was too weak and disunited to stop them. Soon they began to use Lebanese territory to launch attacks on Israel.

In 1982, Begin ordered the Israeli army under Ariel Sharon into Lebanon. The objective was to undermine the PLO and to throw Israel's weight behind one of the sects that might restore order to the country: the Shia or the Maronites, either one would do. It was a mistake to think they could be kingmakers in Lebanon, whose complexities they could never hope to master. The whole invasion was a mistake.

At the time, I supported it, even as I was perfectly happy to give space in the *New Republic* to critics who did not. Michael Walzer was aghast at the entire operation. He was always more skeptical than I was about use of force: it was part and parcel of his principled Left stance. What bothered me most was the slanted coverage from America's establishment press that set the frame for the way Israel's battles were to be reported from then on. Israel was strong, and its main enemy was a roving gang claiming nationhood whose leader was despised by many of the people he claimed to represent. But the broad-strokes narrative wrote itself. Israel was the Goliath versus the Palestinians' David. And Western journalists took it up.

Part of this was the nature of television media. When it came to Lebanon, the film of falling buildings kept coming, and Israel was automatically represented in the worst light, not by its heroic soldiers, nor by its citizens killed by PLO rockets, but only by the destruction it had caused. Part of this was old-line establishment newspaper animus. Katharine Graham had a coterie of foreign correspondents at the *Post*—Jonathan Randal, William Claiborne, Edward Cody, and Jim Hoagland—who dominated reporting on international affairs in the capital and who had a preexisting agenda. They billed themselves as Middle East specialists, and, like much of the old establishment, they had a record of diagnoses to defend. They were unfailingly kind to Arafat—he was lionized by the press as a great liberation leader—and they let themselves imagine him that way for years until his deceptions were too glaring to ignore.

I didn't trust the perception of the Jewish state to either the media or the old-line journalistic establishment. I had a magazine of my own, so I called up people I knew in the Israeli government, and I asked to go to Lebanon to try to find out for myself what was going on.

I started my trip in Israel, which was its own education. Most of the soldiers, many of them reservists, did not like Begin and felt free to say so: "Except for some blatherings from the prime minister," one lieutenant told me, "we heard no jingoistic slogans. It's better that way." The one big demonstration against the war had been mounted by an officer-initiated movement called Peace Now. The same people who demonstrated were signed up to fight.

Lebanon itself was in chaos. It was my first time in a war zone, and its reality contradicted most of the American journalistic reports. People from every faction of Lebanese society told me the problem with the Palestinian militias ensconced in Lebanon wasn't just that they disturbed the peace of the country by using it as a base to attack Israel. It was that they stole from families, harassed women, and commandeered passports and offices; they regularly sacked hospitals and doctors' offices for medical supplies and then took them over as headquarters, using the patients as hostages against Israeli attack.

There were villages of Greek Orthodox in the south who were trying to stay above it or out of it; they were small in number and would have to kowtow to whichever sect ruled the ground. There were Shia, who had first welcomed the Israelis as liberators from the Palestinians, returning to their homes in the south where they'd been pushed out in 1976. There were the Lebanese elite, owners of big pretty houses by the seacoast, who were paying protection fees to the Palestinians to be left alone.

The PLO played the Western observers all the while: the UNRWA, Harry Labouisse's old Palestinian relief mission, was not allowed into refugee camps in case the refugee count was lower than what the PLO reported. In fact, the Palestinian leadership lied about a lot of numbers. Once they reported one hundred killed in an Israeli strike on an apartment building hosting a Palestinian military headquarters and later the number got corrected to ten.

I reported all this in a cover story for the *New Republic*, "Lebanon Eyewitness," with the lead sentence on the cover: "Much of what you have read in the newspapers and newsmagazines about the war in Lebanon—and even more of what you have seen and heard on television—is simply not true." The *Post* reporters hit back. They thought I'd been duped by the IDF. This was not unexpected because I thought they'd been duped by the PLO. I stood by my story: the IDF took me to the battle lines and never hindered me from reporting what I saw and heard.

Two months later, the situation in Lebanon took a terrible turn. The Israelis had chosen to back as their ally in Lebanon the Christian Maronites, whose leader was Bachir Gemayel. These were brutal men, and how Begin and Sharon didn't calculate the consequences of this nastiness beforehand is and was beyond me. Begin was going to crown Bachir leader of Lebanon once the fighting was done, but before that could happen, Bachir was assassinated in a bombing of his headquarters. His brother Amin took over, but he wasn't much. The situation looked uncertain enough when, in retaliation for Bachir's killing, one of his militias massacred hundreds, maybe thousands, of Palestinians and Lebanese Shiite civilians near two refugee camps in Beirut, Sabra and Shatila. These camps were under Israel's control and the killers were Israel's allies.

Sharon, the Israeli general in charge of the invasion, was a tribalist, a man who would do anything for his people. I understood the tribal impulse and the dangers of its extremes because it played inside of me. I think we were drawn to each other. I had been on a list of people Sharon wanted to see, and when we met, Sharon took notes, apparently in case anybody should report or misreport on what had been said. It makes sense: he was a suspicious man. But he was also a cheat, and the Sabra and Shatila massacre was on the most basic level cheating. Sharon's orders to himself were to weaken the enemy as soon and as thoroughly as possible, and this was the result.

He had not considered that it would be a political disaster. Two months after my piece ran, the *New Republic* called for the head of his boss, Begin.

> *When a crime of this magnitude is committed during one's watch, one is honor bound to resign. That is not only our view, it is the view of a large segment of a shocked, outraged and remorseful Israeli society.... This week we write not in praise of Israel, but in praise of its shame.... Israel will not allow itself to be led anymore by those who lead it to the killing ground.*

Martha Gellhorn, the legendary journalist who had reported on the Spanish Civil War, wrote to congratulate me on the piece I'd written about Lebanon. She added, in an appraisal of the extreme condemnation of Israel elsewhere:

> *I'm outdone with the hypocrisy about this [Sabra and Shatila] disaster. A bad misjudgment is treated universally as an Israeli crime, [all] the while no one says a word about US involvement in murder in El Salvador etc. etc.*

The war did not end well for Israel. Sabra and Shatila was a blow to the idea of *tohar haneshek*. Nor did it end well for Lebanon. Once the Israelis withdrew, the civil war continued, this time between the PLO and its former Syrian backers and other factions in Lebanon. By the end of the decade, Syria had used the disorder to make Lebanon essentially a proxy state. Today, it's barely a state at all.

I don't know if the war ended well for me or not. But I know it changed me. Israel was not a perfect country, and it did not have a perfect army. Its leaders certainly weren't perfect. But the war had convinced me that people in Washington and the people giving the American public its information didn't understand what was at stake. They did not grasp the complexities that created Israel's context and shaped its actions.

This flattening of complexities only got worse. A few years after the war, Tom Friedman, who'd won a Pulitzer Prize for his coverage of Sabra and Shatila and then covered Israel for the *Times*, came out with his first book, *From Beirut to Jerusalem*, about his time in Lebanon during the war and Israel after. In it he traced a story he surely didn't intend: the migration of a hard-edged, on-the-ground reporter into a professional pundit who followed the conventional wisdom of his generation and his class.

He gave a scene where he "lay awake in my bed the whole night worrying that someone was going to burst in and blow my brains all over the wall" after a fellow *Times* reporter told him that Arafat's personal spokesman had complained about his filings on the PLO. But he would not—could not—state what the facts told him, which is that Arafat was a murderer and the PLO a sham. Instead, his book was a morality play, a coming to grips with the reality that Israel wasn't perfect, and a piercing of the "Jewish summer camp" mentality of his proudly Zionist youth in the face of the actuality of the Israeli state.

It was my first, though not my last, encounter with a character trait that defined many of the new political and media elite, the first middle-class cohort to have become elite on the basis of learned theory and expertise rather than inherited obligation. It was an elite that my friends and I had helped form, and I'm sorry to say, some of them were intellectually coddled, more interested in how society should be than what it actually was. If reality didn't accord with their ideas, then reality was at fault. For Tom, either Israel was as good as he thought it was, or he became disillusioned with it. This was the blind spot I increasingly took up arms against. It wasn't enough just trying to express Israel's reality in Washington.

Two years after "Lebanon Eyewitness," I was invited to debate on Israel in front of the Oxford Union. The motion was something like: "Israel is the source of problems in the Middle East." Larry Grafstein, who'd graduated Harvard, was then completing his Rhodes Scholarship at Oxford and was head of the Union. He was worried I had no idea what I was in for, and he asked a past president, who was working on his master's at the Kennedy School at Harvard, if he'd be willing to sit down with me for a coffee and talk about it. This was how I met Andrew Sullivan. "You have to understand," he said, "the audience is a bunch of Israel haters bordering on anti-Semites and you're gonna lose." So I shouldn't pull any punches.

Both sides had two main debaters. The two on their side were the PLO representative in London, whose name I forget, and Lord (Christopher) Mayhew, a Labor politician who had worked under Ernest Bevin, the foreign minister in the Mandate period who ran a diplomatic war against the settling of Jewish refugees in British Palestine. You couldn't ask for a finer representative of British imperialism.

With the advice of Isaiah Berlin, George Weidenfeld, and Jacob, Lord Rothschild, I settled on the chairman of the Labor Friends of Israel as my second, and I spent six days in a fancy London hotel preparing. But when I spoke, I spoke without notes, as if I hadn't prepared. I brought along a small cheering section of Jewish cognoscenti: not-a-Lady-yet (Vivien) Clore, David Pryce-Jones, the artist R. B. Kitaj, and Gilbert de Botton. Boris Johnson, then and now a friend of Larry's, spoke from the audience for my side. He was a presence and personage even then—he walked like one even at age twenty—and he spoke wisely, smart-alecky, with humor. It's very messy, the actual debate: you walk out one door and then another door and they're already cheering and booing—Yay. Nay. I made a historical case about Zionism and the bogus claims of Arab nationalisms and I won by a hundred votes, maybe a little less, an unapologetic American Jew with glasses and a rabbinical beard in the intellectual heart of the Old Empire.

✳ ✳ ✳

In many ways, I was a minority voice even among my allies. There weren't many intellectuals or politicians in Europe or America, or even in Israel, who were focused on the complex of nationalities, states, and peoples in the developing world.

One of the few was Fouad Ajami. I'd met him at Leon Wieseltier's first wedding and we developed a strange relationship, an almost tribal understanding though we came from different tribes. He was born in 1945 in Arnoun, Lebanon, a severe infertile place where an old crusader castle still loomed into the sky from a rocky height. He left, went west, studied, and started teaching at the University of Washington, and then at Princeton, before coming to Johns Hopkins.

He met a woman, Michelle, from an East Coast Protestant family and married her. Michelle was able to absorb the Arab ethos—the closeness of family, the concept of having to work for respect—and so freed Fouad to be American while keeping the Arab world in his psyche. It was a two-minded emigration: he wanted to leave the Arab world but he loved the Arab world. He loved Arab culture. He listened to Arab music, Arab songs. He also loved New York whence he commuted to Washington. He was not a typical exile. He held both places in himself and didn't see them through the lens of each other.

He once wrote me:

> *I loved my land—and pitied it. And deep within me lies a memory, at once searing and sustaining, of what it was long ago. It was home—and heartbreak, and all we know. We ached to get away from it, and we grieved when we did. It wasn't that much of a place. And it wasn't even kind. But it was our world.*

Fouad was tied in his heart to the Arab world. But he was an American through and through. This connected us: I love Israel, but I don't want to live in Israel; and I am an American Jew, and maybe a Jewish American. But Fouad came from a place that never had a chance to be a nation: he didn't let me forget how lucky Israelis were. An Israeli is an Israeli.

Then there was the anti-Fouad, Edward Said. He was a Palestinian Christian, but he even had several versions of where he was born. Maybe his mother didn't tell him. And he had an idealized view of the Arab world he had left. He taught literature at Columbia from 1963 until his death in 2003, was a member of the Palestinian National Council, and was everybody's choice as spokesman for the Palestinian cause. He gave an intellectual gloss to the movement, and the radical chic idolized him. Still, being an intellectual didn't prevent him from throwing a stone at Israel from Lebanon, an act that was picked up across Western media.

Said was granted access to intellectual New York in a way that I was not, in part because he was a genuinely serious intellectual and I was—and am—not, but also because even as political support for Zionism rose, intellectual support never did. Isaiah Berlin was an eminence at the *New York Review of Books*, which meant the *Review* wasn't explicitly anti-Zionist. But they were more easily in sympathy with Said because they could imagine that Palestinian nationalism was a product of oppression, bound to disappear as the rational internationalists improved the Palestinian lot, whereas Israel was no longer oppressed, but it was still a nation, a state of a people and not of individuals. And the Left cohort among the intellectuals sympathized with Said from the start: to many of them, Israel was an extrusion of the American capitalist empire.

* * *

Around 1972 or 1973, I took Jesse on his first trip to Israel. We went to the Red Sea vacation port of Eilat with my best friend Ian Fisher, whom I'd met a few years before when Golda and Simcha sent me and a few other Jewish Americans to tour the Golan Heights and we had Ian as our guide. Ian was a commercial pioneer in Israel and an enormously charming man. Around the time we first met, he was dating Mandy Rice-Davies, of the Profumo affair notoriety. She had been a cabaret dancer and the mistress of a slum landlord, and a minister of government had mixed in their circle. The whole matter came out and brought down Harold MacMillan's government. Now she was in Israel, opening a nightclub, and we would all go out sometimes.

Our guide was a handsome and articulate young man named Bibi. He told us about his brother Yonatan, the hero of Entebbe who was killed in the mission; his own service in the army; the wound he'd gotten; and his father Benzion, who had written scholarly books on the expulsion of the Jews from Spain. Benzion had been up for an appointment at the Hebrew University, but his revisionist Zionist politics were anathema to most of the senior history faculty there. He lost out to another scholar at the university, Haim Beinart (the great-uncle of Peter Beinart), whose views were more in line with the prevailing ethos. Denied his chair in Israel, Benzion

Netanyahu went into exile in the United States, teaching at second-rate institutions before landing at Cornell and then coming home to Israel, where he died at 102.

This was the first time I met the future prime minister of Israel. He would look me up when he came to MIT. We'd have coffee, and he'd always pay because I was the older and more "eminent" person. Later, he got eminent himself, but he still picked up the tab, very smoothly. There was a natural honesty between us. There's a truth to him. But it's a truth that comes from an inherited identity that's a bunker identity. He's a man with a family legacy to uphold and avenge. Bibi understood the Arab world because he was a little like them—he was willing to make deals outside of established international norms or rules to help Israel survive. And private deals besides to help himself survive.

Ehud Barak doesn't come from Zionist aristocracy. I first heard his name over dinner with Simcha that time with Norman Mailer: he was the man who planned the Entebbe rescue. A couple of years later, I met him at Simcha's and Vivian's apartment in Jerusalem. Barak is not very comfortable in social settings, and while everybody else talked, he was playing the piano. I knew the piece he was playing, a Liszt sonata, and so he played and I listened. Among his generation, Ehud was the most serious Israeli statesman I knew, at once the most concrete and intelligent.

He was a military hero, the most decorated soldier in Israeli history, and he was intimately acquainted with the Palestinian issue, so he knew what a bullshitter Arafat was. But unlike people of Bibi's political cohort, he saw what was slowly happening abroad: you couldn't discuss Israel without discussing the Palestinians. He knew that something had to change—that Israel had to defuse what was increasingly becoming an inescapable threat to its international reputation. The First Intifada, the series of uprisings in Gaza and the West Bank which stretched from 1987 to 1991, was more proof of this, and during the uprisings, Ehud was deputy chief of staff of the IDF.

I saw what Ehud saw. But I saw my part in the struggle not to make peace with Palestinians but to make war on anyone in America who used the Palestinian situation to make good on an anti-Israel vendetta. Friends, people who believed what I believed, tried to bring me back from the cusp of doing too much for Israel or for writing this or that in its defense: "Don't make 'Marty Peretz' synonymous with one issue," they'd say. "Say that but not in a way that doesn't leave you a way out." But I wanted to own one issue, and I wanted to be in a place that didn't leave me a way out. That was really a motive for me even if I never really thought of that consciously—to leave myself with no room to maneuver. I was a link to, a defender of, a kind of nation that Americans, with their individualism and their freedom from danger, increasingly didn't understand. If it cost me something to defend that nation against Arafat and his Western enablers, then I would take the cost.

CHAPTER ELEVEN

Cambridge: Transitions and Missions

After the sixties, the old Protestant order at Harvard was gone. Nathan Pusey retired in 1971 and was succeeded by Derek Bok, the dean of the law school. Bok was the son of a Massachusetts Supreme Court justice who was a devout Quaker and the heir to a publishing fortune. His wife, Sissela, was the daughter of two Nobel Prize winners, Gunnar Myrdal (for economics) and Alva Myrdal (for peace). A Protestant American academic married into intellectual aristocracy. I thought he was the right person to run Harvard in a time of transition and to shape the curriculum for a newly diversified elite, and he confirmed it for me when he made Henry Rosovsky dean of the faculty.

Henry was one of four Jewish academic arrivals at Harvard who were refugees from the times of troubles at Berkeley and Columbia, where student radicalism was far, far more destructive than anything we saw in Cambridge. Other refugees were the economic historian David Landes and the sociologists Dan Bell and Nat Glazer. Like them, Henry was essentially a conservationist, a builder. He filled the gap left by the collapse of the Protestant veneer at Harvard.

We met in 1967 at John and Kitty Galbraith's chintzy annual commencement party, which featured Ritz crackers and some kind of standard issue cheese. The napkins were more elegant than the food. I was arguing with David Riesman about the Six-Day War and Nitza, Henry's wife, whom I didn't yet know, was agreeing with me. Her family was old Israeli, from before Israel was a state; they owned Berman Bakery, which everybody in Israel knew.

Twelve years my senior, Henry was born in the Free City of Danzig to Russian Jewish parents, very learned folk. Henry's mother went to the University of Kyiv, one of the few women in Russia granted a dispensation to go to university by the czar's minister of education, and she was a real czarist reactionary. She and I really took to each other. It was about roots so deep they allowed us to kid each other with perfect understanding: she would always call me "my favorite Communist," which used to crack us up.

Henry had a huge influence on my behavior, if not my thinking. I looked up to him, and he liked me because, or in spite of the fact, that I was always trying to find my own way of doing things. He was, by his own admission, an institutionalist: he loved institutions, especially great universities. I liked institutions, too, but I was a little suspicious of them. To me, institutions made you forget your background: they tried for majesty; they made you say, "I want to be a part of this." I was wary of that; Henry wasn't. It was how he thought you made the biggest contribution.

Henry's first administrative task at Harvard, before he became dean, was about race. When he arrived at the university, a lot of the students had been advocating for a black studies program, and in the summer of 1968, the Faculty of Arts and Sciences put Henry—whose recreational passion was jazz and who had been one of the faculty pushing for more focus on black culture—in charge of responding to the petitions. Henry assembled a report recommending everything short of a black studies department: a new combined major, increased course offerings, a cultural center for black Americans, an intellectual center for African American studies, and the enrollment of more black graduate students. He stopped short of recommending a department because he was worried it would be underfunded and forced to fend for itself.

But this wasn't what hard-Left students and many of the professors desired. They wanted an autonomous department freed from what they saw as the university's limitations: for example, having a department would mean, at a minimum, the freedom of appointing faculty members. Meanwhile the conservatives on faculty wanted the department separate to ensure its marginality. The faculty called a special session in the days after the University Hall takeover and created the Department of Afro-American Studies, satisfying both the radicals and conservatives.

People admired the way Henry handled the issue. He listened to everybody; he thought that they all had something to say. And once he became dean, Henry used the trust he'd garnered to gather support for his main project: a reform of Harvard's core curriculum, the set of required courses from which all undergraduates had to choose, with the aim of resetting the university's educational perspective for the first time in many decades.

The last time the undergraduate curriculum had been changed was in 1945 with the issuing of what was called the "Red Book." The Red Book was an artifact of that era when aristocrats and their epigones came to Harvard from Andover and Exeter and studied Western civilization in preparation for careers in civil service, business, and academia. An example was William Weld, the future governor of Massachusetts and a neighbor of ours around that time. He was what we used to call a "well-rounded man." He knew Latin plus, I think, Greek, and instead of becoming a professor, he went into politics.

By 1975, the consensus on which the Red Book was built was out of date, replaced by a growing divide among the student body between careerists and idealists. Greek and Latin had been overtaken by science and specialization: the new middle classes that swept Harvard were interested in careers and careers required expertise. Among the idealists, Western civilization was now seen as a source of oppression in the developing world and, in fact, in the developed world as well. In its place were idealized moralities put forward by a committed few and tolerated or dutifully imitated by the rest, who were focused on their careers.

Henry's plan was to correct for this fracture, to institute some sort of universal standard that made room for the new specialties and new idealisms but that had reason and knowledge, not utopian aspirations nor particular expertise, as its guiding principles. It wouldn't mistake "humanities" for "Western civilization" because the human sciences weren't just a Western development. Its assumption would be "the possibility of common discourse among educated people." Its aim would be to help everyone make use of their innate faculty to reason.

It met with tremendous controversy: here was Harvard announcing a new system of values for how to live as an educated person at a time when American values were more in flux than in anybody's memory. But at some level, everybody realized a change needed to be made, or else students would split themselves into idealists and experts with nothing in between. Creating, and recreating, a version of that "between space" is what Henry accomplished.

I supported the reforms. But where I wanted to bridge the specialist-idealist gap, as always, was at the level of the classroom. Increasingly, I was realizing that the changes at Harvard, in the wake of the takeover and the Protestant defenestration, were bigger and more institutional than just temporary disorder. In 1973, Barrington Moore wrote Michael Walzer and me announcing his resignation from the Social Studies program. It was meant as a valedictory note, and it lodged in my mind for years after.

Dear Mike and Marty,

> *There are a great many students at this university who are at least moderately intelligent, who nevertheless have fundamental intellectual weaknesses, and who build up all sorts of pretenses to conceal these weaknesses.... When the false image of themselves is punctured, as indeed it ought to be, the consequence is liable to be extremely painful...One last observation: helping to run the seminar...pushes one in the direction of being a café intellectual with an opinion on absolutely everything. That is unhealthy for the teacher and is a bad model to set before a student. An ideology that provides instant and effortless answers to every serious issue is the last thing we want to inculcate.*

It lodged in my mind because it was such a crystallization of where we were. Immaturity. False images. Instant and effortless answers. This was part of the human legacy of the sixties—or rather, the new world that the disintegration of the old order had announced. I certainly didn't want the old culture back. But what came after, as I was seeing it, was antiseptic, defined not by the gentle, ineffectual old Protestant minders but by layer on layer of administration. It left everybody out on their own, which is part of what encouraged them to take refuge in those false categories, careerist or idealist, in the first place. It was David Riesman's America come to Harvard. Everybody was seeking direction, but nobody was sure how to find it; everybody wanted to be respected, but nobody wanted to be judged; everybody was working off their own script, but nobody was completely engaged or engaging.

In April of 1974, I wrote a proposal for a course to be called "Lives Examined." It harkened back to Max's rather loose, open forum at Brandeis. "It is my assumption," I wrote, "that the 'conduct of life' as Emerson meant it, or at least the conduct of particular lives, may be something subject to scrutiny and evaluation, even to moral reasoning." In my discussions with students, I was seeing them retreat from discourse by saying things like, "This cannot be argued rationally; it is a question of values." This was no substitute for testing their experience against their values and their values against their experience. "The tyranny of undiscussable values now balances out the tyranny of undiscussable facts."

The course really wasn't academic fare. It was about using intellectual tools to develop your own perspective and your own center, in an environment where a center was getting harder and harder to find. This was true of the other class I taught in those days, a junior tutorial with Nat Glazer, who had joined the Social Studies faculty at my instigation. We were talking about America's upper-middle class with some students who eventually would be part of it or govern it. Nat was mesmerizing in class, and I was flattered when he told me he'd learned a lot from me about how to create and run a seminar.

* * *

In Cambridge, I had another role: host of new players in a changing city and university. Our house was not only a lively center of conversation, but also a model of the broader transition at work between an old-fashioned Cambridge and a scholarly one with an underlay of Jewish dissonance.

Our dinners were a Cambridge institution. We had this very long, narrow table so our guests could sit close on opposite ends, and I tried to mix up people. I had a teacher's impulse to seed the group with people of various ages, interests, and backgrounds—academics and public figures, focused practitioners and persons of the world—so the conversation didn't get gossipy or narrow. You never knew what magic, what spontaneous ideas, might happen.

The tradition at our table, no matter who was there, was there should be just one conversation. This was Sissela Bok's policy at the college president's table, and since she had a lot of experience with dinner parties and smart people, Anne and I picked it up too. It was a rule that was not always followed, but it was an opening for everyone to participate. Sometimes it led to superficial topics and sometimes it was more. It was never pompous or deeply ordered, just an organizing principle with the hope something would come up. When public figures or celebrated guests were there, they held the floor. But they had to take questions, and everybody had to up their game. I was mostly quiet but occasionally I'd jump into conversation. Once in a long while, I'd get irritated, and that's where Anne would step in. "Marty," she'd lean over and say, "you are about to embarrass me."

My favorite celebrated guest was Conor Cruise O'Brien: a giant, eloquent, jolly, drunk Irishman with an amazing career. His first burst of fame came in the early sixties when the secretary-general posted him in the newly independent Congo, which was riven by civil war, and he got into a lot of trouble for being too muscular with UN forces there. He was also a prodigious writer, and I grew to like him even more when I read *The Great Melody*, his wonderfully iconoclastic book about Edmund Burke. He would be on our four-pillow couch, in the center of the living room; the party would collect around him, and he'd be in such a happy mood that you were happy too. It was just the kind of mind and manner I wanted to bring into a circle that, because of the pressures and provisions of increasingly specialized academic life, could sometimes get a little rote, a little stale.

Other people who had once filled O'Brien's role were no longer in our lives. Lillian Hellman was on the scene still, and we'd go to dinner parties and cordially despise each other until the cordiality wore thin. We broke up over Roy Cohn. I'd had him to my McCarthy seminar after we'd connected at a fundraiser for Jerusalem. Lillian saw a small item on the fundraiser in the *New York Post*, and she called up Anne and started to rant: Joe McCarthy, Dash Hammett, McCarthy, Cohn. Finally, I picked up the phone and said, "At least I wasn't a fellow traveler for Stalin," and she hung up. We never spoke again. I wasn't the only person she wasn't speaking to anymore. Like Herbert, she wouldn't make room for different loyalties, separate spheres. I had never endorsed Roy Cohn's actions or his politics, but when it came to educating students, I would accept his help. Really Lillian was much worse than Herbert: her mendacity put her in a class by herself.

After we split, she unintentionally did some good: I connected with one of my favorite finds at Harvard over her. Ed Zwick, who has gone on to make literate and ethically informed movies that are commercial successes, like *Glory*, entered my orbit when he came to me for help on his thesis on Lilian. He wasn't in Social Studies, he was in English literature, but he'd written a smart, critical appraisal, and I asked if he wanted to come to the *New Republic* the summer after his senior year. This was in 1974, the year I bought the magazine and its sixtieth anniversary, and I thought a sixty-year anthology was a good idea. I put Ed to work on the book: he spent the whole summer in the basement of the old Victorian house going through old editions. Then he went to Paris on a Rockefeller scholarship. I visited with him, and I took him out to dinner with Mary McCarthy, who spent the whole evening bashing Lillian and flirting with Ed. During the rest of his time in Paris, he and Mary would go see plays together.

My old crush Emily Cohen, who was by then MacFarquhar, came to dinners with her husband Rod. He headed the Fairbank Center for Chinese Studies at Harvard, and she worked at *The Economist* as its China expert. So would Moshe and Michal Safdie, architect and artist, who came to Harvard for him to teach for a year and still haven't left. Teddy Kollek had introduced us from afar, and Moshe did the plans for our remodeled kitchen. In 1982, when Moshe and Michal decided to get married, they did it in our garden.

Larry Summers would sometimes be there. Already he was a wunderkind, one of the youngest tenured professors in Harvard's history. Michael Ignatieff, the Canadian aristocrat and a protégé of Isaiah Berlin, was a regular. I met him when he came to Harvard, broke and in need of a place to live, and I put him up in an apartment in Cabot House for several years. His parents were both famous economists and his grandfather, Count Pavel Ignatiev, was the czar's minister of education who gave Henry Rosovsky's mother her dispensation to go to the University of Kyiv. How the world is small!

Jill and Yo-Yo Ma weren't Jewish, but they were honorary Jews, which is what you become when you get really close to me. They'd bring Nicholas and Emily, their children, to our house for all the big holidays. We'd met right after Jill and Yo-Yo met, when Yo-Yo was at Harvard. He wasn't in my class, but we bumped into each other and became friends. Years later, when they were living in a nondescript town remote from Cambridge, I told them about a house off Brattle Street, Tory Row, that had come on the market. I got them to drive to Cambridge to see it on a Friday, and they bought it on the following Monday. Here was this young, learned, artistic, half-Asian couple surrounded by the old disappearing Protestant elite. They couldn't really afford the house at the time, but it was a gorgeous place, and they grew to love it and the neighborhood.

Stephen Breyer, a law professor at Harvard and then the chief judge of the First Circuit Court of Appeals, and his wife, Joanna, a psychiatric social worker and daughter of Viscount Blakenham, became friends of ours. He was very reserved, and I am not, but he, who came from a much more assimilated, almost aristocratic San Francisco Jewish family, used me a little bit as a Jewish confessional.

Leon Botstein was not quite of this crowd but adjacent to it. He was younger, though his presence represented the same Jewish breakthrough in the American academy. I had met Leon when he was just out of the University of Chicago where he'd studied at the Committee of Social Thought with Hannah Arendt. I hired him as a teaching fellow in Social Studies—he was twenty-two. Years later, after a stint as president of Franconia College, which is now defunct, Leon made a name for himself as the architect of Bard, a college in Annandale-on-Hudson. Bard had fallen on hard financial times but was relieved by Leon's fundraising efforts and by the periodical contributions of George Soros, the most recent of which, pledged in 2021, was a half-billion dollars. For a little while, in the eighties, Henry Rosovsky and I were obsessed with getting Leon the presidency of Brandeis. But he was too inventive for an increasingly flavorless institution, and we failed.

❋   ❋   ❋

I also brought students into my orbit and their ambitions were changing as well. More and more they were bound for finance and administration: the calling cards of the new American elite.

Paradigmatic was Glenn Hutchins. He took from his agronomist father a commitment to fighting poverty and hunger, but because he didn't come from wealth, he was interested in making it. He dual majored in economics and social studies and was an entrepreneur on the side. Every Harvard student got a coupon book to go to concerts, football games, and so on, and Glenn figured out that none of the Social Studies people were interested in those things. So he asked them for their coupon books, they gave them to him, and he sold coupons to students, alumni—anybody who didn't have enough tickets to Fleetwood Mac or the Yale hockey game. Right after his graduation, Glenn went to work for a firm on Wall Street, but then he came back to get his MBA and his JD at Harvard because he thought it would make him unbeatable in business. (It did.)

Glenn's roommate at Dudley House was Jim Cramer. I called Jim originally because I was looking for a reviewer for a book and Mike Kinsley, having read some of the journalism he'd done right after graduating, recommended him. I got his answering machine a few times, used the stock tips he left, and made some real money. I kept calling him, he kept not responding, and finally I left a message saying I didn't care about the book review anymore, I wanted him to look over my investment portfolio. We met at the Coffee Connection, and when he looked at the portfolio, he saw what I'd thought he'd see: the Clark Estates, Anne's business office, was investing in old world products—not only oil but railroads!—which were either stumbling or moribund. He said the stocks to watch were in tech. I said, "Okay, here's five hundred thousand dollars. Invest it." Jim was twenty-six at the time and had no money; he was shocked, but he invested well. I got him writing for the *New Republic*; then I put him in touch with people in New York, and he got a job at Goldman Sachs as a trader. I liked Jim. He was a culturally and psychologically intricate case: he came from the Philadelphia suburbs, and the family was rich but not really wealthy and not elite. Jim was very aware of that at Harvard and after.

I was becoming a figure on campus and not really a categorizable one. I still had my longish bushy beard, and I wore my shirts unbuttoned halfway in the French manner. But I wasn't a certifiable leftist: I drove a red Porsche. I didn't teach full time, and my classes were not too rigorous, yet everybody said they were inspiring. I was provocative and gave my opinion freely and had students do the same. I had lunches, coffees, and dinners with them; I loved some of them, and they loved me back. They were grateful to have someone to talk to who was warm and grounded in a place like Harvard that didn't necessarily give you that feeling unless you'd been born to it. I knew where they were coming from. I hadn't been born to it either.

Henry Rosovsky and Derek Bok were on their way out in the early 1990s. But to clear up one last piece of business, they brought in Henry Louis Gates, who everyone calls "Skip," to take over the Afro-American program. Skip came from Yale, Cornell, Duke, and he was a very sober and serious intellectual possessed of considerable personal charm. The campus political atmosphere was tense: despite Henry's successful reforms to the curriculum, the split between professionals and idealists had by now become institutionalized. The idealists who were practical, if unimaginative, pushed for world health programs and committees on eliminating poverty. The idealists who were hardline took over whatever public culture existed and waged war on each other. The more radical idealists put justice, feelings, and groups over rigor and individuality, and they did it institutionally: identity-based student unions were set up with the imprimatur of the new campus administrative organs. The reactionary idealists defended Western civilization, but they did it coarsely: you got the feeling they were defending the old because it was old, not because they truly believed in it any longer. The genuine liberals and pluralists on the faculty were critical but quiet. There wasn't much they could do with the administration increasingly dedicated to fundraising and afraid of controversy.

This was particularly true when it came to race, and the people who got marginalized were not the radicals, whose small activist groups dominated the discourse, or the conservatives, who had their own favorite professors and small campus publications or clubs, but genuine liberals who were trying to say nonideological things. Stephan Thernstrom stopped teaching a class—or was stopped from teaching a class—on slavery with Bernard Bailyn because the Black Student Association denounced his insensitivity in talking about Jim Crow. They objected to his reading from white planters' journals, original historical documents, saying they gave a "beneficent" version of slavery.

Stephan and Abby, my old friends from our days agitating over Cuba, were moving Right on the issue of race anyway, so maybe the controversy made sense. But other people, far from right wing, were also concerned. David Riesman complained about the atmosphere. C. Vann Woodward, who was at Yale, wrote a piece in the *New York Review of Books* criticizing the radicals and the reactionaries and defending David and Stephan. He was denounced as an overreactor by most of the professors who responded, including John Hope Franklin, the dean of black historians and an eminent and reasonable man, which gives you a sense of how fraught the issue was.

Skip was the right person to address this problem. He was black but not radical; he was committed to scholarship but also a shrewd reader of public opinion. I'd known Skip before he came to Harvard. I liked him, but there was a limit to how useful I could be to him with the black scholars and conservatives who, in many cases, were as skeptical of me as they were of African-American Studies. But we offered a welcoming house, and Henry Rosovsky, Skip's closest ally, was always there, so Skip came often. It was a social base he could rely on—or deny—as he achieved his own mastery on campus.

And he did achieve mastery, because at some level I think he knew the average Harvard student wasn't a radical and wanted to know more about the richness and complexity of black culture. To help him, he brought in star professors with big reputations—William Julius Wilson from the University of Chicago and Cornel West from Princeton, the first generation of black academics trained at the country's elite institutions—and he turned his department around.

I respected Wilson, though I don't think we ever met. He published *The Declining Significance of Race*, a structural explanation for some of the problems in the black community that Glenn Loury had identified in the *New Republic*. He was focused on economics— the shift from an industrially driven society to a financially driven one and the loss of jobs for the underclass that this change drove. He saw racism as the initial cause of black poverty, but he thought these bigger shifts were affecting a population that racism had made more vulnerable.

West was more ideological, a Christian Marxist or Marxist Christian, and a nominal disciple of Richard Rorty. He married Rorty's provocative ideas about the shaping force of context and language to old-school black theology and old-school Marxist dogma. He saw religion as a liberationist vehicle against capitalist structures. He harangued the black middle classes for leaving their brothers and sisters in the inner cities. I couldn't stand him, even when he used to suck up to me. I don't recall whether my dislike became distrust or my distrust became dislike; and I don't recall whether my attitude led him to diss me or me to diss him.

I had a personal triumph around this time that was another kind of high point for the university. In 1993, I endowed a chair for Yiddish Literature at Harvard. The first holder was Ruth Wisse, from McGill University, who was politically quite right-wing, connected to neo-conservatives like Norman Podhoretz. But that didn't affect her scholarship—she is probably one of the two or three subtlest scholars of Yiddish culture I know of—or our friendship. Nor did it affect the significance of her appointment: even one or two decades earlier, it would've been unthinkable for Harvard students to study Yiddish.

When Ruth came on, I had a huge dinner for her at the Fogg Museum. I think Ruth and her husband Len were a bit embarrassed by its magnificence. I made a speech and Cynthia Ozick wrote me after to say: "I was moved in particular by your reference to Yiddish as 'high culture for the masses' – a reminder of Carlyle's incomprehension that the man who cried 'Ole Cloes' in the London streets could be kin to Isaiah."

* * *

In 1991, just after appointing Skip, Derek and Henry retired, and Neil Rudenstine succeeded Derek as President. Rudenstine's ascent signaled something—a change in the elite that had started to manifest twenty years before, now made official. Rudenstine was the son of a Jewish prison guard who had emigrated from Kiev. He attended the Wooster School, an elite private school, on scholarship, then Princeton with the ROTC; he served in the army, received a Rhodes Scholarship, and took his PhD in English literature from Harvard. At a dinner I gave for Shimon Peres, Rudenstine promptly fell asleep: probably he'd had a long day as president of Harvard, but I think all things Jewish put him to sleep. His wife, Angelica, happens to be the daughter of Walter Zander, who spent decades as the secretary of the British Friends of the Hebrew University in Jerusalem and wrote numerous books on Israel. But Neil was an upwardly mobile Jew, slightly older than me, who followed the old midcentury path, studying Western civilization and practicing Jewish assimilation. His main concern at Harvard was fundraising, something at which he excelled, and in this sense, he was a transitional figure from the values of the age before me to the values of the age after.

Harvard has always had a Harvard-centric view of the universe. The *Crimson* refers to people not by their accomplishments but by their class: Henry Kissinger is Henry Kissinger '50. When I first came, the view was almost provincial, a ruling culture so old it was uninterested in what went on outside unless it was in Europe. As I stayed, the view became sharper, more driven by social scientific thinking: more meritocracy, less aristocracy. Now there was a new kind of artifice to replace the old—not an aristocracy of good families but an aristocracy of good intentions. "Social responsibility" was a term one was beginning to hear. "Conflict resolution" was another phrase that meant a lot less than it was supposed to mean. All of these fit under the framework of "missions," which itself was the byword for a new public culture. This is what has become of the utopianism of the sixties: if the world cannot be changed wholesale, we must take it one orphanage at a time.

The grandiose notion of every undergraduate having to have a mission by sophomore year didn't quite square with my belief in the university as the place to learn the conduct of life. The concrete problem, of course, is that some of the most interesting people, the deepest people, are people who don't have missions, at least not at the beginning. Their true purpose may be hard to define, a little out of step with the thinking of the academy, or just developing. More often than not, they are the really interesting people. More often than not, they can't get a foothold without help, and a university built on expertise and utopianism and on specialization and generalization isn't necessarily equipped to give them the help they need.

*　*　*

In 1989, I celebrated my fiftieth birthday with a garden party at 20 Larchwood. Anne had gotten my friends and students together, and they presented me with a book of testimonials. Celebrating the birthday at home was fitting: we'd spent twenty years building our lives here and constructing, in a loose and yet attentive way, a community of people.

While we were together fostering this community in Cambridge, Anne was doing the same through her work at the Family Center, a clinic that she had developed in Somerville, in those days a low-rent town adjoining Cambridge. She was one of those privileged egalitarians, the oppressiveness of whose wealth led them to be passionate about poverty. (Another one of her projects, a hospital in Burundi, has altered the lives of countless mothers and children in revolutionary ways.) By 1982, she had been raising children for almost twenty years, and she believed, without admitting it, what Pat Moynihan believed: family structure was the deciding factor in a person's life. This was true no matter their social class, but with people on the edge of poverty, family could be the make or break.

And, in a way, I was still grappling with the significance of my own family in my life. A positive development was that my brother was a growing presence in my life then. He had attended the University of Wisconsin, where he studied under George Mosse, a truly great historian of modern Europe and of the Jews, and became his devoted student. Part of why he moved to the Right politically, I think, is that his knowledge of Central Europe and fascism is so deep. After college, Gerry became a banker and then, without a PhD in anything, he became a researcher at the Rockefeller University. He is a fine classical musician. When he sits down and plays Bach BWV 887, he is playing the real thing.

My father was never a large figure in my life after I left home—physically that is. Psychologically he was huge. A year or two before he died at ninety-eight, I went to see him and I took Leon Wieseltier with me. We went from LaGuardia to Manhattan Beach in Brooklyn—the same neighborhood Leon came from. My father moved there from Park Avenue after my mother died to be near émigré Russian and Polish Jews. In the cab, I trembled and shook. Leon told me later he was absolutely perplexed by what he saw. After all, this was my strong period: I knew prime ministers, would-be presidents, titans of industry, major philanthropists, and important intellectuals. And here I was trembling at seeing a little, fat man with a too-big tie over a too-little shirt.

All of the ugliness in me came from two things. One was anger at my father. The other was a kind of anxiety at the things that, imitating or responding to my father, I held at arm's length so I could get on with my life in the world: my gayness, my lack of intellectual stature on the level of the people I was closest to, and the way the Establishment saw me as an outsider. It's hard to say to what extent these anxieties drove me. But I never examined their effects either. And so, my feelings at slights real or imagined would build to a boiling point.

At that point I'd explode. It concealed to others those moments when I felt pressed, and it also concealed that I don't, at all, like conflict: I'll leave a room often before I get into a fight. But when I lost control, it obviated the need for a fight—if I was out of control, people would step back. Then I'd move on, and I wouldn't realize that the person I was talking to, screaming at, hadn't moved on and was hurt and angry at my behavior. I was dead to my own effect.

There were people I was close enough to—people who I respected enough, whose good opinion was very important to me, whose judgment I trusted and needed—who I would never risk alienating in that way: Leon Wieseltier, Sherry Turkle, Michael Walzer, Tommy Tisch, Jamie Gorelick, Henry Rosovsky, Yo-Yo, and Al. But this meant that, when I did explode, I often picked on smaller, weaker people. Also, aged fifty, the anger had more outlets, because I had fewer people left to be accountable to. Harry Labouisse had died in 1987 and with him went my link to, and the weight of, that older world where I'd never completely fit. Herbert Marcuse was dead. Max Lerner was nearing ninety. Norman Mailer seemed past his prime. The loss of the elders, if you will, meant that I was now me—unquestioned, in full, an authority figure.

✳   ✳   ✳

At midlife, we went to Paris for a year so Anne could paint and for us to have a respite in a comfortable place. But the trip didn't turn out as we planned. Early on, we were at Le Laurent, a wonderful restaurant owned by Sir James Goldsmith, but I was caught between two women who seemed intent on speaking only to the person on their opposite side, and I had nobody to talk to. I'm not much of a drinker, never have been, but I drank more and more white wine. Finally, I escaped to the bathroom, where the last thing I remember was looking in the mirror. A week later, I woke up. I'd fallen and hit my head. Eventually they'd found me lying there, and I was taken to the hospital in an ambulance.

The kids, thinking I was going to die, had flown over and no doubt the magazine staff was wondering if they'd be looking for jobs. Anyway, I didn't die. The doctor who saved my life was

Didier Grosskopf, who naturally became a friend. The kids went back home, and the *New Republic* kept publishing, but the concussion changed things. For one, I lost my rich English vocabulary for months; I would find myself speaking in Yiddish without realizing. I couldn't put my left arm into a shirt or a sweater. Anne didn't trust me to cross the street alone. Once coming back from lunch, I forgot my address and couldn't tell the taxi driver where to go. I got out and walked back and found my way in the rain. For the first time I felt, not my age, but arrested in my momentum by something I couldn't ignore.

✳ ✳ ✳

Once, years earlier, I was walking on the beach in Truro with Ed Zwick. The salt was in my eyes, and the wind was whipping the tops of the waves into white flecks like it did in Anne's paintings. I saw Anne and the kids up ahead. It was almost time for dinner and just as we were getting ready to go into the house, I stopped Ed.

"Make room for this," I said, "because life moves you past things, and then they're gone. Take some seconds because things change—and you'll lose the meaning, and it will never be back just this way. You don't care about this now but believe me—you will."

It's impossible to crystallize those moments. You lose them too fast—they move by, the world shifts. Life in my fifties was like that—I was at a peak of influence, comfort, ability, and the dark spots were there but still marginal. And yet the world I had come up in, the world I knew, was shifting. The hub of the shift, its nexus, was New York.

CHAPTER TWELVE

New York: Capital

New York in the seventies was different from the city I remembered. The shift of America's economy from industry to consumption hadn't been kind to its urban spaces or its unionized workers. Neither had Robert Moses, whose New York highways cut through old neighborhoods and broke them, forcing the migration to the suburbs and making refugees of the city's poorest inhabitants. The Grand Concourse, the old neighborhood for Jews, Irish, and Italians, was now home for Puerto Ricans and Dominicans. Unlike us, they were contending with a landscape where synagogues, churches, and community centers were being replaced by gangs, drugs, and chain stores.

I didn't come to New York for intellectuals anymore. My new friends were in finance, and I met them through my work for Israel and for Jewish cultural institutions. I was on the board of a few Dreyfus funds through my connection with the chairman Howard Stein, who had been the financial head of the McCarthy campaign. Dreyfus was my real introduction to the dynamics of finance. What attracted me was the democratic aspect of it, where you could have small investors put their money in funds and see returns: a shift driven by many of the Jewish arrivals on Wall Street. Actually, Howard was a violinist who had gone to Juilliard, and he created a very friendly, cozy, gemütlich environment. But we weren't consciously Jewish: the funds were the project of people who came, and invested, naturally together.

Larry Tisch, who I also knew through Jewish concerns, was not a democratizing influence: he was a corporate titan, and as Dreyfus remade Wall Street from the bottom up, he was remaking Wall Street from the top down. We'd stayed in touch since we met in 1967, and his youngest son, Tommy, and I had become close friends. Whenever I was in New York, I stayed at the Regency on Sixty-First and Park Avenue, the flagship of Larry's Loews Corporation that he and his brother started with a resort in New Jersey. They'd made that one resort into a chain that stretched as far south as Florida. But then Larry moved a step away from their product. He began buying the controlling shares of failing companies with promising products and turning them around. He became one of the most aggressive investors of his generation. In 1969, he bought the Loews movie chain, dismantled many of the old downtown theaters, rebuilt them elsewhere, and made the old lots into apartments in time for the real estate market boom. He bought CNA Financial in a hostile takeover in 1974, when hostile takeovers in pursuit of profit margins were a revolutionary occurrence.

Larry was a singular figure on Wall Street, keeping a cool head as money was inundating the markets and everybody was heady with what they could buy. He was religiously interested, very charitable, and modest in his personal habits and tastes. He and his wife Billie had four sons, three in the family business, and all of them good people, which isn't easy when you have that kind of money. I know it was a close marriage. Larry gave back to the city: NYU Tisch, Tisch Hospital, the New York Public Library, the Metropolitan Museum of Art. He was an old-fashioned service provider with an eye for investments, and he had a bold, no-nonsense gamesmanship about him: he wasn't a corruptible man.

In 1986, Larry took a controlling share of CBS. CBS was in terrible shape when he stepped in, a touchstone of the media culture but trailing in rankings behind ABC and NBC and hemorrhaging money. The vultures were circling, and it looked like the network might go to a cohort headed by Jesse Helms, the reactionary Republican senator from North Carolina. The financier Ivan Boesky, a friend of mine, was also rumored to be interested. Bill Paley, the CBS founder, who was still a force on the board, brought in Larry as a white knight.

With Paley's blessing, Larry did what everybody knew he needed to do but somehow couldn't believe he would: cutting jobs to make the network profitable again. Dan Rather, who'd taken over the anchor chair from Walter Cronkite a few years earlier, wrote an opinion piece in the *Times* against the layoffs. Don Hewitt, who'd created *60 Minutes*, made a public statement saying the same. More and more, this intra-elite animus was par for the course. People in the press increasingly tended to be sixties idealists gone institutionalists, and from these institutions, they intended to hold the people in power to test their ideals. Big business was an easy target: it had become less about production and industry and more about consumption and return, focused ruthlessly on the bottom line and shareholder value.

But the real symbols of this change were not corporations—they were hedge funds. One of the most successful was run by another friend, Michael Steinhardt. Michael and I had met in 1979, after the *New York Times* ran an article about a financier who had taken a year off his hedge fund to pursue other interests: "As a Jew whose fealty to Israel is deeply felt, he explored a variety of ways to create new American investments there. He had hoped that…work with the city might materialize, public service being high on his list of morally meaningful activities." He seemed like an interesting person and so I called his office to arrange a meeting.

We met at the Grand Central Oyster Bar. The menu is mostly *treyf*, seafood and pork—a challenge for me but not for Michael, who doesn't keep kosher. Our conversation was on Jewish matters, and we hit it off—two very active, passionate Jews who don't obey most of the rules, even the Jewish ones.

Michael had grown up in Bensonhurst, off Bay Parkway, by Coney Island in Brooklyn. His father was in the diamond business and the gambling trade, which is to say he didn't always make money legally and ended up in prison. Like me, Michael went to college at sixteen. His father used the money he had made selling stolen jewelry and gambling to send his son to the Wharton School of the University of Pennsylvania. Michael started his career as an investor by putting thousands of his father's dollars, which he received in the form of hundred-dollar bills stuffed in envelopes, in the market. After college, he did a stint on Wall Street when Wall Street, like Harvard, was mostly genteel old Protestant scions with their principles, principals, and public trusts, existing like they'd always existed.

In 1967, Michael broke away from the firm he was working at to form a hedge fund, which, as everybody now knows, is an investment firm that makes high-risk investments promising high rewards. It's not democratic financing, like the Dreyfus funds, because you have to have enough money to be let in: it's for pension funds and firms and people interested in leveraging their wealth through aggressive investing. It's elite, like Larry Tisch's investing. But unlike Larry's, it's a step removed from an actual product. Michael's was one of the first on Wall Street—he was, in this world, a pioneer.

Michael ran a lean shop, an idiosyncratic shop: he and his employees wore Bermuda shorts and pullovers. But nothing else was casual. Michael's intensity and his rigor from nine thirty to four o'clock, when the stock market was open, were frightening to behold. His investors expected returns to the tune of 20 or 25 percent, almost three times the annual performance of the S&P index for that period. To beat the market like he did, you had to get good information, and, because of his earnings, Michael was first on the list of calls brokers made to see who wanted to sell or buy what. It was an inbuilt advantage in a market that increasingly ran on information. That wasn't illegal. But sharing that information with other firms to make the same trades in a bid to control the market was. Politicians were under pressure from the media to regulate some of the murkier looking plays. In 1991, Michael's firm and a few other funds cornered the market on treasury bonds and the Treasury Department started a federal investigation. They reached a settlement where Michael paid a fine but didn't admit wrongdoing.

The harder price got paid by Ivan Boesky, of the "greed is good" mantra. Ivan grew up in Detroit, the son, like me, of a middle-class Jewish tradesman. In this case, the family owned a delicatessen, which it called a restaurant. He had bounced around Midwestern universities without getting his BA but somehow managed to get a JD from Michigan Law. Then he came out to New York to make his fortune. Ivan and I didn't initially know each other through finance—just through financiers. We hardly talked about business; our conversations were about Judaism, art, and the news of the day. It was something different; it relaxed him and let him express his curiosity and a certain rigorous, inquiring religiosity. He gave millions to the Jewish Theological Seminary, the rabbinical school of Conservative Judaism, and on the weekends would go and study there—Ivan more often than me.

Ivan was an arbitrage trader: he ran bets on which companies corporate titans like Larry Tisch would take a controlling stake in and which new opportunities hedge fund leaders like Michael Steinhardt would wager on for his investors. With these bets, Ivan took the new financial instruments a step further. He wasn't just wagering on an outcome of a product; he was wagering on an outcome of a negotiation between producers and investors—the variables were that much more complicated and good information was that much more important.

Ivan got capital and investment for some of these plays from Michael Milken, who was pioneering another Wall Street innovation: junk bonds. These were bonds issued by companies with lower credit ratings—risky but with big upside. Milken's operation persuaded these companies to issue junk bonds to investors, and he then underwrote the risk on the bonds. Some of the issuing companies were small players who used the bonds to grow; others were growing firms looking for takeover targets, firms that couldn't get traditional financing for such risky plays.

Ivan used the capital Milken gave him to bet on takeovers—a lot of them led by firms financed by Milken. This was a murky area, which they muddled and muddied even more, because Ivan would also use Milken's capital to buy up shares in a company that Milken would want to take over, making it easier for Milken to do so. They were operating in a vacuum; there were no laws against this sort of thing because nobody had ever tried it.

These were Wild West days on Wall Street. Money was being made and excess was in the air. But resentment was brewing, and regulators were coming under media pressure to apply stricter standards to the activities of these new geniuses. Ivan was high profile: aggressive, self-promoting, twisty, diffident, and seemingly aloof in his public presentation from any effect his attitude or actions might have. He was an obvious target. In 1986, the Feds arrested him for insider trading. He became the poster child for a changing financial system and went to prison for two years. By that time, I was part of several of his ventures and when they cratered after the indictment, I found myself one of dozens of people who were both plaintiff and defendant because two of the firms were suing each other. How does that happen? Somehow, as everything toppled around him, Ivan made sure none of his people would be left in the street financially.

Sometime during his prison sentence, Ivan called me: his son was graduating from Princeton, and there was nobody there to watch him walk. The family, like any family in that position, was a mess. So, I went to Princeton and represented them. It wasn't that I thought Ivan was innocent—though I did question whether what he did was a crime when he did it. I did it because he'd been a good friend.

What drew us to each other—Ivan, Michael, Larry on one hand and me on the other? We were all middle class, from a strong culture that was an outsider culture, in the first generation when that culture could assert itself in American institutions. We weren't constrained by old obligations because we were coming into a world that didn't want us anyway. We had each other's backs because we knew the kind of resentment arrivistes, and Jewish arrivistes, unleashed.

Most of all, we had the sense that wealth and success weren't enough: we were supposed to use them to give back to our society and to our people. Does that sound romantic? It was romantic. We loved America because America's upper echelons allowed us in. We loved high culture because we thought it made people more thoughtful and humane. We loved the ideal of public service because only in a secular democracy could marginalized cultures thrive. We were the first ethnicity to break through into the ruling class institutions following the wane of Protestant influence, and we saw those institutions as the key to our flourishing. If you trace the arcs of many Jewish careers, they hover around this nexus. That wasn't, however, the way they were seen right then.

The financial center was leaving the city behind, creating fallout in the lives of New Yorkers not on the way up or the way down but just trying to live normal lives. It was a divide that more and more people realized needed to be bridged with political action. In my life, the person who charted the course between the city's financial life and its political one was Eric Breindel.

Eric had been my student at Harvard—brilliant and passionate, quirky and contradictory, and full of push and pull. He wasn't a particularly handsome boy, but he was a distinctive one: he had a demarcated, even chiseled face, and a kind of inner strength to him, a magnetism. Two of his girlfriends at Harvard were Caroline Kennedy, who is currently the ambassador to Australia, and Benazir Bhutto, who twice served as prime minister of Pakistan before her assassination in 2007. And then there were the others, all Jewish girls, because he was thinking of marriage.

His family was old-fashioned in a way I understood. His parents were Holocaust survivors who had become quite wealthy; they loved America, hated the Soviet Union, believed ardently in Zion, and were quite right wing. His father was the obstetrician to the Lubavitcher court, the Orthodox sect some of whose adepts had accrued huge wealth and influence in New York and all of whom had a lot of babies in fulfillment of the commandment. The outlier was Eric's sister, who was very Left. At her wedding at the family apartment on Seventy-Sixth Street and Fifth Avenue, I wheeled Eric's grandmother into the living room to witness the ceremony. She saw the canopy, a Mexican blanket, and she said to me, in loud, clear Yiddish, so that anyone who comprehended could hear, "That is not a canopy." (*Dos iz nisht keyn chuppah.*) Then the rabbi, a woman, came out, and she said, "This is not a rabbi." (*Dos iz nisht keyn rov.*) Then she saw the rabbi was pregnant and she said, only in more primitive words, "This is not an obstetrician's office." (I can't reconstruct the Yiddish on that.)

Eric felt pretty much the way his grandmother did. He was, in many aspects, much more adult than his cohort, even in his love of America, which was a very immigrant love, a love I felt too. Like me, his passions were politics and journalism: he was almost elected editor of the *Harvard Crimson*, but he lost in a brutal contest with Jim Cramer. And he went with a crowd who couldn't understand his obsessions—America, Israel, Communism—just as many people in my crowd couldn't understand them in me.

His best friend at Harvard was Bobby Kennedy Jr., a smart boy and a bad influence. Bobby took a course with me and one with

Robert Coles, the star child psychologist who was quiet about his Jewishness, and once when we were talking about inherited identities, Bobby asked me, "Is Robert Coles Jewish?" He was socially savvy: he knew I identified and Robert didn't. I somehow responded calmly and held my tongue. I was the adult in the room. Another time, at the graduation party we threw for Eric, one of Bobby's cousins, Maria Shriver, began to carve her name onto our eighteenth-century dining room table until Anne caught her at the task: I guess she thought it would be an honor for us to have her name on it. Caroline Kennedy, Eric's one-time girlfriend, whom I liked, was watching this cousin do the carving, and Caroline looked so embarrassed. But for some reason, she didn't stop her. Still, Eric liked the Kennedys, he was drawn to them, and he and Bobby Kennedy became drug mates at Harvard.

Eric moved very fast, and I was not the only "eminence" he looked to as he mapped his path. He was a genuine human; he never hid what he believed in, but he also knew how to use those beliefs to mesh with powerful people. Pat Moynihan, who was back teaching at Harvard in between stints in the Nixon and Ford administrations and his Senate run, was a mentor. Norman Podhoretz was another mentor. Eric didn't have the Democratic Party in his veins in the way of Jews who came up when we were a marginalized people, and he wasn't a convert like Norman: he was a conservative all the way through. But like Norman, Eric held his politics close to him, even religiously; unlike Norman, he didn't let them interfere with his friendships.

After Harvard College, Eric went to Harvard Law School and then to Washington to work as an aide for Moynihan. It was very clear, given his passions and the people he'd lined up behind him, that he was headed to a career in government. But not long after he came to Washington, D.C., he got caught buying five packets of heroin for $150 in a drug sting at a Holiday Inn just outside the city.

Eric called me and I called Jamie Gorelick, who represented him at his arraignment. Once he was out of jail, I gave him my Georgetown apartment to live in as a place to recover. It was a tough, tough thing: it was in the papers and not just the *Washington Post*. His family, a proud set of people, had to read about it; his career in government was derailed. But he didn't dwell on the loss, at least to his close friends. What we talked about, and we talked a lot in the next few months, was how he should get back on his feet.

Part of his recovery was personal. He had started seeing Lally Weymouth, Katharine Graham's daughter, who was on her way to becoming a wonderfully funny right-wing type. Lally wasn't really Jewish, but she had a Jewish grandfather and that made it almost okay for Eric. Lally gave Eric the personal stability that allowed him to find his professional footing again. The place where he found it opened up thanks to one good deed by Norman Podhoretz, and it wasn't an auspicious, or even a respected, place. It was the *New York Post*.

When Eric started there, in the late eighties, the paper was a tabloid that leaned Right: Rupert Murdoch had purchased it from Dorothy Schiff in 1976, then sold it again in 1988 because of a conflict of interest with his television channels. Max Lerner was still its one resident liberal writer, and it was just coming off the editorial tenure of James Wechsler, a longtime liberal who kept the page honest Democrat. But most of all, the *Post* was popular: it would cover, as it covers now, popular culture and local interest stories about sex, divorce, and petty crime like the soap operas they were. It would cover subjects the *Times* wouldn't touch. *Post* reporters were more aggressive, less polite. And it was onto something, a feeling in the air, the way average people were experiencing New York's economic divide, as already gutted neighborhoods got left further behind and all these disruptions and resentments got grafted onto the easiest target: tribal animus.

The stories were operatic and tragic. In one case, a fifteen-year-old girl named Tawana Brawley, who was discovered in a garbage bag, her body covered with scrawled racial slurs and excrement, accused a group of white boys of kidnapping and raping her. Al Sharpton and Louis Farrakhan championed her cause; the black community was incensed. No one was ever indicted in that case because it turned out there never was a rape: it was a made-up story, orchestrated by Brawley, perhaps to avoid punishment by her mother and abusive stepfather. But this was not a typical tale: if the Tawana Brawley case was a fiction hyped up by incendiary figures like Sharpton, there were plenty of examples of events that warranted indignation. The mostly white press, abetted by the tabloids, cheered as a jury tried and convicted five black defendants from the projects for the rape of a jogger in Central Park; years later, it turned out they were innocent. In Howard Beach, Queens, a twenty-three-year-old black man was set upon by a group of white men outside a pizza parlor and ran for his life across the Belt Parkway where he was run down by a car. A white subway rider, Bernhard Goetz, shot four unarmed young black men and was cleared of a racially motivated crime because they were trying to rob him.

But on the editorial page of the *Post*, Eric helped the paper articulate what its natural constituents—middle class, outer borough, practical, sometimes ethnic—felt: mostly fear and surprise that the city wasn't doing more to prevent the disorder that had to be prevented before any of its root causes could be addressed. Eric said this, again and again and again, and eventually, he did more. His impetus was two ethnic, almost tribal, clashes that happened blocks from each other in Brooklyn between 1990 and 1991, and both shook Eric, a Jew, a conservative, and the son of survivors.

The first was the Flatbush boycott. A black woman had gone into a Korean-owned store and when she came out, she said she'd been assaulted by three employees. The store said she'd refused to pay for what she wanted to buy and denied her story. A couple of local community organizers, black nationalists and veterans of the black "people power" movement in Brooklyn, organized a boycott of the store. There followed eight months of "scorched-earth" protests: every day protestors stood outside, jeered at the workers who went inside, intimidated customers, and sometimes threw stones. And it spread beyond the store where the incident happened. When the crowd first gathered and started throwing stones, a Korean passing by had gone into a nearby shop for safety; the protestors stoned that shop, too, and demanded it close.

The second was the Crown Heights riots, a conflict between blacks and Orthodox Jews. Two children of Guyanese immigrants had been run over by a car, part of a procession belonging to the rebbe of the Chabad sect, Menachem Schneerson. One of the children, Gavin Cato, died and the other was injured. Although a grand jury eventually refused to indict the driver of the car, the immediate circumstances were confused, and the incident hit at accumulated resentments that had built in the neighborhood. A score of young black men pulled the first Jew they could find, as it happened a student from Australia, off the street and beat and stabbed him in a vicious attack. He died later that night at the hospital. Then, for three days, the rioters besieged Jewish houses and stores, which they identified by the mezuzot on the doors, and looted them.

Both incidents were handmade for political theater and, like in the Tawana Brawley case, the sensationalists took full advantage. Al Sharpton and Sonny Carson, the notoriously anti-Semitic leader of the Korean grocery boycott, led a march through Crown Heights. In a eulogy at the boy's funeral, Sharpton criticized Jewish merchants in Crown Heights for selling diamonds from apartheid South Africa, and he also said: "All we want to say is what Jesus said: If you offend one of these little ones, you got to pay for it. No compromise, no meetings, no coffee klatch, no skinnin' and grinnin'." Meantime, among the banners hanging to commemorate Gavin Cato at the funeral, one read: "Hitler did not do the job."

Frankly, the ultra-Orthodox are hard to like. They're closed off, self-righteous, unneighborly; they've stayed in neighborhoods other Jews have left but have not made friends with those around them. Secular Jews, Jews who believe that ghettoization is impotence, have little kindred feelings for them. But nobody doubts that the Orthodox have a right to be Orthodox, and this is what the riots called into question: maybe a Jew couldn't be a Jew in America. It wasn't the attacks so much, though they were heinous—Jews were used to hate, even in New York. It was that the city's response was muted. David Dinkins, New York's first black mayor, had relied too much on the black activists to get into office, and he was unwilling to criticize people like Sharpton and Carson who'd been involved in his mayoral campaign.

The *New Republic* covered all of this critically, but we were a Washington-based magazine. Eric had a mass circulation paper with vast influence, and he cared about the Lubavitcher. For him, they were, if not family, the people who had kept his family prosperous. Eric had the authenticity of real passion behind him: he would hammer and hammer and hammer for a cause, and you knew that he meant it. He would go as far as he needed to protect what he thought needed protecting.

Dinkins was up for reelection in 1993 and while Eric went after him in print, he did two other things behind the scenes. First, he convinced Rupert Murdoch, who'd sold the *Post* a bit earlier, to buy it again, knowing that Murdoch would put money into a paper that stood powerfully for conservative concerns. Then he started working to convince Murdoch to back Dinkins's most powerful challenger—a former federal prosecutor and Republican named Rudy Giuliani who was running on the Liberal Party ticket in order to get a foothold in an overwhelmingly Democratic city.

Convincing Murdoch to back Giuliani was tricky because he'd prosecuted Ivan Boesky and Michael Milken, two of Murdoch's friends. Murdoch wanted to back the Conservative Party candidate instead. But Eric knew how to reach Murdoch—the same way he appealed to Podhoretz, to Moynihan, and to me. If you're older and hold to a set of values, you always worry that they're fading in the younger generations—that people will forget. Eric had grown up with older values, and we, his elders, knew we could trust him to maintain and sustain what we believed. When Eric told Murdoch that, despite all his instincts, he needed to back Giuliani, Murdoch was willing to listen. The *Post* endorsed Giuliani, and it was probably decisive: he won Staten Island and Queens, the boroughs where the *Post*'s readership was strongest, by enough to make up for losing the Bronx, Brooklyn, and Manhattan. And so, he won the city by almost three percentage points and more than fifty-three thousand votes.

Eric went on working in conservative media as a vice president at Fox. But he was best as an interlocutor with the mayor, creating a mode of talking about the city, a focus on order, that gave Giuliani the public momentum he needed to take New York in hand. And from New York, through Fox and through the city's preeminence generally, a new set of political attitudes began to emerge. These attitudes were grounded in the apprehensions and realities of people from Staten Island, Queens, and parts of Brooklyn; attitudes that gave Giuliani the political momentum to clean up Times Square and to institute policing for small infractions to prevent bigger infractions—steps that are now controversial but that then seemed to us to be making the city livable again.

At the same time as Eric was asserting his conservatism to order the city, the Democrats were adjusting their party to respond to the conservative ascendence. The roots of the adjustment came from New York, from people like Michael Steinhardt and Mort Zuckerman, and from Washington, from people like me.

*　*　*

In 1985, a group called the Democratic Leadership Council formed to push the party toward the center after it had lost four out of the last five presidential elections. Many of the financial people in the DLC were Jewish and many of the political people were Southern because both groups shared a basic distaste of the party's leftward lean. Michael Steinhardt was involved, and so was Mort Zuckerman, who now owned two magazines, *The Atlantic* and *U.S. News & World Report*. Al Gore looked like the obvious candidate for the DLC to back: he was young; he was Southern, to make up for Democratic losses in the region; he was liberal but not Left, to correct for the last twenty years of Democratic mistakes; and the policies he supported were designed to appeal not to fractions of the electorate but to the majority.

New York would be decisive in the 1988 presidential primary, and to boost his chances, Al was scheduled to meet Rabbi Shlomo Halberstam, also known as the Bobover Rebbe, the Grand Rabbi of Bobov, Poland, and head of the largest Orthodox sect in New York. Rabbi Halberstam, now deceased, was a descendant of the Ba'al Shem Tov (the Master of the Good Name), the founder of the entire Hassidic movement, who lived from 1698 to 1760. Thousands of black-coated men (no women) gathered outside their leader's house for what was actually quite a long time while the senator and the rebbe were no doubt discussing the state of the universe.

Suddenly they emerged and a roar went up from the crowd. The candidate said nothing. And then the Bobover Rebbe spoke in a whisper, without any amplification, and at length. A Secret Service agent standing next to me muttered to himself, "How is this crowd supposed to hear what the rabbi has to say?" "Don't worry," said one of the Hassidim near us. "The rabbi speaks, his people hear." Indeed "his people" did hear. After the primary, I asked one of the campaign workers checking the Gore numbers how the Bobover shtetl in Brooklyn had done for my candidate. "Very well," he answered. "Almost unanimous."

But Al, in retrospect the strongest candidate in a general election, was knocked out in the New York primary by Jesse Jackson, who collected a strange combination of general-Left energy, black-Left activism, and free-floating Democratic populism. Jackson was eventually stopped by Michael Dukakis, my old debating opponent over the Cuba question twenty-six years earlier, who still had zero charisma and lost to George Bush Sr. But, though Al's 1988 run for the presidency hadn't taken, he—we—still saw in the DLC a chance for him to exercise influence in preparation for 1992. Then, in April 1989, coming out of a Baltimore Orioles game, Al's six-year-old son Albert was hit by a car and nearly killed.

Al spent every night for about four months, as a sitting US senator, in the hospital while Albert recovered, and the family said almost nothing to the press except for short, dignified statements. This was a very conscious choice, and it had to do with his father, who was an impressive man but not a warm one. Al was determined to be a father, first, to his son. At the very same time, my son Jesse was in the hospital for an operation, and Al found the time to call him twice, which says a lot about Al. He kept the family close while Albert got better, and he decided not to run for president in 1992. Instead, he wrote a book, *Earth in the Balance*, about climate change. "This is not only a good book," I wrote him about an early draft, "it will be an important book." He was the first major presidential candidate or presumptive candidate to have a book on the *Times* bestseller list since John Kennedy.

The DLC's standard bearer in 1992 was an unlikely one: a Yale Law School graduate who'd been governor of Arkansas for almost a decade. Bill Clinton was not a visionary about society like Al; he was a salesman. And he stepped into an open field. Mario Cuomo, the governor of New York, was an icon for liberals but couldn't decide if he wanted to run. Paul Tsongas was running, but he was hobbled by being the second Greek American presidential candidate from New England in four years after Dukakis, by being perceived as too socially liberal, and by fears that the cancer he had beaten a few years before might return. In any case, George Bush looked unbeatable after the First Gulf War.

The *New Republic* backed Clinton. Some people attributed that to Sidney Blumenthal, and this might be so. I hadn't liked Sidney since Palmer House, but he was a clever journalist, one of Rick Hertzberg's favored hires. When Rick left for good in 1991, after his second stint as editor, I picked Andrew Sullivan to replace him. Andrew inherited Sidney. Sidney had been on the Clinton train before I knew who Clinton was, and he introduced Andrew to Bill. (Eventually, in the summer of 1992, Andrew took Sidney off the Clinton beat when he caught him faxing copies of articles to Hillary for her approval before we ran them—but that was later.) Almost immediately, Andrew was seduced, like lots of people, including me for a short time. We put Clinton on the cover the week after Andrew met him. The magazine called him "the anointed." Actually, even though I wanted Al, Clinton's platform and his background made him everything I had been pushing for: a Democrat from a conservative state, someone friendly to finance, and one who would move the party to the center.

When Clinton needed a vice presidential nominee, he chose Al: he was wholesome and popular, he had all of the foreign policy seriousness Clinton lacked, and he'd served in Vietnam, which Clinton had not. Anne and I were all in for Al. But we were less certain about Clinton. When you give a serious amount of cash, as we did that election year, you take a risk: either you get what you want or you set yourself up to be kicked if you are not already kicking yourself. And we'd had some misgivings about Clinton from the start.

After Clinton won, and before he took office, there was talk in the nascent administration, I suppose thanks to Al, about an appointment for me, though not for any position of policy significance. Insiders seemed to settle on me for emissary to Copenhagen (since 1975, six or seven of the ambassadors to Denmark have been Jews—I'm not sure why), but nothing came of this. The first Democratic presidency in twelve years was an opportunity for the people I taught, the people who had made Washington their locus, to really serve. The last days of 1992 and the first of 1993 saw a flurry of letters from me to Al and his good-natured, attentive, sometimes interested responses: the subject was stocking the new administration. Jamie Gorelick became defense counsel and Tony Blinken chief foreign policy speechwriter for the National Security Council. Tom Williamson became the solicitor of labor at the Department of Labor and Glenn Hutchins an economic advisor to the White House. Pretty quickly, I fashioned myself less as a recommender and more as a conduit, calling Al's attention to the new research at Cambridge I knew about and to journalists who knew what was going on all over the world.

We tried to get some kind of role for Gene McCarthy. Al went to Clinton asking him to give Gene a cabinet position, and Clinton brushed him aside. I asked Al again, Al went back to Clinton, and again the president brushed him aside. I asked Al a third time, Al went to Clinton, and Clinton said, "I heard you the last two times." And that was it: Clinton was a Fulbright man and like Fulbright, a triangulator. McCarthy was a truth teller and so would not have thrived in a Clinton administration.

Clinton didn't much care for history. The photo of sixteen-year-old him and Kennedy in the Rose Garden in 1963—an image of the modern Democratic hero anointing his inheritor (so the retelling had it)—was all that mattered. He was not malicious like Bobby Kennedy, devious like Joe Kennedy, or opaquely manipulative like Jack. But he was shallow and needy; he thought in images, in photo ops. There was none of the density of history to his Democratic Party.

Early in the administration, Al asked me about the Supreme Court. I said they should talk to Steve Breyer, who was on the First Circuit in Boston. Al called me in Italy, at the villa of I Tatti, where Anne and I were staying for a three-month Harvard fellowship that was really more of a vacation, since I was charged with no responsibilities. It was strange because I was there, it was strange because it was advice that he didn't need, and it was strange because he must've known I'd say Steve. (Though Al isn't strategic that way.) Anyway, I contributed what I could. I told Al to mention that Steve Breyer had a Kennedy connection: he had served as counsel to the Senate Judiciary Committee when Teddy headed it, which I knew Clinton would like. And, at Al's request, I called Steve, who was in the hospital recovering from a bicycle accident. Clinton and Breyer met, and he was nominated and confirmed a year after Ruth Bader Ginsburg had been appointed. Neither the press nor the White House made anything of the fact that both justices were Jewish. It was a small sign of how far American Jewry had come since Louis Brandeis.

Whatever shadiness the Clintons were involved in—the Whitewater land deal; the suicide of deputy White House counsel Vince Foster, about which unpersuasive but still damaging conspiracies were aired; and the rumors of affairs covered up not just by Bill but by his wife—couldn't compare to the Kennedys. But the new post-sixties journalistic elite believed in holding their political counterparts' lives to a different standard, and the Clintons didn't have the Kennedy's elan as a shield. Instead, they had self-righteousness: one of those traits of the new educated leadership class I was seeing more and more often. They'd been told they were special early at Wellesley, Georgetown, and Yale; but they weren't inheritors, so they had to scrabble and claw to get to where they were. This combination of ideological certainty and real effort meant that they thought their ideals justified whatever means they used to make those ideals a reality. And they were very defensive if someone—a reporter, a journalist, a commentator, or another politician—suggested otherwise.

The old Democratic Party, the liberal midcentury party, was receding, getting older. In June 1992, Max Lerner died. He'd been sick with cancer for a decade. I hadn't seen him at the end. It was too painful to see someone I'd been so enmeshed with, who'd been the closest thing in my life to a father figure, prepare to go. I have a letter from him from June 1990 that says: "We seem to have a harmony of mind and spirit that I cherish, laughing together at the same things, scorning the same people and causes, identifying strongly with the same dreams and visions. Bless you for being who you are."

I wrote about him in the *New Republic*—not personally (I couldn't bear it) but politically.

If Max was mesmerized by anyone, it was Franklin Roosevelt, the aristocratic scion whose mission was to include the excluded in the national life once dominated by his own class. And Max knew that the process of inclusion was unfinished, that it needed to include not only classes but other people and races. Max brought an immigrant's love for America to the politics with which he grappled; and, though I am not an immigrant, it is a love I can grasp and feel. An immigrant's patriotism— how old-fashioned the word now sounds—is not a sentiment in the abstract. It is a comparative judgment, America viewed against every place else. Max would try to explain this to his Marxist and faux-Marxist critics, and they wouldn't understand. Herbert Marcuse, once in my hearing, charged Max with "false consciousness," and the editors of Dissent *were not much less derisive. They said he was part of the great American celebration, to which he retorted, "And isn't there much to celebrate?" America, he used to say, is the only fabulous country.*

Already Max's immigrant love for a fabulous country seemed old fashioned. And a year later, Irving Howe, another figure with an older sensibility, was dead, too. Irving was never someone I'd particularly liked. But he had a way into my heart through Yiddish, and there was an authenticity to his loyalties that I respected. A few years before he died he wrote me with praise and friendly suggestions for Leon's literary section, "probably the best book section of its scope in America...the one major competitor, though probably more influential in the literary-intellectual world [the *New York Review of Books*], is – I suspect – starting to slip, in ways too complicated to go into here." Who, what, could replace a person who cared about politics and about culture at this level, with this depth, in this way? But Irving came from a rich, thick world that ran on older social bonds— and those bonds were attenuating fast.

* * *

In 1998, Eric Breindel died from the HIV or AIDS he'd contracted from infected heroin needles. His funeral was at the Park Avenue Synagogue on Eighty-Seventh Street, which was closed to traffic. The NYPD was there with a full honor guard. Norman Podhoretz was there and Rudy Giuliani, Rupert Murdoch, and Pat Moynihan. Larry Tisch was there and Mort Zuckerman, Henry Kissinger, and Ed Koch. A few of us, Eric's mentors, spoke; there was a five-minute limit that everybody held to but me—I talked for twenty. ("Marty Peretz can clear a synagogue faster than the PLO," ran the joke, or so I was told later.) It was a rainy March morning, and after the funeral, some of us went out to the cemetery in New Jersey to say the kaddish and shovel dirt on the grave: Tom Tisch, me, Leon, Eric's parents, his sister, and Lally Weymouth, who loved him with a disciplined and yet uncontrolled love.

The city that was Eric's subject was a world removed from where it was at the end of the seventies. Finance had rejuvenated New York and then America, and politics, influenced by the financial boom and its new elite, was moving back toward the center. But the progress came with losses that most of the people I knew—good liberals raised in stable communities of traditional values and sent into the wider world of growing institutions—were not prepared for.

The new prosperity was about buying, not about loyalties to the little structures and societies that had shaped my generation. When your individuality is tied to what you buy, not where your loyalties lie, defining the self becomes a preoccupation; so does finding meaning. Increasingly, providing that meaning became the purpose of politics. The Democrats of Clintons' cohort came with the idea that society was a maze to be worked through in search of *collective* meaning. The Republicans of Eric's cohort decided the opposite: to them, meaning inhered in the local, the traditional, the tribe. Meantime, the broad American middle, which was neither communitarian nor traditional, would vote Democrat some years, Republican others, or not vote at all. And the lower-middle and lower classes—who lived in the still-broken neighborhoods; who were minorities but also increasingly poor whites; who were most susceptible to a hyper-consumer culture that marketed more than it educated—were left behind. So were people like Henry Murray's old student Ted Kaczynski, the Unabomber, and Timothy McVeigh, the Oklahoma City bomber. They were rebels against the society, actors out of the discontents and despair that alienation brings.

There were nascent signs even then of the rough beasts this new society would create. In my files is a letter from me to Fran Lebowitz from the mid-1980s about a Sharpton-esque figure of the Right: a real estate inheritor who had spent the eighties playing off tribal resentments, most famously placing an ad in the *Times* calling for the death penalty for the alleged, and eventually proven innocent, assailants of the Central Park jogger. I only caught the superficial whisp of this figure's draw, the garish consumerism, not the tribal politics that he so seamlessly joined. But I caught something all the same:

Dear Fran,

Looking through the catalogues the other day I came upon this effort at autobiography by Donald Trump who, as you will see from the blurb, "lives in Trump Tower in New York City, in Greenwich, Connecticut, and in the fabled Mar-A-Lago mansion in Palm Beach, Florida." Is this not something you would want to do a job on? Lord, what this man has done to New York.

First to New York, then to the country. We didn't know it, but even then, he was slouching toward Bethlehem to be born.

CHAPTER THIRTEEN

A New, New Politics: Communalists and Reactionaries

The first taste of the times to come arrived with the Clintons, who brought to Washington, D.C. a new ideology. It was the top-down institutional version of the bottom-up street politics of the Palmer House, wrapped in the language of corporate expertise that Wall Street had helped introduce to America. It lacked the New Politics' racialism but was equally idealistic, totalistic, and emotionalistic. In her famous 1969 Wellesley commencement address, Hillary Rodham used words that could've been spoken by Herbert Marcuse:

> *We are, all of us, exploring a world that none of us even understands and attempting to create within that uncertainty. But there are some things we feel, feelings that our prevailing, acquisitive, and competitive corporate life, including tragically the universities, is not the way of life for us. We're searching for more immediate, ecstatic, and penetrating modes of living.*

Twenty-four years later and by now the first lady, she was still trying to solve the spiritual crisis faced by those of her class. In a speech at the University of Texas, she said:

The discontent of which I speak is broader than that, deeper than that. We are, I think, in a crisis of meaning.... What does it mean in today's world to pursue not only vocations, to be part of institutions, but to be human?

What was needed, she went on to declare, was "a new politics of meaning":

We need a new ethos of individual responsibility and caring. We need a new definition of civil society which answers the unanswerable questions posed by both the market forces and the governmental ones, as to how we can have a society that fills us up again and makes us feel that we are part of something bigger than ourselves.

Like most movements of ideas, there was an intellectual foundation for this one: Michael Lerner, no relation to Max, who became known in Washington as "Hillary's guru." Twenty-five years earlier, he had been at the near center of the Free Speech Movement; he then migrated to SDS and black liberation. Once it became clear no revolution was happening, he took up psychology, looking for revolution in personality rather than politics. He founded a progressive-Left Jewish magazine called *Tikkun*, meaning "to repair the world," and then started translating his psychology back to the political sphere. Now the political revolution wouldn't overturn the state, the political revolution would work *through* the state; people were lost and atomized, they needed government to prepare them to spend more time doing good for others, to create a more caring society.

In service of this ideal of solidarity, government would be "mandating" changes in the workplace, not to make it less dangerous or unequal the way the unions wanted, but "to make it less stressful, more concerned about workers' intelligence, creativity and ability to cooperate with others, and hence ultimately more productive." The state was joining with your employer to mend your soul and maximize your output in a sort of communalist utilitarianism.

In the academic and intellectual sphere, there had been an obsession with the communalist side of this equation since the early eighties, led by people like Cornel West who was now a kind of academic Al Sharpton, a philosopher-performer who dabbled in rap music and street politics. West and Lerner, who had become a rabbi, coauthored a book called *Jews and Blacks: A Dialogue on Race, Religion, and Culture in America* that proposed "spiritual" dialogue and "psychological" solutions as opposed, I suppose, to empirical analysis or reasonable debate.

"The Republicans know business, but the Democrats know the new management theories," a high-up Democrat told Leon Wieseltier for the piece he wrote on Lerner's "politics of meaning" in June of 1993. Lerner's intellectual anchor was W. Edwards Deming, who made his name deriving management lessons from the postwar rebuilding of Japan and applying them to the management of societies at large. To make workers more productive, Deming said, you had to work psychologically, getting away from the "I" and to the "we": a vision of work as an orchestra in which every member worked harder because the conductor made them feel that they were being heard as part of a larger whole. Corporate bureaucracies and government agencies like the Defense Department took up Deming's creed of uplift in service of productivity; and Deming and other consultants who held the creed became gurus. Lerner was the political messenger, applying Deming in service of social solidarity. But references to Deming also came from Robert Reich, the secretary of labor, and from writers and policy thinkers to whom the White House listened.

At the *New Republic*, we thought that you couldn't preach a politics of utilitarian solidarity and call yourself a liberal. Liberals were supposed to care about individuality and freedom. Leon pointed this out, and the White House didn't appreciate it. I read in the Style section of the *Washington Post* on May 6, 1993 that Michael Lerner and Hillary were talking about what they called "the *New Republic* disease." In context, this illness seemed to be cynicism, but it wasn't explained, and I wrote her a polite letter asking what she meant. She never wrote back.

The first major policy initiative of the Clinton administration was giving every American health insurance: an ambitious effort to pull Americans closer together. In practice, this meant mandating them to enroll in a health insurance program through their employer or on their own, with premiums and prices for medical procedures set by insurance alliances and overseen by a national health board.

From the beginning, this was Hillary's purview, a fulfillment of the promise during the campaign that the first couple would be "two for the price of one." There was a lot of confident fanfare and an effort to make complicated phenomena seem easy. Intellectual honesty is not always a component of political programs. But health insurance was a snake pit of problems, contradictions, and complexities all around. There were myriad different interests to reconcile—doctors, nurses, hospitals, old-age homes, insurers, people with healthcare, and people without.

Hillary's handpicked point person for the task did not come with a background in reconciliation. Ira Magaziner was a management consultant, an expert in industrial policy and another exponent of the Japanese vogue for productivity maximization. Management consulting had existed to advise businesses on how to grow and organize employees for almost a century. But the field had mushroomed in the 1980s when the growth of financial markets and the proliferation of financial transactions meant they needed to make more decisions at faster rates to stay competitive. Consultants didn't know much about politics or policymaking. But they did know how to help corporate leadership get what it wanted from workers, which is why Magaziner got hired.

Magaziner had been featured alongside Hillary as a young student leader to watch in a 1969 *Life* magazine story. This cohort of sixties idealists had migrated toward management and then brought management into government, so they had the ability to impose their ideas through the state in the name of both social solidarity *and* economic productivity. This was a parody of the midcentury Democratic ethos I had come from: the fusion of capitalism and democracy that had created postwar peace and prosperity. Its project was not to free people to purchase and participate or even to mobilize them to solve the world's problems, like the Kennedy version. Its project was to shape them into better workers and citizens, which smacked to me of Germany and Russia in the twentieth century.

The healthcare process played out predictably, considering the backgrounds of the players and the theories that drove them. Hillary and Magaziner convened a panel of healthcare policy experts that worked in secret, even as doctors and health policy professionals sued in court to open its deliberations to public view. Their own advisors urged them to let Congress in on the deliberations. Donna Shalala, who headed the Department of Health and Human Services, recalled later that "A lot of us told [President Clinton] that we thought [the approach] was screwy, that he should draft principles, go up to the Hill.... [B]ut when the president and the first lady decide they want to do something...unless it's illegal, you support it." When Hillary did talk to members of Congress, they reported that she was impressive in her expertise but had no interest in feedback.

When Clinton and Magaziner rolled out the plan, the pushback was immediate from their own party, which had a majority in the House and the Senate. Pat Moynihan, now chair of the pivotal Senate Finance Committee, whose care for the poor was never in doubt, asked Hillary to commit to something gradual and provisional. He pointed out that the last major Democratic expansions of social protections, Medicare and the Social Security Act, had passed with sweeping majorities—an endorsement from the country her husband didn't have. Jim Cooper, a conservative Democratic congressman, asked for a plan that wouldn't compel employers to pay for insurance and didn't promise universal healthcare immediately. Hillary's response to Cooper was "We'll crush you." This was hubris, and when it collided with reality it vanished like smoke.

At my house and at the *New Republic* we were pretty disappointed in the Clintons that first year. When it came to the causes we'd supported them on, causes that we thought increased people's freedom rather than mandated what they did with it, they caved or they compromised. They'd tell us, for example, that the compromise of "don't ask, don't tell" would lead to the immediate end of discharges of gay servicepeople—in fact, the discharges doubled. When Andrew eventually testified against the Defense of Marriage Act at the Senate, it was that very day that the Clinton Justice Department issued its opinions that there was nothing constitutionally problematic with it. This was a real gut punch. For Andrew, who had written *the* piece for gay marriage and who had championed Clinton, it was a personal betrayal.

Clinton was a public opinion pragmatist, like John Podesta and Sidney Blumenthal—young idealists of the sixties who'd gotten savvy and successful. They wanted a better world, and they wanted personal success, and nothing in their experience had convinced them they couldn't have both. If push came to shove, though, they'd go with success. He was protean; you couldn't get a handle on him. When he introduced the National Performance Review, which used the Deming-Lerner lessons of productive uplift, he said it was an example of "government being run more like a business," which, along with his betrayal of the gays, was part of his rhetorical pitch to the Right. And, even as Hillary prepared to universalize healthcare, Bill had pledged to halve the deficit in four years, which is plainly impossible.

These were suddenly two wings of the Democratic Party we'd helped into being: collectivist corporate leftists like Hillary and public opinion pragmatists like Bill. I didn't like either set of principles. Where had we failed? After all, this was the first administration filled with the new American elite, the types of students I'd been so hopeful about when they came to Harvard twenty-five years earlier. The better ones, like Jamie Gorelick and Al Gore, were liberal incrementalists, civil servants devoted to improving peoples' lives, humanist technocrats. Other people's students, like Hillary and Magaziner, were idealist managers: what they seemed to have taken from their educations was utopianism and self-certainty, unexamined and unintegrated—everything I'd tried to push back on since Barrington Moore had identified it for me in his retirement letter in 1973. Others were like Podesta and Blumenthal, careerists with good feelings about themselves and an eye to public opinion polls. To call them disappointments was an understatement.

We couldn't do much about the character of the people in the White House. But the healthcare proposal was the kind of thing the *New Republic* was made to fight. And we did.

Our writer was Betsy McCaughey, a specialist in healthcare who, in early 1994, got in touch with us wanting to write a piece about the law. She was smart and aggressive, and she saw in Hillary's plan the kind of totalistic thinking—the moralist insistence about values, the aversion to compromise—that she didn't think government should be in the business of promoting. The piece she wrote for us was called "No Exit." It argued that a bill constructed in this kind of secrecy would end up with doctors and patients subjected to a single unaccountable bureaucracy.

Betsy's piece was a provocation: a worst-case scenario. She was convinced it was a certainty, and she wouldn't change a word of the article, even over the part that claimed her doomsday scenario "would" rather than "could" happen. It came out a couple of days before Clinton's State of the Union address where he would champion the reform bill, and the shockwaves were immediate. We were Washington's premiere liberal magazine, and we'd been Clinton's early champion. Now we had turned on him, giving Republicans a liberal cudgel with which to beat him. Democrats who were doubting the plan in private and being hammered by their rivals for it in an election year had an excuse to jump ship.

There was backlash against us from the Left, and we published rebuttal after rebuttal to Betsy's piece in the magazine. We backed Jim Cooper's more moderate healthcare reform plan. But the White House never considered it. By the fall, Hillarycare was finished and Republicans had taken over Congress for the first time in forty years.

In the years since, we've taken criticism for Betsy's article, which treated as a certainty what was an unproven possibility. I don't know that I'm proud of the article, but I'm proud of the outcome. I think the administration was trying to ram a bill down America's throat, and we helped stop it. And I think that Hillary's methods demanded such a response.

Three months later, on a nice day in May, I was in the Rose Garden for a reception for Steve Breyer after his Supreme Court nomination. Joanna Breyer and I were talking when Hillary came up. Joanna introduced me as Marty Peretz, the editor of the *New Republic*. She looked me straight in the eye, said "Oh, I know," turned her back, and walked away. Later I learned from a White House source that she deliberately took me off the lists of state dinners for Vaclav Havel and Ehud Barak. I have an image of it in my head: Hillary crossing names off a guest list while Bill fooled around. I was dead to her, even if maybe she could have used my help some other time.

* * *

In Andrew Sullivan, I had hired a real provocateur: someone as temperamentally opposed to orthodoxy as I was, even if he was a little bit in thrall to an orthodoxy of his own. In retrospect, making Andrew editor was my riskiest move as owner, though I didn't see it that way at the time. In 1989, Mike had quit. Rick came back in, and we fought. Rick was brilliant, but it took him forever to do anything and the manuscripts would pile up. Also, he was reflexively Left, which sometimes I couldn't stand. I wrote him from Paris: "Our political differences—less than they were five years ago and ten—are givens... but if I have to be the only person responsible for getting the issues and viewpoints that I care about into the mag I am going to be a very unhappy person...."

"Marty, mon vieux," went his reply. "If you are going to insist on trying to micro-manage the magazine from Paris instead of using your sabbatical to ponder the Big Picture and explore new places and pleasures, that's alright with me...but when you get in a mood to nitpick and recriminate, how about mixing in a bit of commendation? ...I mean, JESUS H. FUCKING CHRIST!!!!" That was a pretty typical response.

One morning after I came back to America, I invited Andrew to breakfast and offered him a deputy editor job, a post in the wings where he could wait for the editorship to open up. Rick could see the writing on the wall and didn't much like being helped by a twenty-seven-year-old, so he jumped to the *New Yorker*, where he could write about politics for a more traditionally liberal audience in a less combative place. And I made Andrew editor.

"But I'm gay, everybody knows it," Andrew said when I offered him the editor's job. I told him not to worry about it, nobody talks about this stuff, it'll be fine. It did turn out fine, more or less, but people absolutely spoke about it. He was probably the most prominent openly gay journalist in America: there was a whole round of stories and a profile in *Time*. "Dear Marty," he wrote me,

in all the maelstrom of publicity, I forgot one thing.
Thank you for the honor of choosing me to edit this

magazine. 28, British, Catholic, homosexual: these
are not qualities normally associated with a job such
as this, and that didn't really dawn on me until the
last couple of days. I'll do my best to live up to both
your achievement at the magazine, and to its history.

I didn't hire Andrew because he was gay. But I also didn't think twice about it—once, but not twice. He was very smart. He would cause trouble. He might expand the magazine's horizon. Really I do these things by instinct. It was not like I didn't know there were plenty of people in Washington who didn't like me and who might use the opportunity to hurt me by referencing my own private life. Midge Decter, Norman Podhoretz's wife, couldn't stand our stance on gay marriage and hinted in one of her pieces in *Commentary* that I was gay. This was hypocritical considering how she would scold me any time I took out against one of her friends for some public act: "[*Commentary*] is frequently very stern," she once lectured me, "but we are not personal. Nor do we engage in insinuating crudity." Really, Midge? The Podhoretzes were, in their mind, fighting for civilization even as in practice they were arguing for a very narrow definition of it. Their insinuations worried me a little, until Anne pointed out that none of *Commentary*'s readers would understand a veiled homosexual reference anyway.

Some on the Left, meanwhile, had taken to outing closeted public figures as a way to advance the gay agenda. It was not clear to me what good was to be achieved in this way, and I took Andrew aside and said, "If you want to write a piece that favors outing I'd be troubled because there are people who'd want to say that about me and this would give them license." Instead, he wrote an essay condemning the practice on principle: revealing your sexuality is a personal choice and there's no reason to compromise someone's privacy to advance a political cause. A year in, he wasn't just crusading for gay marriage, he was printing a cover about gays in advertising—a sexy cover, with a guy who was not quite dressed, to push gay life into the mainstream cultural sphere. I was proud when he printed that: we were at the edge of something that mattered.

Andrew wasn't just pushing gayness into the mainstream; he was pushing conservatism, too. We were all very sad when the magazine's resident Tory, Henry Fairlie, had died the previous year after a fall in our lobby ended a magnificent career of drinking, smoking, and fucking. When Andrew became editor, he showed himself to be a harder Tory than Henry—a fierce journalistic warrior with an intellectual agenda to push. Henry and Andrew came from the same Burkean tradition that favored organic social change. But deep down Andrew was a real conservative who saw a tragic dimension to change itself: he thought people were happier in tribes than in societies; he thought liberalism robbed them of their wholeness. This was a view that our readership tended to dismiss—and Andrew didn't want to let them dismiss it anymore.

He brought in writers who were doing controversial work: studies of Christianity and research in the sciences and biology that didn't have obviously egalitarian outcomes. He published Camille Paglia, a feminist theorist who picked intellectual fights: she hated Susan Sontag and called Hillary a "bitch goddess." He championed Bob Wright, a staff member with provocative views on evolutionary biology and genetics. Andrew ran Bob's piece "Feminists, Meet Mr. Darwin," which criticized prominent feminists for ignoring biological realities that Bob said separated men and women.

The greatest controversy was when Andrew asked Charles Murray, a card-carrying member of the conservative intellectual establishment, to publish an excerpt from his new book *The Bell Curve: Intelligence and Class Structure in American Life*. *The Bell Curve* made the case that biology and culture were better predictors of success than socioeconomic factors. The excerpt Murray wanted to run was on black IQ.

We'd talked in our meetings and our pages about race and about the crisis in the inner cities after the Korean boycott and Flatbush riots and took our usual complex middle ground. Rightists deplored the culture of hip-hop music, drugs, and broken families. Leftists saw the ghettoization of black neighborhoods, poverty, and disproportionate incarceration rates for blacks as a failure of social policy. We thought both sides were right on certain emphases—but that they overemphasized them. We thought everyone deserved a better environment, which meant we needed better social policy but also that when popular music talked about rape, theft, and battery, there was also a problem of worldview, of culture, and of expectation. Stanley Crouch, never one to shirk, was particularly good on this, calling out rappers who glorified violence by name. We took everybody on—mostly prodding the Left, because the Left was our audience, but never embracing the shibboleths of the Right.

Murray's piece, "Race, Genes and IQ – An Apologia: The Case for Conservative Multiculturalism," was something different. It used a statistical study of race, genetics, and intelligence to argue that group differences were so important that they made human beings more different than similar and human values relative. Murray thought his research showed that different racial and ethnic groups had different heritable traits—whites had higher IQs than blacks, and blacks had more artistic "vitality" than whites. Genes, he said, coupled with culture, made differences like these impossible to bridge. His philosophy of "conservative multiculturalism" was to accept what each group can do.

Practically speaking, this meant no more affirmative action, no more worrying about the inner cities, and no more efforts at integration: let the tribes coexist in peace, and let the outliers in each tribe—whites with a sense of rhythm, blacks who excelled at math—rise and thrive in the free American open. Murray's was the mirror image of Michael Lerner's vision, a particularist response to a collectivist one. Lerner pointed to politics as the ultimate solvent; Murray said politics could solve nothing. Lerner escaped from individuality through the solidarity of the state; Murray escaped from individuality through the solidarity of the tribes. Lerner used utilitarian corporate systems to justify and apply his statism; Murray used social scientific systems to justify and apply his tribalism.

The staff was aghast. Opinion ranged from "ugly provocation" to "immediate threat." Leon was furious, and so was his deputy editor, Jesse's best friend from high school and college, Alex Star (who, as an editor at Farrar, Straus and Giroux, took five minutes to reject this manuscript). Leon said: Publish a review of the book, but don't run the piece itself. We don't run Marxists here; we shouldn't run social Darwinists. Andrew said: Our readers read Marxists and Marxist derivatives already. If we don't run Murray they'll never read him at all—and Murray is a person who matters.

The decision was complicated but not hard. The book itself was a bestseller, but I was convinced that it wasn't among our readers, for many of whom it was a foregone conclusion that the argument was both wrong and foul. I agreed with Andrew that if we'd run just a review, coming from where we came from on the intellectual map, it would've been more or less what everybody else had been saying: an easy dismissal. The point was to open a discussion. I was happy to publish dissents: we always had, but not to cater to people's axiomatic feelings. When you do that, you're giving up belief in your readers' power of reason. Nothing is more undemocratic than that. If Murray was a charlatan and a determinist, as Leon said, then all the better for readers to see that through carefully examining Murray's argument and the arguments of his dissenters. How else would people have all the information to decide how their society was working and how it should work?

I actually thought Murray had a serious point. The Clinton's new-age psychological corporate-speak didn't take seriously that people come from specific cultures in which they are raised. In a country of immigrants, cultural, ethnic, and tribal politics is real—and tricky. Republicans increasingly spoke in those terms, crudely. Democrats were not really engaging with it outside the most slap-dash vote-getting categories: blacks, Hispanics, Jews, and even the hodgepodge category of whites. Murray's was a jarring way to remind people of what happens when you administer a society from the top down as the new Democrats were increasingly wont to do. When you deny the existence of some of its core social realities, they come back at you in a more toxic, more reactive, more assertive, more politicized form: a form designed to appeal to people who feel that their reality has been disenfranchised. I said as much in a piece I wrote in the magazine. I wanted liberals and leftists to consider that Murray's book was a stand-in for something bigger: a canary in the coal mine.

> [We] are fast learning, we are being forced to learn, to
> see behind every face and behind every phrase the group
> from which it emerges. This is a sad development. It
> was not so long ago that one's race or religious beliefs or
> ethnic origins could fully block even the most remark-
> able individuals from the paths of achievement....

*The regime of racial and ethnic set-asides in educa-
tion and employment makes victims of others who, on
simple standards of merit, would have won the places
reserved now by custom and law for members of particular groups. We have thus far been spared the historically laden nightmare of having legislatures and courts
decide what constitutes membership in these groups.
Our luck, however, may not hold out. In an economy
in which good jobs and scholarships are ever scarcer,
someone will finally have to decide: What constitutes
being black? Will one grandparent do?*

A quarter century later we still see "behind every face and
behind every phrase the group from which it emerges." And the
backlash from people who feel that their social realities are being
denied elected a president in 2016.

The piece was greeted with a storm of criticism from within the
magazine and without, all of which we published. Stanley Crouch
compared Murray to the racist Tom Buchanan from *The Great
Gatsby*. Skip Gates said Murray made social action predetermined to
fail. Leon savaged Murray for letting science determine philosophy.
Glenn Loury took the same line: it was one thing to talk about
the science—he supported talking about the science—but it was
another thing entirely to turn science into a moral system.

The controversy over *The Bell Curve* ended the friendship
between Leon and Andrew. They had been close, gone together to
gay bars, and instructed each other in their religions. But Leon cares
about principle, and Leon's response to a perceived betrayal is ferocious. Extra ferocious, I would say. He started a siege, and it came at
the worst time because Andrew had just been diagnosed with HIV.
He couldn't tell anyone: it was the height of the AIDS epidemic and
if word got out, he could be deported, sent back to England in the
full glare of publicity. And the idea of going back home to die was
unthinkable.

He eventually told me—in desperation, I think—and I helped
him get on a list for one of the new cures being tried. He got lucky:
it ended up being a cure rather than a placebo and saved his life. But
he was ill, and ill in secret, and he was increasingly alone. When we

supported gay marriage, some on the gay Left barred him from the community because they didn't support marriage as an institution. Really the issue was that he was a conservative. His gay social life ended: he was kicked out of gay bars, drinks got thrown at him, and he was smeared as a collaborator. He became a deeply alienated man. He also became a daring editor: he published pieces like he had nothing to lose; he thought he might be a dead man anyway.

✳ ✳ ✳

Bill Clinton got reelected in 1996. Like a good pragmatist, he had gotten very practical in 1994 when the Republicans swept Congress and, together with Newt Gingrich, he was making comprehensive laws. That year, the *New Republic* threw itself behind welfare reform, a bill that included the national health insurance program for children, an idea that Donald Cohen, my friend from Brandeis, had come up with at Yale. The welfare bill passed after three Clinton vetoes wore down the Republicans' more extreme proposals. I didn't mind supporting the Clintons when I thought they were right, and I'd do it again today. Within fifteen years, the program covered over seven million children. But the bill didn't do anything to solve the root causes of inner-city decay: it was a compromise between centrist Democrats and conservative Republicans focused on economic growth.

By 1998, the Democrats' political capital was being drained into the sink. The president's dalliance with intern Monica Lewinsky was fanned into a full-scale scandal by a no-holds-barred media. The same people who in the sixties had held corporate chieftains to account were now applying scrutiny to their counterparts in politics. And now hardly a day goes by that some politician or corporate executive isn't embroiled in a sex scandal.

Politically, I was not interested in the Lewinsky scandal. I already didn't like Bill Clinton and nothing we found out about his sexual mores surprised me. I'd seen him at Karenna Gore's wedding, probably a year before the scandal broke, dancing with the wife of one of the Koch brothers, and his hand was all the way down her back. The entire room saw it. I was standing next to James Murdoch, and he was so scandalized he was actually slack-jawed, which was both funny and sort of how I felt.

On the other hand, I thought the Republicans were sanctimonious hypocrites when it came to Clinton's sex life. Like the Podhoretzes, card-carrying intellectual ballasts for the Republicans, they said they were fighting for morality even as they weaponized people's personal lives against them. That isn't moral, it's totalitarian. Clinton had had sex and naturally he lied about it: what was so unusual about that? The tactics of Kenneth Starr's prosecutors in uncovering the sex that had led to Clinton's testimony had bordered on the illegal. Re-traditionalizing society wasn't the government's duty any more than communizing it was. It only gave politics too much power.

I worried about Al. In the *New Republic*'s editorial endorsement of Clinton's second term, in 1996, we'd mentioned him as the morally serious president-in-waiting. Now, Clinton's scandal put Al in danger with voters in states he would need to carry the Electoral College in 2000. It was a waiting game at this point, to see who Al's challenger would be. He needed to craft a campaign that emphasized the economic boom the Democrats had helped create while maintaining distance from the circus Clinton had created.

The *New Republic* was thriving. Now it wasn't just the eminences who read us. Andrew had made us hip—really, made us a part of popular culture in a way we hadn't been before. Young people read us and were inspired: I learned later that John McWhorter, who began writing for us as a contributing editor in 2001, was stimulated by reading Stanley Crouch and Glenn Loury in our pages.

But Andrew, finally tired of the fighting, left the magazine in 1996. In his place I hired Michael Kelly: an intrepid, charismatic, and serious reporter who'd made a splash with his Gulf War coverage. Kelly was an Irish Catholic from Boston and a Democrat. It was a good change for the place after Andrew, and in the beginning, everybody seemed to like Kelly.

But he was a nut. He had a vendetta against the Clintons, a vendetta that was unrooted in anything but personal dislike. At the *New Republic*, our vendettas were supposed to emerge from our philosophies. But Kelly was convinced the Clintons were crooks— maybe true—and that Al had engaged in improper fundraising—

which was absurd—and he said so in our editorials. Al was pretty calm when Kelly made this accusation in our pages; he didn't see it as any existential threat. Anne was furious and kept pushing me to fire Kelly. I was calmer than Anne, less calm than Al, and I held to my noninterventionist approach: your bullshit goes in, so does mine. That's until Kelly wouldn't run my unsigned editorial defending Al from his accusations. Then I fired him and replaced him with a senior editor at the magazine, Chuck Lane.

Chuck was a Harvard graduate who'd cut his teeth reporting in Latin America. He was a skeptic, the way anybody would be having come up through those trenches. Unlike me, Chuck didn't like dazzle, and it was his misfortune to be saddled with the controversies that arose from our publication of Steve Glass, an immensely talented young writer who was also a habitual fabricator. Before Andrew left, we'd had a problem with Ruth Shalit, who'd exaggerated (okay, falsified) enough facts for her story about affirmative action at the *Washington Post* to make Andrew issue a retraction. Afterward, Andrew appointed Steve as a fact checker, and soon he was writing features. His articles, especially one about the changing demographics of cab drivers in D.C., were incredibly well written, with hosts of colorful characters and persuasive insights. But complaints about the veracity of his reporting followed every piece. Michael Kelly dismissed the accusations, ferociously. But when Chuck became editor, he started investigating, and that's when it all came out: Steve had falsified at least one part of most of his stories.

We retracted his pieces; we issued apologies. The staff was shattered. Chuck said in a letter to me around this time, "I can't honestly say...that I've felt like the architect at TNR for the last few months. More like the fireman, putting out the organizational blazes..." Steve became a cautionary tale. After he was drummed out of journalism, he went to law school and passed the bar exam, only to be disqualified on ethical grounds. (How many lawyers can claim they've never told a lie?)

A lot of people who'd disliked us at least since Betsy McCaughey's piece, who saw us as unreliable liberals, now had reasons to point to a trend. And in a way they were right. The potential for error was a built-in risk with the way the magazine worked—this was a competitive place full of ambitious and intelligent people who wanted to impress their readers and each other. People like Steve and Ruth, who had something in them that made them willing to cross lines, were dangerous people in such a place. But most of all, they were dangers to themselves.

Through it all, Leon's back of the book was a guarantee that half our product was always top intellectual quality. Some people went to the back of the book and never ventured to the front. He was my insurance policy and because of him I could take the risks I wanted in the front part of the book. Leon could drive me nuts by not running people I wanted him to run or at least to try out: there were plenty of intellectuals, some of them now quite famous, who he put off and put off and put off or didn't even answer their phone calls. For a deep intellectual, he was strangely fixated on celebrities: he never missed Shirley MacLaine's or Barbra Streisand's calls.

But week after week, the back of the book was the most serious literary section in the country. Leon had Jed Perl on art, Martha Nussbaum on philosophy, Lee Siegel and James Wood on literature, Sean Wilentz on history and politics, and David Bell on European intellectual history. He even had Stephen Breyer on Louis Brandeis. His assistants—Adam Plunkett, Alex Star, Louis Menand, Adam Kirsch, Ruth Franklin, Jeremy McCarter—were smart, smart, smart and dedicated. If you read the *New York Review*, you had the sense of being in a very particular world, a clique: Upper West Side or Bloomsbury, politically Left or liberal academic. Leon's section wasn't like that. People from all beliefs and backgrounds were treated; ideas got fought over like they mattered. In Leon's mind, one way to keep critical silliness at bay—one way to maintain the cultural health of a society—is to be a merciless critic of what other people quietly accept. Leon did that, brilliantly: he rejoiced in good work; he skewered bad.

Leon, who's a textualist, abhorred the new postmodernists who thought context was all there was, and in 1996, he ran Martha Nussbaum in an attack on Judith Butler for her reduction of human society to systems of capital and politics. And he also knew how to stir and stir up the conservatives: ten years later, he ran her again on Harvey Mansfield for his reduction of human society to traditionalist systems of gender and masculinity. And I was proud that, even though Harvey was a friend, my magazine ran the piece.

In a way, even then, the section was a little out of time. Granted, if you were literary or literary aspiring and wanted to be abreast of *the* book section that wasn't afraid to praise and censure no matter the name, it was the place to read. But Leon's guiding stars, namely Isaiah Berlin and Lionel Trilling, were a little bit out of time themselves. If the pluralists could explain a philosophically rich way to think about values, they couldn't explain, at least in a way that I understood, what was happening now in America. The postwar world was no longer quite what they had thought it was.

Around this time, Caroline Kennedy's brother John came to see me about a project that was very much about this new commercial era: the idea for a political magazine that sat at the intersection of politics and popular culture, what would become *George*. He came to see me two or three times and was very respectful. He didn't understand a lot of what I said, and that was, I think, because he didn't know what he wanted. He wanted to have a hip magazine. But he knew there was something to not going the hip way, and I don't think he ever got over the equivocation—he got Norman Mailer as a contributor, but the first issue also had on the cover a model dressed as George Washington.

George wasn't successful, and it folded in 2001, two years after John's death. But it was an effort toward new journalism for a new society of consumers and individualists, and I didn't quite know what to make of it. I knew our latest crop of stars at the *New Republic*—Hanna Rosin, Jon Chait, and Ryan Lizza. But my own students at Harvard were less journalistic, and the value loci of that generation of writers was less legible to me. They seemed so detached from the loyalties, to peoples and causes, that I understood. Which I suppose said as much about me as it did about them, about the growing distance between me and the culture writ large.

The theory of the sixties seemed a long way off—and so did the aesthetics. Norman Mailer wrote an awful book, *The Gospel According to the Son*, a reworking of the story of Jesus Christ. Our up-and-coming young book reviewer James Wood wrote a brutal pan: Norman had made Jesus over in his celebrity image and not very well either. He presented examples of other biblical fictions better told. We ran it as the cover, with Norman on a cross as Christ, and the headline: "He Is Finished."

A month or two later in Provincetown, I was entering into a restaurant when Norman suddenly appeared in front of me. I remember I grinned, partly because I hadn't seen him for a while, since before the story ran, and partly because I wanted to see how he'd respond. He punched me in the stomach.

I didn't punch back; I just pushed him away. Norman was seventy-three. I was fifty-nine. It was like we were back in the sixties: it felt like an old anecdote even as it was happening. But really it felt like a goodbye. Norman was an immensely talented writer but a bullshit artist and a very pampered guy; he was abusive and selfish and because he was Norman Mailer nobody said anything about it. His politics were crazy, and we were no longer close. But he had been good to me early when he was a celebrity, and I was a nervous twenty year old. He was part of how I'd grown up. And he was a throwback to an older politics, an older culture, and an older social configuration. He wasn't in the thick anymore—his ideas didn't much matter. And, right then—this was part of the poignancy of the goodbye—it felt like the time might be mine.

CHAPTER FOURTEEN

Millennium: In the Thick

I was not one of those people who was surprised at the sudden evanescence of the Soviet empire. To me, Communism was the most extreme derivation—the most brutal to be sure—of the "One World, We Believe" fiction that my teachers at P.S. 28 had tried to establish as the norm in the minds of American children. It was clear to most of us kids on the Grand Concourse that this did not describe the world as we knew it. In the eighties, I developed a new course on nationalism at Harvard to make my case. In those days, nationalism was thought to be completely irrelevant, a thing of the past. I didn't think so. Pat Moynihan also looked at the Soviet system and its structures with the eye of a sociologist and said that it couldn't sustain itself. By the end of the eighties, we were beginning to seem prescient.

No doubt Ronald Reagan, by pushing Mikhail Gorbachev into a corner with his stance on Star Wars and in negotiations over nuclear weapons, was doing his best to put the Soviet political system under stress. He must have been surprised at how successful he actually was. In his broad-strokes way, he had given Gorbachev momentum to reform his country. But by 1989, Reagan was gone and George H. W. Bush, who made decisions as a foreign policy pragmatist of the patrician school, was in the Oval Office.

Like most aristocrats who don't go Left, Bush's main concern was order and the same was true of James Baker, his secretary of state.

They were happy that perestroika had opened up the Soviet economy to Western investment. But they didn't think America needed to get involved in the politics of the old Soviet region. Neither did the *New Republic*'s readership—but for a different reason: leftists and liberals were skeptical of nationalism, which they identified with atavism. I had to push back:

> It is a sad fact that Mr. Gorbachev's allies in the West, who sincerely believe in the cause of progressive reform in the Soviet Union, seem to wish that these nations remain mute…. Why can't these irrepressible ethnics at least wait, they almost say, until the democratizing reforms are in place before they do their chauvinist mischief?

> Why indeed? The answer is relatively straightforward…. Communism tried to crush the ethnic particularities under its rule and induce cultural amnesia so that the formal ethnic structures of the Union would be without content.

Meantime, with the Soviets leaving the region, the Middle East was breaking open, too. The dictators were losing a patron and looking increasingly shaky. But the Bush policy was the same here: in the worst-case scenario of Saddam Hussein's invasion of Kuwait, America would act, but afterward it would retreat again, and leave the pieces it had put in motion to sort themselves out.

In 1991, we saw where that led, with the First Gulf War, a war which the *New Republic* and new Democrats like Al Gore supported but whose aftermath left a bitter taste in some of our mouths.

The cause of the bitterness was the Iraqi Kurds. The Kurds were a non-Arab people who could trace their place in the area of Turkey and Iraq back a millennium. They had been promised statehood in the settlements reached after the First World War, only to have it yanked away from them by the British. They saw that the Kurds' land overlapped with the region's biggest oil fields, and made the land part of Iraq, a de facto British protectorate with a majority Shia population and a Sunni monarch at its head. The British had instituted some measure of protection for the Kurds. But when Saddam came to power, he treated them like he treated anybody who wasn't a Sunni and wasn't an Arab: he persecuted them, exiled them, and killed them. The Anfal genocide, which occurred between 1988 and 1989, as Saddam brought his war with Iran to a close, killed between 50,000 and 182,000 Kurds—and all because certain groups of Kurds had allied with Iran.

There was no real hope for the Kurds unless they had their own state, and after Saddam's defeat in Kuwait, they saw their chance. They declared independence and braced themselves for the inevitable retaliation. These Peshmerga, in Kurdish "those who face death," were battle-hardened fighters. But they were fighting on flat terrain open to bombardment, and Saddam attacked them savagely, pushing the fighters back to their mountains and slaughtering civilians in the recaptured towns. The *New Republic* urged action. I thought this was Biafra all over again—but worse: we'd given these people hope, and they'd acted. Now we were leaving them to die.

Bernard-Henri Levy was a champion of the Kurds, and so was Fouad. Al was behind us, as was James Woolsey, the CIA director, and Reaganite Republicans like Jeane Kirkpatrick. None of us were enough of a force right then, and Bush and Baker didn't seem much bothered: they were busy talking to the Saudis about the regional endgame, talks that certainly didn't involve the Kurds or what Saddam did to them.

I always thought the Saudi ambassador Bandar bin Sultan got along so well with Bush and Baker because they were all aristocrats: they recognized in each other the same interests. Bandar's advice was in the aristocratic interest of order: don't get bogged down in another interethnic quarrel. Instead, focus on the real underlying issue in the Middle East, which, in Bandar and the Saudis' view, meant getting the Palestinians a state of their own. They had an ally in Chas Freeman, Bush's ambassador to Saudi Arabia, who'd always been suspicious of Israeli influence—maybe Jewish influence?—in Washington and who saw Israel-Palestinian relations as the hinge on which the region turned. I thought this was nonsense: it ignored the legacy of colonialists and the faulty borders they'd drawn. But the Saudis didn't want to look at that reality because it was a potentially destabilizing one. And Bush listened to them and focused on Israel instead.

In the first year of the Clinton administration, there was a moment of hope when Yitzhak Rabin seemingly secured a peace with Arafat. There was a picture on the front page of all the major newspapers of Clinton pushing the two together as they shook hands on the Oslo Accords. Arafat had attained full respectability in his always iffy claim to represent the whole Palestinian people. I cannot count the number of offices and homes in which I saw his portrait on the wall—even at the vice president's residence in the Naval Observatory.

I was invited to the signing ceremony. But I didn't go. Leon was horrified. Even Al, in a late-night phone call, urged me to come. Still, I refused. I didn't think it would come to anything. I thought people were deluding themselves about Arafat's intentions. In my view, he wanted to enter Jerusalem as a conqueror, and he wouldn't settle for less. Nothing Israel might give him would ever induce him to let go of his war, not if he thought he had any room to maneuver. And in the Clinton administration's foreign policy—with its combination of ideals, inattention, and polling fixations—there always seemed to be more than enough room.

Two years later, in November of 1995, Rabin was shot dead by a right-wing Orthodox fanatic, and it all collapsed. By June of the next year, Shimon Peres, Rabin's successor as prime minister, had been defeated by Benjamin Netanyahu. The peace process, at least as envisioned by Rabin, Peres, and the Labor Party, was dead.

As prime minister, Bibi had all the virtues and flaws of a right-winger, the ones that I had seen in him early on. He had been a consultant in America—he'd worked at Bain Capital—and he knew a lot about privatization and efficiency. As finance minister under Begin, he started the economic boom that continues to this day. That was the plus side. On the minus side, he was narrow: if you weren't obviously in his ideological camp or vociferously with Israel, he had no interest in you. We were friends in the way that one is friends with the prime minister of Israel. "Dear Bibi," went a note from me, urging him to notice more the concerns of American Jews, "reformed and conservative Jewry in America make up the bulk of deeply energized American Zionists. These are the Zionists whom the US government conjures with. They, too, are your allies in urgent moments—if only you would have them." He is not a crude warrior type like Begin, but he shared Begin's ideology, maybe at a deeper level considering the trauma and sacrifice of his family.

My eye was on Ehud Barak. When Rabin and Arafat signed the Oslo Accords, Ehud was put in charge of implementing them. So, he had a direct and serious notion of what compromising with the Palestinians actually looked like. He hadn't, like Bibi, grown up in an ideological cocoon: he spent his life in the army; he was tough enough, and practical enough, to be a leader who could actually solve the problem. I, for one, never thought that the Palestinian problem was the Middle East's major crisis. But the Western media and political class never tired of discussing it. I thought Barak could put Arafat in a corner without pummeling him and could possibly make him give up on his dream of ruling Jerusalem.

As the Palestinian issue inflated and then deflated in the early years of the Clinton administration, Eastern Europe came to the fore again. By 1992, the Soviet Union had officially disbanded. But again, America's focus was elsewhere.

Bill Clinton had gotten elected on the slogan "It's the economy, stupid," which was a fair reading of the national mood. The American inclination right then was inward, after a decade of financial swings that had created recessions and recoveries and that had chafed group resentments. With his hands full on the domestic front, Clinton foreign policy in practice amounted to turning the reins over to the free market and its operators. The most notable of these was a kind of emblem of this new era, its hopes and delusions and the structures that got set up to hold them in place: George Soros.

Soros is an interesting man: generous, idealistic, and egomaniacal. He sees himself at the center of the universe in a way that's shaped by the trauma of a particular inheritance, a brush with brute force—the Holocaust. He's created a foundation that's given billions of dollars to unimpeachably good causes and to people who I respect, like Michael Ignatieff, as well as people I respect and love, like Leon Botstein. And in the process, he's become a kind of hero of the One-Worlders. His son Alexander, I am told, is a bit more Jewish, more particular, than his father and sits on the board of the Center for Jewish History, which means Soros didn't force his children to be like him. But when it comes to his own ideals, he is clear and uncompromising.

He was born between the wars, in Hungary, to assimilationist Jews who changed the family name from Schwartz. His father survived the Holocaust by working with the Nazis under duress, buying the furniture of Jews the Nazis were deporting. His mother was "quite anti-Semitic, and ashamed of being Jewish," Soros told Connie Bruck of the *New Yorker* in 1995. "Given the culture in which one lived, being Jewish was a clear-cut stigma, a disadvantage, a handicap—and, therefore, there was always the desire to transcend it, to escape it." (Note: "always" is the word he uses.) After the war, he came to England, where he attended the London School of Economics and studied under Karl Popper. Then he came to America to work on Wall Street, and in 1970 he founded Soros Fund Management, a competitor of Michael Steinhardt's hedge fund and also a target of the federal collusion inquiry into the Treasury bond markets.

Soros went on making money, and today he is said to be worth more than $8 billion, which puts him at 234th in the Bloomberg Billionaires Index. But this is after giving away more than $30 billion to philanthropy—and 1993 was the year he stepped into his philanthropic own. He looked at Eastern Europe breaking open, and he saw an opportunity. He used his money to start the Open Society Foundations, inspired, apparently, by Karl Popper's book *The Open Society and its Enemies*. Soros's was an aggressive brand of philanthropy: rather than adopt the customs of a particular society in hopes of changing it, he funneled money to universities and national foundations to open up these societies, using the force of the market. And this funneling synchronized with Soros's financial interests, since he ran an international investment firm that could benefit only from a relaxation of borders and currency flows, the free market counterpart of a free society. If states were secondary, then not only culture but capital flows could be universal: barriers to movement, of people and finance, could be stripped away. It was a view as hostile to nationalism as it was to labor unions. But most people weren't talking about it that way. Not then.

Soros sounded me out for advice about the Foundations, and it even seemed like he might want me to sit on his board. The discussion was very polite and lasted for about fifteen minutes, and we never spoke about it—or much of anything—again. I did write him a long letter offering advice. One point in particular jumps out now:

> *A warning: if you want to widen the ambit and orbit of such a center on a permanent basis you should take precautions that it not be seen as too personalistic an institution. You would not want a Yeshiva of one rebbe.*

Reader, he did not take my advice. "By having these foundations," he told Bruck for the *New Yorker* profile, "I was sort of able to play God, right? I was something above it, outside it, benevolent, farsighted, godlike—O.K.? If I become an investor, I come down to earth, you know? I'm just a player."

And Soros was playing God for a particular purpose, an echo of his mother's stance about Jewishness: "I am escaping the particular," he said in the same interview. "I think I am doing exactly that by espousing this concept [of open society]. In other words, I don't think you can ever overcome anti-Semitism if you behave as a tribe.... The only way you can overcome it is if you give up the tribalness." His line on Israel was the logical extension of this stance: "I don't deny the Jews their right to a national existence—but I don't want to be part of it." It's an interesting position to take, in part because it's so hardline, so inextricably set against how many people, and not only Jews, think about themselves. The uncomfortable fact, the difficulty for Soros, is that to the extent Jews identify with Jewishness, most are identifying in some way with a particular culture, which comes from a particular tribe: a tribe and then a culture and then a nation with religious beliefs, ethnic habits, moral standards, and intellectual inheritances.

Soros's approach, like Hillary's on healthcare, was top down, straight out of the management manuals the Clintons had read. So, to them his instincts were trustworthy. Here is Strobe Talbott, Clinton's deputy secretary of state, talking to Bruck about Soros's foreign policy,

> *I would say that it is not identical to the foreign policy of the US government—but it's compatible with it. It's like working with a friendly, allied,*

independent entity, if not a government. We try to synchronize our approach to the former Communist countries with Germany, France, Great Britain— and with George Soros."

According to the article, Strobe actually grinned when he said this. I, by contrast, felt like throwing up at this equation of Soros with NATO. Relying on Soros's money didn't actually solve the regions' problem, which was above all political. If Orthodox Jews, Koreans, and blacks were having trouble getting along in a place as stable as New York City, imagine what it would be like in these newly awakened Eastern European nations.

We found out soon enough.

❊   ❊   ❊

In the presidential election year of 1992, reports of mass killings of Muslims started coming out of the former Yugoslavia. My friend Vlado Dedijer had told me that his country had been like the Soviet Union in miniature, a patchwork of ethnic and religious communities living side by side, kept from each other's throats only by socialism and the dogmatic will of the dictator Tito. Now that Yugoslavia was gone, that fragile equilibrium was breaking.

The biggest state in the new Yugoslav federation was Serbia, led by Slobodan Milosevic, a former Communist Party apparatchik who found a new lease on power as an ardent Serbian nationalist. In 1992, the Muslim Bosniaks voted to secede completely from the Yugoslav federation to form their own state. The Christian Orthodox Bosnian Serbs resisted: they were afraid of ending up in a state where they were a minority, and so their leader, Radovan Karadzic, formed a Serbian state to compete for the same territory. It was a one-sided conflict: the Serbs, backed by Milosevic, were slaughtering Catholic Croats and Muslim Bosniaks. It was state power in the service of tribal animus, and the result was the worst atrocity in Europe since the Second World War.

The world was horrified by the pictures in the news. Clinton saw the crisis and did his best to look away. He had been humiliated in Somalia already, and he didn't want another military adventure to sink his already low poll numbers. As the deaths mounted, all on one side, excuses for inaction piled up from the White House: Yugoslavia was too complex to think about interfering; the evidence for who was at fault was too murky. Underneath all that, you could tell, Clinton's stance was fatalism, which he articulated at least once: "Until those folks get tired of killing each other over there, bad things will continue to happen." This, readers will notice, is very like what Fulbright said about Biafra.

Prominent liberals pushed back on Clinton, even people less muscular than me on the use of American force. Susan Sontag went to Sarajevo, where she staged a performance of Beckett's *Waiting for Godot* and wrote dispatches for the *New York Review*. Michael Walzer urged intervention in the *New Republic*. But we, the magazine as a collective, had a special responsibility: we had helped put Clinton in the White House, and this, we figured, gave us the right to say what we wanted. By early 1994, with the administration on the defensive over healthcare, there was no better time to push for it. So, we mounted a campaign.

We sent a twenty-two-year-old journalist, a Yale graduate named Samantha Power, to Bosnia as a war correspondent. Samantha was Irish, and she believed from her own people's bitter disappointments with the British Empire what I believed about the American Empire now: that it was our responsibility to do what the British couldn't or wouldn't the last time this happened—to protect the peoples that the new world was allowing to break free. The *New Republic* carried many of her compelling dispatches from Bosnia.

In early February 1994, when sixty-eight people were killed by a mortar shell explosion in the market at Sarajevo, we ran an editorial called "The Abdication." We put the first paragraph on the cover:

> *When blood is spilled, it is the responsibility of those who spill it, and the responsibility of those who could have stopped its spilling. For this reason, the carnage in the market of Sarajevo shamed also the White House, which should have been shamed long ago. Bill Clinton's dilatory, casuistic response to the great crime*

in the Balkans was not only shameful, it also marked a
moment in the history of American foreign policy. This
administration is transforming the only superpower in
the world into the only abdicating superpower in the
world. Poor Bosnia, it should have found itself a trade
war. Trade wars we fight. Wars of genocide we watch.

I worked on Al all I could, not that he needed it. But I laid it
on thick. "Anne and I know that you are not the one who is making
these decisions," I wrote in a letter. "But we also know that it is not
in you to make the kind of decisions which have been made."

As if all this weren't bad enough, rumors of another genocide were coming out of east Africa, in Rwanda, where the Hutu
tribe were slaughtering the Tutsis, with whom they had formerly
lived in relative peace. A superpower whose leaders didn't want it
to be the world's policeman anymore was confronted with crises
that demanded immediate action with Bosnia and Rwanda. How
could the United States escape its historical responsibilities? Tired
of making impossibly fine distinctions between more and less legitimate interventions, we used Rwanda to draw a line. In May, as the
death toll rose, we published an editorial—"Why Not Rwanda?"—
which made the case that, because the conflict was between two
peoples in the same state, as opposed to the Yugoslav war between
peoples of different declared states, a clear and easy distinction
existed between the cases:

> *In international law, most notably the UN Charter,*
> *war to redraw recognized national boundaries is the*
> *"bright line" across which no actor in the interna-*
> *tional system is permitted to go...If the Serbs succeed*
> *in violating that bright line in Bosnia, the results*
> *could range from a demoralized, destabilized Europe,*
> *to wider war involving Turkey, Greece, Russia and the*
> *United States.... For better or worse, Serbia's sending*
> *of troops and arms into Bosnia is simply of greater*
> *import than the conflict in Rwanda...encouraging*
> *international chaos throughout large and strategically*
> *vital parts of the world.*

Did I agree with this? Not entirely. To me at the time, Hutus were as bad as the Serbs, maybe worse, because they were using the power of the state against its citizens. But if we could have one humanitarian intervention, I thought it should be in Bosnia. That was the stance of the magazine, and finally Bill Clinton came to agree. But I didn't feel right about Rwanda at the time, and I am more embarrassed, more mortified about it now.

In the midst of the genocide in Bosnia that year, I was proud to receive an honorary degree from the Chicago Theological Seminary, which had an African American religiosity that I intuitively recognized from the civil rights movement. This is what I said in my speech, in which I also argued for a similar response in Haiti, where the military regime was murdering its political enemies and creating a refugee crisis:

> *If lives are to be saved in Haiti and Bosnia, and if some decent politics are to have a chance at survival there, only American arms will make this possible. No one else will. It seems to me ironic and tragic that Haiti, where the US has intervened so often in the past and so malignly, now waits to be rescued by Americans. This is a country which wants and needs the Marines [and] whose democracy will not be restored without the Marines. And those Marines do not go, not because they would not be welcomed in the oldest black republic in the world, but because Americans themselves do not have confidence in what at last the American idea really means. The innocent children of Sarajevo and Kigali and Port-au-Prince are the real victims of our own narcissistic ideological battles over identity and possibility.*

In 1995, after a year of delay, Clinton intervened: NATO bombed the Serbians, forcing Karadzic to retreat and Milosevic to withdraw from Bosnia. Richard Holbrooke, at that point deputy secretary of state, negotiated the peace: it was a triumph, for him, for the country, and at some remove even for the *New Republic*.

The agreement stopped Milosevic but didn't strip his power or his territorial ambition. Even before the Bosnian ceasefire, he was moving on the Albanians of Kosovo, who occupied a "semi-auton-omous" republic in Serbia itself. The Kosovar president, Ibrahim Rugova, had played a careful hand during the Bosnian War, but he was increasingly trapped between Kosovar Albanians who wanted a state of their own and a Serbian minority in Kosovo who natu-rally saw Milosevic as their leader. President Rugova asked the UN for help, and then he petitioned NATO, just as Milosevic's Serbs marched in.

Russia had come in on Milosevic's side, making noise about NATO interference. Because Russia had a seat on the Security Council, the UN was, as usual, paralyzed. A resolution in favor of intervention, which the US had obtained in 1995, would be harder to come by a couple of years later. We pushed for action in print, Al pushed the president in private, and finally, in early 1999, Clinton decided to forgo the UN resolution and bomb Serbia. Russia didn't make good on its threats, and Milosevic retreated again. Despite this success, UN Secretary-General Kofi Annan argued, as he visited the refugee camps, that "the Security Council should be the sole source of the legitimate use of force," blatantly ignoring the reality that had the Security Council been the sole source of the legitimate use of force that year, these refugees would all be dead.

We made a big thing of this nonsense in the magazine: we thought it was the opposite of how responsible American leader-ship should sound. Our man in Kosovo was David Rieff, son of Susan Sontag and Philip Rieff, a strict reporter, cold and clear. Now twenty-seven, Samantha Power had come back to Harvard after five years in the field and started writing pieces about her expe-rience—brave, motivated, intellectual, dazzling, and idealistic but rooted in reality—that we began publishing in the magazine. They were collected in a book, *A Problem from Hell: America and the Age of Genocide*, which after being turned down by publisher after publisher was finally published by New Republic Books, in partner-ship with Basic Books.

The book articulated the thesis that preventing genocide was the minimum standard the world's only democratic superpower should expect itself to maintain: it made the case for the kind of global order, rooted in minimalist interventionism, over which the American Empire should preside. Her hero was Raphael Lemkin, the author of the term "genocide." She made her case, Lemkin's case, by setting out the times and places where intervention could have made some difference: Armenia, Cambodia, Iraq, and, of course, Germany. She was brutal about the lame reasons policymakers gave to excuse their inaction: they "overemphasized the ambiguity of the facts"; they suggest the "futility, perversity, and jeopardy of any proposed intervention"; or they humanitarianize and globalize the crisis with references to the "international community," blunting the moral truths of the war itself.

This was not talk that resonated with the so-called liberals in the White House because it described so accurately their rationale for waiting a year to stop the Serbs. The Clinton administration foreign policy professionals were more rationalist than pluralist, more about systems than about people. Clinton's second secretary of state, Madeleine Albright, was cut from the same Jewish cloth as George Soros. She'd been raised a Catholic and became an Episcopalian. But when she was nominated for secretary of state, an investigation by the *Washington Post* revealed she was Jewish. I could tell Madeline was Jewish back when she was an undergraduate at Wellesley and the roommate of my friend Emily Cohen. When the story came out, she acted like it was a big surprise and said her parents, Czech Jews, hadn't told her. I didn't think it was a scandal to be discovered as a Jew. But I guess Madeleine did because Emily called to ask me not to write about it. She knew I would be very sarcastic and sardonic, and of course I was.

Madeleine had the kind of desperate universal mindedness, the driving, aspirant urge to escape inheritance, that conceived of the world as a series of administrative problems to be solved and organizational issues to be worked out by rational people. The holders of this faith didn't believe, as I did, that the worst sin in the world is coercion, to march people and peoples in lockstep. Looking back, I realize that lack of distinctions, lack of history, was everywhere in that period—hope was high and context imaginary or imagined. The philosophy seemed to be that everybody was friends—that distinctions, differences, didn't matter.

Around this time, I got a call from Emily's husband, Rod MacFarquhar, who'd heard that the Clinton administration was encouraging Yo-Yo Ma to go to the handover of Hong Kong from the British to the Chinese and perform. Rod, who after all was one of the preeminent experts on China, said, "I know you're a good friend of Yo-Yo's. Can you arrange for me to have a meal with him so I can explain why this is a terrible thing?" So, we gathered a small dinner party—six people: Anne and me, Rod and Emily, Yo-Yo and Jill—at the table in our kitchen. And everybody at the table was making the case to Yo-Yo (Jill didn't need the case made) about how terrible this was and how it would give legitimacy to a totalitarian Communist state.

And it was an interesting divergence in views between me and Yo-Yo, between someone raised on politics and someone raised on culture, because Yo-Yo respected the argument but didn't listen to it. For Yo-Yo, there was almost never a reason not to play music, because music, itself, can start to mend differences—and if you keep music out, you're only hurting everyone. For me, art can't be disassociated from its political context if the context is a coercive one. I think I'm right. There's a photograph of Yo-Yo and Jiang Zemin, and it makes me wince. I wonder what Yo thinks now.

Looking back, I realize something else: at what was the apex of my influence, I felt, more often than not, alienated—out of step from people who, nominally at least, were supposed to believe what I did. Most of these people were rationalist universalists or even polite liberals, not the type to have been caught dead at the New Politics Convention thirty-odd years back. But I *had* been caught dead there, and I always remembered it, always remembered the feeling, and the basic axiom I'd taken from the whole messy debacle: when distinctions were allowed to break down—in language, in belief—trouble wasn't long in coming. If you let in everything, you end up with nothing.

❋   ❋   ❋

It looked, in the summer of 2000, like Al would be the next president. I was both in the thick and not: Al's campaign was not like others I had been involved in.

Anne and I and all four kids made contributions. I talked to Al a lot, though I called less than I might have because I wanted to be respectful of his time. I never thought of myself as a political advisor, even though my files testify that I was full of suggestions in writing about policy and strategy. Really, I was an emotional advisor: I knew Al, knew what he could and couldn't tolerate, and that was what made me valuable. So, I was near the top of the campaign, with constant access. On the other hand, for all of the intensity of my belief, I always felt marginal. The political professionals in his campaign were mostly Southerners, smart but not cerebral, and I think Al wanted me there because I was a break from these Southern pols, his father's people, against whom he'd been in perpetual but well disguised rebellion his whole life. Running for president was something Al wanted—and not just as a fulfilment of his father's legacy. He was going to run in his own way, and I was part of that.

But I was never comfortable. And the professionals were never comfortable with me.

I was never quite sure why they weren't doing certain things. Why, particularly, didn't Al go after Ralph Nader, who was running a quixotic third-party campaign that would only siphon votes from the Democratic candidate? In the end, I think this would've shifted it in Florida, where it ended up mattering more than any of us could have ever imagined. But it wasn't really a mean campaign: that wasn't the mentality. Especially if you look at the campaign from the perspective of 2016, where both of the candidates were very mean indeed, or for that matter 2020. Bush wasn't mean to Gore, and Gore wasn't mean to Bush.

Al knew from the beginning that he was in for a tough fight. One summer in that small stretch of years, he came to our property in Truro. The Secret Service shut down maybe one-eighth of a mile beach, much to the dismay of the neighbors, and Al and I talked about the state of the race. Not once did I hear him underrate Bush. "Take him seriously," he told me one night over dinner. "He's not, no matter what they say, a dunce." As Anne and I were driving back home that night, she—who, unlike me, had only contempt for Bush (I can always find reasons to like Republicans)—observed, "He never knocks his opponents."

Al didn't knock his friends-cum-enemies either, even when they made the electoral fight tougher. He wouldn't, for example, speak to me candidly about Clinton, who had handed him a tough political challenge: How do you be your own person, take credit for the good economy, and censure your predecessor for bad sexual behavior, all at the same time? He wouldn't speak to me candidly, I think, in part because of his natural discretion, in part because he knew I disliked Clinton, and he knew it would only precipitate a useless argument. He knew me for a troublemaker, most comfortable when I was fighting. But he was playing a long game, and he exhibited tremendous self-control.

I don't know how much I thought about what I would do if Al won, whether I would go to work for the government or maintain my independent stance. Unlike with Clinton, this time there was the possibility that I would have the option of something serious, more than just ambassador to Denmark or something. I wasn't sure how to feel about this. Perhaps I would be witch hunted, which is too heroic and misplaced a metaphor but captures my fear: I was gay, and then only a few people knew. But under the glare of publicity, a few people can turn into a lot of people. That would hurt not just me but Anne as well. It might be enough, maybe more than enough, to be editor of the magazine with a direct link to the president of the United States.

In 1999, I appeared on *Charlie Rose*, and Charlie pressed me as to whether the *New Republic* had lost its edge. Charlie and I never got on: he told me once I was too combative with the other guests, which always struck me as the point of a serious show of ideas. I answered his jab with what I thought: "We look forward to being at the center of the next presidency, with Al Gore in the White House." A year later, when Al was nominated, I told the *Washington Post* about the *New Republic* under a Gore presidency: "My guess is we would be involved in a tense and dense encounter with the policies of the administration if they win." I didn't really mean "if." When it came to Al winning, I was sure it was going to happen.

Even my ideological enemies thought that would be the case: "OK, Marty, You Win" went a piece in *The Nation* in August 2000.

I guess we have to hand it to Marty Peretz, Al Gore's tutor at Harvard and informal adviser ever since. All his political dreams are being consummated. In the fall of 1967, exactly at the time Gore was learning political science at Peretz's knee, hundreds of young leftists gathered in Chicago for a National Conference on New Politics.... Peretz helped bankroll the convention...[and its unraveling] prefigured not only the itinerary of Peretz from fashionable rad to the rabid neocon owner of The New Republic *but the later mime of that shift, embodied in the rise of the Democratic Leadership Council, which was born in 1985.... At the level of effective policy, the battle was won in the Clinton/Gore era.*

What were my motives so close to the apex? My motives were that Al was a smart, decently inclined, and an honest person. I thought he'd make a better president than anyone else on the horizon. We didn't talk about Israel a lot, but I knew he would be all right. There was also Al's choice as his vice presidential nominee, Joe Lieberman, who was not quite a friend but an ally and who was and is as Jewish as anyone I knew and know. He was not only Al Gore's vice president but the first Jewish nominee in a major party, and this says something about Al Gore's Zionism.

I trusted Al's instincts abroad: he had pushed and pushed and pushed Clinton to intervene in Bosnia and Kosovo, to his own detriment within the White House. And, domestically, he was the opposite of a utopian; if he was for a program, it had to do something specific and significant, and if he thought the program measured up to that marker, he would keep pushing it. He was a liberal incrementalist, not an idealistic manager; a humanistic technocrat, not a utilitarian communalist—the best of the generation I had tried to help educate.

I knew him well, and I trusted his decency because Al is a deep feeling man. The press kept mocking that big TV kiss of Al and Tipper's at the convention, but I think it was real. They were a normal family: when Al was vice president, his kids refused Secret Service protection, and Al said that was against the law. They fought him, and he sort of gave way. Tipper, for her part, had to have it, but she had a big hat she'd use to leave the residence at the Naval Observatory to do something normal, like go shopping.

Apart from Al himself, any number of my protégés stood to gain from what a Gore administration would bring to Washington. Jamie Gorelick was the number two at Justice, the frontrunner for attorney general in a Gore administration. Merrick Garland, whose career Jamie had helped catapult, was now on the D.C. Circuit Court of Appeals, the traditional jumping off point to the Supreme Court—where he would be now if not for the Republican majority in the Senate during the Obama administration, which refused to even consider his nomination in 2016. Tom Williamson had been the chief lawyer in the Labor Department—he left in 1996—and there'd be a place for him. In 1999, Larry Summers was named Clinton's treasury secretary, and in a Gore presidency he might stay on in the position or take over the Federal Reserve. Nita Lowey was in the House of Representatives. Chuck Schumer had just become a senator from New York. Zeke Emanuel, who was at the National Institutes of Health, would probably have a policy position. Glenn Hutchins, who'd worked in the Clinton administration, might come back for Al, too.

All these people had come through Harvard, and some through the *New Republic*—they'd been in my classes, and they'd come to the editorial meetings, or interned there themselves. They were the Democratic Party as I'd tried, in my way, to help form it over the past quarter century. They believed in progress, certainly more than I did, and they were also expert practitioners who specialized in sensible policy pitched to America at its broadest.

❋ ❋ ❋

It felt to me as if, on the verge of sixty, the circle of my life was about to close. Anne threw me a birthday party in the catacombs underneath the Brooklyn Bridge, a place you can't go now. It became a lavish thing. It was just a raw, beautiful stone space; it didn't have any lights, and we had to put them in. It was my style: a little out of step, a little more real than one of the elegant alternatives. But the event was also elegant, in its way. And everybody came—old friends, new friends, feuding friends: Ivan Boesky from La Jolla, the Alters from Chicago, the Safdies and Koerners from Cambridge, Leon and the *New Republic* people from Washington, the Dinitzes from Israel, the Granetzs, Grafsteins, Ackmans, and Steinhardts from New York, John Callahan from Oregon, Ira Rosenberg from California. Al was there, too, and it took almost an hour for people to get down to the space because there was so much Secret Service. Leon Botstein toasted me, and so did Jamie Gorelick. And so did Anne. She gave me a bouquet of flowers, each of the flowers different, and she identified them in her talk. Together, she said, it was a garden.

Yo-Yo was going to play an awful, sweet, saccharine French romantic piece that I was embarrassed to love. But he left his Stradivarius cello in the trunk of a cab that afternoon. He'd been exhausted—he'd played a concert at Carnegie Hall the day before, a Friday—and he'd simply forgotten the cello. By the time he realized he didn't have it, the driver, who had no idea who Yo-Yo was, had sped off. And so, the police put out an alert. Between two and six, it was all over the networks, and the AP picked the story up: Stradivarius, made in Venice in 1733, worth $2.5 million (who knows how much it's worth now) lost in a cab. The police used Yo-Yo's receipt to track down the driver to a garage in Queens, and Yo-Yo got the cello back by 5:15, before the party. (Do you take a receipt from cabs? I don't. But Yo-Yo does.) "Somehow magic happened, and I have my cello," is what Yo-Yo told the AP. Before he played my piece that night, Yo-Yo played the "Tennessee Waltz," and then I introduced the crowd to Al: the next president of the United States.

In one way, the night was a kind of victory for a faith I had in people that I never gave up—and a defeat of my father, who'd never gotten beyond the mistrust and never wanted me to. In another way, the sheer improbability of all of these people from all of these eminent places and institutions here to honor a middle-class boy from the Bronx was a victory for the other part of my faith: break the rules; be iconoclastic; be distinct from the Establishment but be smart enough to be taken seriously. Those two parts of that night, the love and the pugnacity, put together: that was my imagining.

And now I knew, with a sense of a little bit of wonder, that that imagining, that push, had brought me *here*. Of course, there were signs, even then, that here might not be where I thought it was.

* * *

There were failed campaigns to boost subscriptions at the *New Republic*, which were flagging—we'd peaked at one hundred thousand with Andrew, but afterward circulation had fallen off. There was staff turnover: I'd appointed a new editor, Peter Beinart. He was the son of South African Jews who'd moved to Cambridge, and his stepfather was Robert Brustein, who'd been the *New Republic*'s theater critic since before I'd bought the magazine. Peter had gone to Yale, gotten a Rhodes Scholarship, earning a Master of Philosophy in international relations, and he came on staff during the Bosnian intervention. He was also a Zionist. In a sense, he was perfect, maybe even too perfect: on some inarticulable level, it felt too setup. Remember, I hadn't come from Cambridge. And neither had Rick, Mike Kinsley, or Leon. We were all smart people, but we didn't come perfectly minted. Peter, on the other hand, never had to break in. He'd come from the new American postwar institutional elite, and that was his definition of the world. All the rest of us had had different environments to draw from. I'm overstating this now—everything looks clearer, in retrospect—but on some level, I wondered about what that might mean.

There were changes in the Democratic Party I saw as problems. That June, Hillary Clinton had announced her candidacy for senator from New York. Pat Moynihan was giving up his seat. Nita Lowey, who was planning to run if Hillary didn't, stepped aside. Moynihan gave Hillary his blessing. I couldn't understand why Pat was surrendering so significant a spot. And, even more, I couldn't understand why he was endorsing her when I knew he disliked her intensely. I said to him, "God, why are you giving this up?" which was not an invitation to a discussion. But I knew what the change meant: the preeminent liberal of the party was being replaced by the preeminent manager. Her next stop, so everyone said, was the presidency.

Finally, there was the media coverage of the presidential campaign. The race, looking back, was relatively centrist on the big economic and political questions, and so it became very much a race about character. There wasn't as much to say about George W. Bush beyond the midlife conversion to Evangelism and the successful Texas governorship. Al, on the other hand, had a record of twenty-five years in government you could analyze. And the beat reporters at the *Times* and *Post* needed copy: the big papers were still afloat financially, but they also were, much more than they had been thirty years before, about selling a product. So, they picked Al's record apart to fill white space between the ads. They were thoughtlessly vicious. They mocked Al for all sorts of things: one of them the kiss with Tipper; another being that he'd claimed, rightly, that he was central to the growth of the internet. It didn't matter that Robert Kahn and Vinton Cerf, who had worked on the internet since its inception, pushed back against the pushback with a public statement that said, in part, that "Al Gore was the first political leader to recognize the importance of the Internet and to promote and support its development.... No other elected official, to our knowledge, has made a greater contribution over a longer period of time." The narratives got pushed; the labels stuck.

In retrospect, the signs did mean something. The apex was over, as quickly as—almost before—it came. Fourteen months after Yo-Yo played the "Tennessee Waltz," everything had changed.

Jim Cramer and I were fighting our way through an internet endeavor we'd come up with together: thestreet.com. It was not exactly together. You never could keep up with Jim, and that wasn't always a good thing. The fact is that Jim is a genius—a mad genius, like most geniuses are. But we were on to something new, an actually big idea: use the internet, which nine years after Al's bill was becoming ubiquitous in American life, to give immediate financial news, and charge for it. At the time, it was looking like when the company went public its worth would be in the stratosphere. I remember saying, around this time, to my friend, the investor Gerry Cardinale, "Who woulda thought I woulda been a multimillionaire?" He grinned because he understood exactly what I meant: Gerry from Allerton, Jim from Philly, Marty from the Bronx—middle-class boys who'd gone through the higher institutions of American life but never quite lost the roughness, making good. But thestreet.com tanked. The internet had too much free-flowing information: there was no reason for people to pay for a subscriber service. Jim was moving on, upping his TV appearances, which eventually would lead to his own investing show—the climax of the democratization of finance he'd always, somehow, predicted and embodied.

Ehud Barak won the Israeli election against Bibi Netanyahu and became prime minister. The most decorated military leader in Israeli history immediately began a push for a peace with Arafat. Unlike Bibi, Ehud wasn't a defensive player. He saw Arafat was a thorn in Israel's foot, and, using the capital he'd accrued through his whole life, he was trying to pull it out. But now Barak was embattled: Arafat had refused to compromise at the negotiating table, and late that year he launched the Second Intifada, responding to the supposed provocation of Ariel Sharon visiting the Temple Mount. It lasted for four and a half years, until a few months after Arafat's own death. It inflamed Israeli Jews, many of whom believed they were in a negotiating process with the Arabs, and also inflamed the Palestinians, who seemed not to understand they were being led down a warpath that would entrap them more.

And Al—Al had just lost the presidency.

The election had been horrifically close the whole way. My memory of the night is standing with Larry Summers in a suite in Nashville as the results came in: first we were up, then down, then Florida called for Bush, and Al was about to concede. But then the news came in that the margin of votes in Florida—less than two thousand—automatically triggered a recount. The legal gymnastics—over the course of more than a month, each day a kind of agony—ended at the Supreme Court. And then, finally, the loss was declared.

Anne and I had been watching television just as the Supreme Court gave its ruling, the final ruling, that stopped the recount in Florida and, in effect, handed the presidency to Bush before all the votes were counted. We saw Al going into his car, picking up a phone—and the phone rang in our bedroom: he was calling for me. Anne began to cry. I probably did too, mostly for Al, a little for myself—maybe a lot for myself. This was my closest moment to power, and I had been eclipsed—and a little part of me knew that, even if it wasn't something I'd ever let myself think into words.

Al took the defeat with dignity. He told his supporters, "Our disappointment must be overcome by our love of country."

Here's something I let myself think about now: imagine what kind of political hay Al might've made from the Supreme Court decision. But he took it stoically, in contrast with Hillary sixteen years later, who wanted to blame anyone but herself: racist white people, white men, white women. This was also in contrast to the other Democratic dynasty besides the Clintons, the Kennedys: until they died you could still hear Schlesinger and Goodwin talking about Bobby Kennedy to the tune of "If Only." And, of course, in contrast with Trump in 2020, who tried to invalidate the election itself.

In July, about six months after Al's loss, Anne and I went with Al to a summer place in Spain on the Costa Brava we'd rented many times. Because vice presidents lose their Secret Service protection after six months, this was the first time Al was without his. We went to Barcelona to pick him up; he was coming off a commercial plane from Beijing and he had a hat on—sort of pulled down. We went back together, and he was down, very down. We were trying to keep him up, and so we took him out to a café on the beach. There was some town festivity going on with fireworks. And suddenly the fireworks erupted—from far away—but the sound was very, very close.

Intuitively, we all ducked to the ground. We thought it was gunfire. We thought we were in danger. Where were the Secret Service guys? Really, somewhere in our brains, we thought we were still in the thick itself. But we weren't.

CHAPTER FIFTEEN

Post-Millennium, 2001-2010: Cast Out

In September, a month after we got back from Spain, the planes flew into the towers, and it looked like history had come around in a different way. Save for Pearl Harbor, it was the first foreign act of war on American soil since the British burned the White House in 1814. But who, really, was responsible? Everything was confused. The waiter came over and said, off hand, that the Russians had hit the towers. Elsewhere people were saying it was the Zionists—or the Saudis, who had lost control of the Islamists they'd been backing. And on the fringes, on the internet, they were saying it was an inside job.

People I was close to in Washington had a different explanation. Nine days after the towers went down, Leon and I signed an open letter to George W. Bush, reprinted in the conservative *Washington Examiner*. It called for a "comprehensive strategy" in response to the attacks that targeted Al Qaeda but recognized that Al Qaeda was part of a broader, bigger web of Middle East interconnections.

The letter was organized by Bill Kristol, and the signatories were the big neoconservative players: Norman Podhoretz and Midge Decter, Richard Perle and William Bennett, Francis Fukuyama and Jeane Kirkpatrick. Leon and I, along with Stephen Solarz, a friend from Brandeis and a former Democratic congressman from Brooklyn, were the only certified liberals who signed. It was a boilerplate statement, probably written by William Bennett. But I stood by what it said.

In retrospect the key paragraph in the letter was this one:

> *We agree with Secretary of State Powell's recent state-*
> *ment that Saddam Hussein "is one of the leading*
> *terrorists on the face of the Earth...." It may be that*
> *the Iraqi government provided assistance in some*
> *form to the recent attack on the United States. But*
> *even if evidence does not link Iraq directly to the*
> *attack, any strategy aiming at the eradication of*
> *terrorism and its sponsors must include a determined*
> *effort to remove Saddam Hussein from power in Iraq.*
> *Failure to undertake such an effort will constitute an*
> *early and perhaps decisive surrender in the war on*
> *international terrorism.*

The administration was moving faster than we knew. The night of 9/11, George Bush had asked Donald Rumsfeld to look into a connection between Al Qaeda and Iraq. By September 15, Rumsfeld was proposing targeting Iraq.

Many people I knew had doubts about the Iraq War. Anne was strongly against it. She had limited patience with American crusades abroad, and she saw Iraq as another one of those—not close enough to the ground, too moralistic. But Anne was a peacenik from a long way back. I knew we'd disagree. Laura Obolensky thought we were nuts: she was French, and she'd grown up in the shadow of Algeria and Vietnam, wars started by men who thought they could control more than they could. Michael Walzer was a little horrified by the invasion: he thought that if you wanted to help an oppressed people, you worked with them; you didn't take the lead and impose freedom from above. Al, for his part, opposed the war because he worried about the aftermath: "The events of the last 85 years provide ample evidence that our approach to winning the peace that follows war is almost as important as winning the war itself" was his line, prescient in retrospect. But Al's bigger focus was now global warming. He had taken out the old slide show he'd used to sketch the dangers of climate change when he first got interested in the issue and was now taking it on the road to new audiences: he was making a different way for himself.

The Left, of course, opposed the war. But the Left was in ugly disarray, emanating more heat than light, opposing not just the invasion of Afghanistan but the liberation of Afghan women from the Taliban's fundamentalist government on the logic that rescuing the women would strengthen the "Great Capitalist Satan" that was America. In response, Michael Walzer wrote an essay in *Dissent* that must have been harder for him to write than for his readers to read, accusing the Left of self-hatred and ending, "The Left must begin again."

After 9/11, the neoconservatives were in political ascendance. I had always been a little repulsed by them, not just by their emphasis on social control and on American power for power's sake and on their rigidity that made most of their positions hostage to the needs of their movement, but by the fact that they were actually tribal: they passed their politics and their roles in public life on to their children, Norman to John, Irving to Bill. But I had personal connections to the movement, people in it who I trusted absolutely. The first was Charles Krauthammer, the most original of the conservative thinkers—harsh but gentlemanly. He may, in the end, have trusted the ability of America to shape the world too much, but he never hungered after power: American force, for him, was a vehicle to achieve others' freedoms. That's how I felt, too. The other was Fouad Ajami who was not a neoconservative but whose lifelong project meshed with neoconservatives' ambitions and their worldview. The Middle East was Fouad's home ground, and he had been growing his ideas on it for twenty years: for secularism and democracy and for a strong Western presence to prod the region forward.

And I had other reasons to support the neoconservatives' project after 9/11. Though the right-wing political types who clustered around President Bush cared more about deterring aggression and projecting American might than they did about preventing genocides and freeing peoples, their commitment to a systemic approach to the failed states of the Middle East matched with the course of action I'd been urging for ten years. Russia was still withdrawn from the region; dictators' holds on colonial states that the Soviets had supported still looked fragile. We had turned our eyes away in the nineties, under Bush and Clinton. Now, under a new Bush, I thought we, the last superpower, might finally exercise our moral responsibility to support the peoples and nations the tyrants were oppressing. Finally, I carried a grudge from the First Gulf War: I thought, after the Kurds, we owed Saddam his head.

Really, I never contemplated that we might lose. This is an admission, to paraphrase Donald Rumsfeld, of how much I didn't see, and how much I didn't know I didn't see.

Though I did see one thing, even if I didn't see its full implications: it's difficult for a country to fight a war when it's not socially united.

At the magazine, there wasn't a lot of internal opposition even if there wasn't a lot of enthusiasm. When I would talk up the war, or Leon or Charles would, a lot of the staff would sort of just say, "Oh, yes," and that was that. Peter Beinart articulated our stance for the invasion in print, and Leon went on *Charlie Rose* to make the case. Paul Berman supported the war and didn't mind attacking other liberal American intellectuals for backing away. Really, the Establishment was pretty united behind it. It was a patriotic moment.

We didn't know then what we know now—that the administration was pushing connections between Iraq and Al Qaeda without enough evidence; that Saddam Hussein was bluffing when it came to weapons of mass destruction; and that time for further weapons inspections would have clarified things. And there was a reason we didn't know this: a tragedy of the Bush administration, or at least a fundamental disjuncture, is the talent and decency it collected in its middle ranks set off against the arrogance and idealizing at its top. Talent and decency abounded: Juan Carlos Zarate, an old student of mine, was a vital part of the administration, working in counterterrorism first at the Treasury Department and then at the National Security Council; Rory Stewart, a Tory politician, intellectual and adventurer of astonishing capacity, who I would know later, was a provincial administrator in Iraq; and Condoleezza Rice, at the highest levels, was a formidable public servant. But mostly, the ideologues and public relations people ran the show. It was a kind of extension of the Clinton White House's aloof managerial tendencies except now the philosophy wasn't soft communalism but patriotic hawkism.

The war's trajectory reflected this disjuncture: there was "shock and awe" and the president piloting down to the deck of an aircraft carrier to declare victory, even as, away from political theatrics, the situation on the ground devolved. Paul Bremer, appointed by the White House to administer postwar Iraq, disbanded the Iraqi army and sent four hundred thousand seasoned fighters into unemployment, essentially creating the militant opposition to American occupation in the time it took to make a pen stroke. The militants bombed the UN mission and forced it to withdraw. (Samantha Power wrote an agonized biography of Sergio de Mello, the head of the mission who was killed in the attack.) Then they attacked coalition forces and the Shia, who had access to power after their long persecution under Saddam but whom the Sunnis feared would exact revenge on them. The Shia responded to Sunni attacks by organizing an army backed by Iran, eager to make a regional power play at America's expense.

The administration response to the shifts in those early years was summed up by Donald Rumsfeld, who told reporters asking him about lootings in Baghdad after Saddam's fall, "Stuff happens." Around that time, I met Rumsfeld at a dinner party and to my own surprise, he spent the evening angling for my attention. I imagine he did it because of the magazine's stance in favor of the war. He struck me as the kind of man who makes plays for himself: not a cynic and not a believer in causes but a pursuer of power who doesn't much look at collateral damage.

But we, at the *New Republic*, were believers in causes, and this cause was in trouble. Peter, Leon, and I had pushed hard for the invasion; we had put the credibility of our liberalism and our pluralism, what Leon and I had developed at the magazine for twenty years, behind it. And it didn't seem to be working. We brought in, as we always brought in, dissents and debate: in 2004, we devoted an issue to Iraq, with the headline "Were We Wrong?" on the cover and varying answers inside.

On one level, Iraq was an operational failure. But it was more than that: it was the failure of a foreign policy ideology, neoconservatism, and the failure of an analysis of the Middle East on which that ideology's real-world success rested. A lot of the neo-cons—

Paul Wolfowitz, Richard Perle, Lewis Libby, Ken Adelman—were Jewish. But I don't think their backing of the war had to do with Israel: it's hard to see how Israel benefited from the American war in Iraq, especially as things went south. I think it was just a case of smart people in thrall to an ideology. They had a total analysis of deterring terrorism and promoting democracy through regime change. Iraq was the acid test of that ideology, and it failed.

Iraq actually was the last test of reforming the Middle East along the lines of the order set up at the Versailles Conference. We now know that reform is impossible: none of the countries drawn there can function because the map drawers made states that were not consonant with the peoples living inside them. Iraq is the starkest case: there are so many sects, and it's so rich in natural resources that, when order is taken away, the conflict between sects becomes explosive. Eventually some people in Washington cottoned to this new reality: the division of Iraq into separate states consonant with peoples (Kurds, Sunnis, Shia) was a late theme in the war. But by then, it was too late for new ideas from Washington: the violence continued, and the regional consequences were becoming difficult to reverse. Iran had used its new influence in Iraq to become the driving power in the Middle East, and it was bent on expanding its remit, bolstering alliances with Syria, Hezbollah, and a newly aggressive Russia. The possibilities for freedom I had seen in the region in 1991 were contracting.

In 2004, in an effort to run against the war, the Democrats chose John Kerry: a higher-good internationalist and a rational institutionalist, negotiation-not-intervention prone. He was a sign of the new ascendance of these types in the party after the debacle that Iraq had become. I've known John a long time, and in private, he is a kind man. But as a politician, I never could stand him. He seemed to me to be so fake, so full of himself, always puffing himself up. I hated his attitude toward his Jewish roots, always for me a test. His brother, Cameron, is a convert—actually a reconvert—to Judaism and president of a synagogue. Sometime between when I met him and when he ran for president, it became clear that John's grandparents on his father's side, instead of being German, were German Jews, and that shook him up. His grandparents' brother and sister, the ones who did identify, died in concentration camps, but his line survived. The lesson was the same as Soros's: assimilate, don't associate, and save yourself.

John knew how I felt about him, but he forced our reconciliation before running for president, out of some imagination of how powerful the *New Republic* editor and staff were, or just because he didn't want to be sniped at from its pages. He paid for lunch, which was his gesture, and I went along with it and laid off him in the *New Republic*. I was never happy with myself for that: I felt like a hypocrite. I don't remember who I voted for in 2004, and I don't think that's an accident, my not remembering. Since I lived in Massachusetts, it didn't matter anyway.

Iraq had created a breach in the Establishment we hadn't seen since Vietnam, and the same types of people who had taken advantage of the breach forty years before were taking advantage of it now. It wasn't a coincidence that, at a YIVO dinner right after the war started, George Soros turned a paean for Imre Kertesz, the Hungarian Jewish Holocaust survivor who'd won the Nobel Prize in Literature the year before, into a screed against Israel. By the time Soros had finished his speech, maybe more than half the crowd had left the Pierre Hotel. But it was a sign, like Kerry's nomination, of a change in the assumptions of the people and the institutions around me: in what they would and would not allow themselves to say and believe.

More signs were seen. Tony Judt wrote a piece for the *New York Review* the week the Iraq War started that began, "We are witnessing the dissolution of an international system," and followed it up that November with "Israel: The Alternative," making the case for a one-state solution. It was like we were back in 1962. Judt's piece calling Israel an "anachronism" in a world of states could have been written by Hannah Arendt. The fact that many of the same people who had backed the Iraq War were ardent supporters of Israel had given Arendt's argument a way back into the discourse, however unrelated those two stances were. As the neoconservative edifice started to look shaky, attacks on its constituent parts increased. Stephen Walt and John Mearsheimer made the case explicitly in "The Israel Lobby," a piece published in the *London Review of Books* in 2006: American foreign policy had been hoodwinked by warmongering capitalists, and those villains were Israel-supporting Jews. Later, the piece was expanded into a book, *The Israel Lobby and U.S. Foreign Policy*, that contained about ten derogatory references to me in its five-hundred pages.

I was increasingly marginalized because I was part of the system that had stumbled. The irony was not pleasant: almost forty years after I'd helped mobilize a political community to end a tragically failing war, I was defending a different, smaller, failing war, with no panacea in sight.

Iraq wasn't Vietnam. It wasn't a fire engulfing American society; it was a murk removed from most Americans' lives. There were too many institutional players operating without transparency: the ideologues, the generals, and the profiteers like Halliburton and Blackwater and outside players like Ahmed Chalabi. And on the ground, there were the Sunni, Shia, and the Kurds. It made for a confusing cast of characters, and it was difficult to see what they were all doing. The Iraqis we were supposedly trying to help attacked our soldiers and each other; American mercenaries mowed down Iraqis in Nisour Square. There was no Osama bin Laden—he got lost in Afghanistan. And there was Abu Ghraib, where American soldiers not only tortured Iraqi prisoners but made pornographic videos of themselves doing it, a grotesque mockery of American liberationist ideals. Seymour Hersh poked his head up to break the story for the *New Yorker*, and, as with My Lai and Vietnam, he was right. I hate to admit it.

In December 2005, Gene McCarthy died. Gene had opposed Iraq from the beginning: he thought the Bush people were bullies, he despised the inflation of the government away from the control of regular people, and he saw empowering the Pentagon to fight a multiyear foreign war as another step in that direction. Gene saw a lot of things early, and that's a lonely place to be. I wrote a long piece for the magazine when Gene died, and afterward Teddy Kennedy wrote to thank me for the conciliatory reference I had made to him:

> *Whatever our differences over the years, I've always felt we had far more in common. In many ways, that '62 campaign seems like only yesterday—I had no idea you were with Stuart Hughes at the time. I also loved the story that Gene was present at the creation of*

your brilliant leadership of TNR. I was at the cathe-
dral because Gene's name will be forever linked with
our family. In spite of the '68 campaign, I admired
Gene enormously for his courage in challenging a war
America never should have fought, and his life speaks
volumes to us now as we face a similar critical time
for our country.

Gene's life did speak volumes. But now there was no one like
him on the political stage, nobody to help restore the trust of Americans who increasingly looked to their government and saw incom-
petence, corruption, stagnation, and failure.

❋   ❋   ❋

At this time, there came a precipitous drop in finances of the *New
Republic*. The internet, having failed to make me millions with thes-
treet.com, was now draining the revenue out of my magazine. It had
never lost money the way it was now losing it. Free news, free commentary on the internet, was eating into our margin. The market,
more even than before, did not value the slow and reasoned thought
that was our signature. I couldn't use new money to make up for the
magazine's shortfall. This meant we were in trouble.

I got advice from people who wanted to help—Marc Granetz
was one of them—but the finances increasingly didn't make sense.
I had to find some kind of way out, and I found it, first, in Larry
Grafstein. We saw each other a lot socially, and I told him my troubles, first casually, then less casually as things got worse. Larry, in
a low-key way, went around talking to people, figuring out who
might and might not help. Michael Steinhardt was a might: he liked
the *New Republic*, he agreed with what we were trying to do, and he
was willing to bankroll us as long as he had a partner to help him
make up for the shortfall. The partner he chose was Roger Hertog.

Roger's parents were Jewish immigrants, and he had grown up
near me on Walton Avenue in the Bronx. He'd become wealthy in
asset management and then retired to devote himself to his passions
in Jewish scholarship and establishment right-wing politics; and he
has funded the American Enterprise Institute, the Manhattan Insti-

tute, the Institute for the Study of War, and the New-York Historical Society. Roger's tough. I can think of only one person who actually likes him, and that's Ruth Wisse. But it's an ideological affinity—she likes Norman Podhoretz too. He's a suspicious man, and he brought this suspiciousness to our partnership on the magazine: he thought we were out to get money off him while we pulled an ideological trick on him by using his money to fund liberal journalism. That suspicion was only compounded by Leon, who became a saboteur in my relationship with Roger: anytime we tried to impose some financial guideline, he would work covertly to undermine it.

By now, Leon was fifty and had married a second time, to Jennifer Bradley, a young *New Republic* intern from Texas who went on to become an expert in urban policy. He had come out of whatever emotional wilderness he occupied in the nineties when his father had died, and he was jolted out of his distractions. Leon's father was not a pleasant man, but he loomed large in Leon's life, and Leon decided to honor his memory by reciting the Kaddish, the Jewish prayer for the dead, three times every day. He began a scholarly search into its history, and the book that came from this search, Leon's first, brought him the National Jewish Book Award and a National Book Award Finalist nomination. And it pulled him into a productive, respected middle age as a Washington eminence. He was still Leon, only more confident in his evasions: he wouldn't call you back if you needed something from him, but if he needed you, he'd call you in the middle of the night.

For all the difficulties, Michael and Roger did a good job of cauterizing the magazine's losses and the bleeding slackened some. But the fundamental problems, the internet chief among them, weren't becoming any more manageable and, a year or so in, Roger, with Michael's passive assent, started looking for the exits. Again, Larry came in, this time with his good friend from law school, Leonard Asper, who'd become CEO of his father's company, Canwest. I liked Asper. His politics were broadly liberal, broadly pro-Israel, and broadly centrist in foreign and domestic policy. Canwest bought the majority stake in the magazine, and for a few years it looked like we were going to have the space to reset.

Peter Beinart had left the editorship in 2006 to write a book defending and extrapolating our foreign policy philosophy during his tenure. We had pushed very hard for what we believed in, but it hadn't been the six years we'd thought it would be, to put it mildly. We did improve in certain areas—Peter, prodded by Anne, had been making sure more women writers were featured in the magazine— but by the time he left it was clear our reset was urgently needed. To run the magazine during the reset, I brought in Frank Foer, a really deep intellectual who had grown up with the magazine and cared about bringing a younger crowd back to it.

Frank's pitch was simple: in an era of quick digitization, where real analysis was getting squeezed out, we would be the place to come to for serious thought. In 2007, Frank, Leon, and I went on *Charlie Rose* to make the case for our new, rebooted magazine. We talked a lot about the internet, and about the incipient 2008 campaign already choking on false media narratives, ads, and sound bites, so much worse even than eight years before. We said we would be the intellectual antidote to the noise.

But later that year, we got brought up short by the accelerating financial crisis: the overinflated real estate market crashed, and Canwest had to file for the Canadian equivalent of Chapter 11 bankruptcy. All of a sudden, we lost our space to breathe. This time Larry stepped in directly: he and Bill Ackman, backed by Michael Alter and Gerry Cardinale, formed a consortium to buy the magazine. They cut losses, dramatically; they got more subscriptions, especially more subscriptions online. The goal was to break even and then cautiously grow from there. But there was no mistaking this for the austerity moment that it was. Leon and Frank felt starved for resources: Leon's line was "too small to fail." Frank was tired because we laid off staff, and he had to do more with fewer editors, fewer fact checkers. We moved to smaller offices, on Fourteenth Street. Laura Obolensky retired, and that was a little bit of a sign that the people who had put up with me for the longest were done putting up with me now that things were on the downswing. Even though I was editor-in-chief, I was no longer footing all the bills. Leon was trying to devise ways to keep the magazine going if I ended up selling it completely, and there was a lack of trust between us.

We lost star talent. James Wood left for the *New Yorker*. "I know exactly," his handwritten letter said, "how much [Leon] and you contributed to the career I have had so far in America: everything." The staff—even the good ones: Ryan Lizza, Jon Chait, Michael Crowley—weren't well-paid. I'd taken a Yale graduate named Jamie Kirchick under my wing, a real talent who shared my confrontational journalistic approach and cared about Israel and issues of free speech. But he got laid off to cut costs. It showed how little control I had in what had been my world.

As my alienation from the magazine increased, so did my emotional distance from Cambridge. Sometime in this period—it's interesting, I don't remember the exact year—I stopped teaching at Harvard. I was still a fixture in Cambridge, but the university was no longer the place it had been. The trends Barrington Moore had seen were accelerating to the point where the public face of the university was something I didn't recognize: hyperspecialized on the one hand and hyper-idealized on the other. I didn't know Mark Zuckerberg, but he is surely the emblem of the specialists taking over the world. I did know Homi Bhabha, who represented the so-called idealists.

Bhabha was a poststructuralist critic in the tradition of the anti-imperialists, and he'd been influenced by Edward Said. He was very popular, very respected, and he seemed to me to be just as anti-humanist as the structures he was teaching against. He was interested in systems; individuals didn't have a place in his theory. Also, he wrote absolutely impenetrable prose, as if in possession of some arcane knowledge inaccessible to his readers, a sign that he was a phony and a snob. (This is not unrecognized by others: in 1999 he placed second in *Philosophy and Literature's* Bad Writing Contest; unsurprisingly, Judith Butler was the only writer deemed worse.) Once, when I asked his wife, who was Jewish, why her family from Germany settled in India rather than Palestine, she told me that Palestine was "too provincial." He was a sign for me of everything that was going wrong at Harvard.

For a while, I was optimistic about the university because of Larry Summers. His appointment in 2001 as Harvard's second Jewish president seemed like a small sliver of silver lining to Al's loss: he was alive to the visceral challenges the university faced like no one since Henry Rosovsky. Yo-Yo Ma summed him up best, quoted by me for the *New Republic*:

What I like about Larry is that he understands that nobody knows everything; not he, not you, not me. But he also understands that one cannot have a coherent view of the world without trying to know what the other knows. Larry's is an analytic mind, and yet he makes so much room for the cultural and emotional sphere, even the irrational—that which is ultimately human.

As president, Larry was active and lively, popular with the students because he still taught courses. He tried to modernize Henry's core curriculum, rolling out a new model called GenEd to bridge the growing divide between scientists, humanists, and postmodernists on faculty. He contracted with Google to digitize Harvard's library. He started an initiative to connect Harvard's growing Boston campus with its Cambridge center. He pushed Cornel West out for not teaching or publishing the way a full professor was expected to do. And he fired underperforming deans, including the dean of the faculty, William Kirby. But this sort of leadership made enemies on the faculty, which didn't like Larry's managerial approach and looked for opportunities to cut him off at the knees. The Kirby firing, compounded by some earlier remarks about women's aptitude for science that were construed as offensive, was used as an excuse for a no-confidence vote. The *Harvard Crimson* was for Larry; the students were for Larry. But the faculty won. Larry resigned, Derek Bok came back in to replace him for a year, and the search committee for the new president looked for someone who wouldn't rock any boats.

The person they found was Drew Faust, a historian whose closest friend on the faculty at Harvard was Homi Bhabha. Under Drew, trends at Harvard continued as they had before Larry: the gradual dissolution of the center I'd cared about, the one that was less about the split between specialization and ideology, the one that was more about the "conduct of life." In 2008, they abolished the core curriculum, and the new requirements are quite impoverished.

The campus culture changed, too. The *Crimson* represented not just left-wing student opinion or very liberal student opinion, the way it had for half a century. Now it was all about personal sexuality and personal identity, what my generation would call politi- cizing opinion about lifestyles. To me, it was not an improvement: protest had commodified itself, along with the rest of the culture. The voices were louder and more radical, but the complaints were largely symbolic. It was as different from the off-the-grid activisms of forty years before as you could possibly imagine.

❋ ❋ ❋

In 2007, Al won the Nobel Prize for his work on global warm- ing and the documentary, *An Inconvenient Truth*, which showed the world in clear words and blazing pictures the danger Al had always seen. We talked less these days; I was part of the political portion of his life, and he'd moved on. Our differences over Iraq had made us more distant, too, as had my ignorance about climate change: I knew it was an important issue, I trusted Al about its significance, but it wasn't where I lived. Still, I went to Oslo to watch him accept his Nobel Prize. Al had come through a wilderness, he had reinvent- ed himself, and I loved him for it.

During the ceremonies at Oslo, word came from the United States that Roger and Ginny Rosenblatt's daughter Amy had died suddenly of a rare and undetected heart condition, leaving behind a husband and three young children. I left immediately for Wash- ington, before Al had been honored, and I went to see Roger and Ginny. It was a shocking situation, and situations like that bring out things in people you didn't know were there. Roger and Ginny came down from New York to Bethesda, Maryland and moved in with Amy's husband, Harris, and their children, and they helped raise them. I couldn't, can't, imagine such a thing: getting back into the business of raising kids in my late sixties. I admired them, and I was grateful that they were my friends, which is a good feeling to have when you're older. It makes you feel, no matter what else is happening, that you've made some right choices somewhere.

My children were another source of joy. My son Jesse was making movies: a drama based on an Ian McEwan story, "First Love, Last Rites"; a few years later, a comedy, *Our Idiot Brother*, starring Paul Rudd. In 2007, Evgenia, a staff writer for *Vanity Fair*, wrote what I think is a definitive piece on media coverage of the 2000 election and the way the fixed narratives impacted the candidates. By that year, Evgenia and her husband, David, had a son, my first grandchild, Elias, who, when he was three, went to one of Yo-Yo's concerts at Carnegie Hall. From the stage, Yo-Yo mentioned his friend's four-year-old grandson in the audience. "I'm three, Yo-Yo!" Elias shot back. A few years later, I took Elias to the medieval sculpture hall at the Metropolitan Museum of Art. He loved all the works except the statues of Mary. "I don't like Mary pregnant," he told me, echoing me at the Cloisters sixty years before, "because that couldn't have happened."

This was around the time I first met Barack Obama. We met through Michael Alter: they were both from Chicago, they played basketball together, and Michael was quietly a big backer. We talked primarily about Israel. I'd heard about his speech that winter at a Cleveland Jewish community meeting playing for Jewish support and wanted to press him on some of his statements. In that speech, he was tentative, defensive even, about his ties to his former pastor Jeremiah Wright, about his much looser ties to Louis Farrakhan, and about accusations that he lacked an appreciation of Israel's political reality. He also said he thought Iran, now America's chief regional adversary, was a hinge for Middle Eastern stability. He felt that a practical peace was possible despite its moves in Iraq, its alliance with Hezbollah and Syria, and its perennial animus toward Israel. He talked about resetting American policy in the Middle East toward new cooperation and understanding.

This seemed to me a willfully broad-brush reading of the Middle East, its deep and entrenched inheritances, and of tribal and religious differences more generally, and I wanted to push back against it. Obama seemed disinterested in our meeting—we all stayed standing—and a little cold, willing to listen but guarded.

In any case, I was thrilled that he was beating Hillary Clinton. Compared to the Clintons, Obama seemed like an open book. In 2008, there was real consensus at the magazine in favor of him. Cass Sunstein, Samantha Power's husband, called Obama a "visionary minimalist" who would find consensus between Left and Right. I think we all believed that. I'd grown up waiting for the election of a black president, and I had tried to see it into being, however briefly, quixotically, or unrealistically, at the Palmer House forty years before. Pretty quickly, I became passionate about the Obama candidacy, and, like I always did when I was passionate, I made it my business to reassure people.

I wrote a lot that year, almost always to the center-Left and center-Right and almost always in Obama's defense. I thought the Reverend Wright controversy was absurd: it didn't surprise me that this scholarly, thoughtful, serious man had spent his formative years searching for a place to belong and had found one at this lively Chicago church presided over by this coarse minister with conspiratorial ideas.

I went down to Florida to campaign for him among the Jews. I debated Fred Barnes at a Jewish Federation meeting in Miami. Still, I don't think the Obama people much cared for me: Dan Shapiro— the Jewish honcho in the campaign, later ambassador to Israel— stopped having people ask me to do events after a while.

In January, the night before Obama's inauguration, the magazine threw a party. It was a patriotic concert, and it started with religious Christian music from the eighteenth century. I almost cried; it was such a good time for a patriotic moment. Yo-Yo played with the Silkroad Ensemble. Rahm Emanuel, Zeke's younger brother and the new White House chief of staff, came. Charles Krauthammer came. John Kerry, now the chair of the Foreign Relations Committee, came. Walter Isaacson was there; so were Larry Summers, Michael Alter, and Samantha. Rahm said that the *New Republic* "was required reading in our house. And it will be required reading in the White House." I wrote a post the next day on the *New Republic Online* titled, "Required Reading, Again." The night felt like a new consensus, eight years after Al. But there were signs that it wasn't. My own friends aside, this group at the party was a second-tier political crowd. The Obama folk had gone someplace else.

Was I gaga to believe in this as a new beginning? I think now that I went along with the Obama phenomenon because everyone else in my world did. My more skeptical friends thought he was a smart man and a smart politician, cool under pressure, but not a visionary. But for most of us, Obama provided a blank screen to project our fantasies. For me, it was the fantasy of renewed American purpose and a revitalized American center after eight years of flatlining. In retrospect, it seems disappointment was inevitable.

There were more signs after the inauguration. In February, Obama selected as the chair of his National Intelligence Council Chas Freeman, still an enemy from the Bush I days, who'd only gotten harder in his positions; he was a big backer of the Mearsheimer-Walt book because he saw Israel as upsetting American realpolitik in the Middle East. And people like Freeman, people in "small" positions, can do great damage because they're the ones controlling the flow of information from the ground. I pushed back on the nomination, and Charles Krauthammer joined me from his perch at the *Washington Post*. Freeman eventually withdrew, publicly blaming me and his other critics as part of the Jewish Washington cabal. In a statement he said: "The tactics of the Israel Lobby plumb the depths of dishonor and indecency and include character assassination, selective misquotation, the willful distortion of the record, the fabrication of falsehoods, and an utter disregard for the truth." This was absurd. I could write in the *New Republic*, but I couldn't get a secretary of state on the phone the way he could. I don't think I ever had a concrete influence on anything.

The big disillusionment came in June, when Obama gave an address at Cairo University called "A New Beginning." He extended an olive branch to "the Arab world," citing John Adams's remark that the United States has "no character of enmity against...Muslims" and the meaningless fact that Thomas Jefferson kept a copy of the Koran in his personal library. "So long as our relationship is defined by our differences," went the key line, "we will empower those who sow hatred rather than peace."

The top-down idealists were back, only now their stage was the much larger one of foreign policy. In their view, erasure of differences in rhetoric could lead to the erasure of differences in reality— this is how the intractability of the Palestinian leadership, Hamas, and Iran could be overcome. In practice, the next year when Iranians started mass protests, their government murdered them, and the president of the United States didn't say a thing. The administration's approach was clear: in the interest of "peace" in the Middle

East, which meant a détente with our new regional adversary Iran, America would step back from its humanitarian commitments.

Eventually, news leaked out of the White House about who these decisions were made by: thirty-year-old speechwriters and political advisers like Ben Rhodes who had no historical memory and a lot of certainty; well-educated, privileged people who'd come up in institutions like the one in which I'd taught; and idealist experts like some of Hillary Clinton's cohort but newly emboldened by the Establishment's failure in the War on Terror. They seemed to think that they were better—more moral, more pragmatic—than the people who disagreed with them because anybody who disagreed was probably on the wrong side of Iraq, and so on the wrong side of history.

Not everybody in the administration was like this, of course. Antony Blinken was deputy national security advisor and would become deputy secretary of state. But, as with the last two presidencies, the terms of governing were set in the West Wing, by the ideologists and polling experts. This was something that had been growing into the norm for fifteen years—but it had grown up underneath and around me: the email blitzes, the technological mastery, the staged events that had helped the Bush administration sell the Iraq War and had helped Obama win the election. The Obama administration was an advanced stage of that, powered by thinner idealisms and better polling data: the methods were sleeker and less obviously corporate, and there was less philosophizing and more sloganeering. The Bush Freedom Agenda, which at least had a kind of logic, however utopian, had given way to the Obama project of "hope and change," unattached to any object or goal, shallowly rooted in one-world universals I remembered from 1950.

Running underneath my alienation from all of this was the most painful element of what felt like a betrayal of the notion, the dream, that the black culture that had run through W. E. B. Du Bois, through Ralph Ellison, through Richard Wright and the Harlem Renaissance would ally with Jewish émigré culture: two minority peoples, with the elite Protestants as their allies, remaking America. Now here was a president, our first black American in the White House, who seemingly disassociated from all of the grounded loyalties that rooted me and the Democratic Party I'd come up with.

My view was not the view of the established media. Obama had a protective cohort of older journalists, Fareed Zakaria, Nick Kristof, and James Fallows, who would always try to make the best out of whatever the White House was doing. I think Obama's managerialism and universalizing aspirations appealed to them. Zakaria could be trusted to provide cold rationales for letting the mullahs slaughter people in the name of "stability." Kristof would report on suffering anywhere, everywhere, but he'd never work through the hard questions his reporting unearthed: if people were suffering in South Sudan and the "global community" wasn't stopping it, did we need American bombardment or American troops, and if not, why not? To him, saying the right things and accomplishing them in reality were one and the same, which made him a perfect defender of Obama. And James Fallows, now at *The Atlantic* and a certified "wise man" of American letters, was a gentle and righteous sop for whatever establishment thinking was at in any given moment. He had never been original, and nothing in him had changed since I'd known him in Cambridge years before.

There was a new breed of younger commentators to whom criticisms of Obama were worse than unrealistic or ill-meaning—they were immoral. I remember reading a piece by Ezra Klein, an already prominent commentator in his late twenties, criticizing Andrew Sullivan and the *New Republic* for taking after Hillary over her healthcare policy:

> *Maybe if articles like "No Exit" hadn't been published, and editors like Sullivan hadn't been out to get the Clintons, the Clintons wouldn't have acted as if articles [like] "No Exit" were being published, and editors like Sullivan were out to get them.*

The argument was, in essence, an argument against journalistic investigation, and it was ridiculous. But it pointed to a trend. A new generation, who'd been toddlers or unborn when Communism ended, who'd come up expecting prosperity and peace, felt cheated. Now we had Iraq. Now we had the financial crash. Now we had a backlash.

My near and dear ones would ask me: "Why don't you step back some? We've gotten what we wanted, a new generation, a liberal generation, a hopeful generation—why don't you relax your grip, let them make their own mistakes, move with the times?" People I didn't love but who I respected were signaling my marginality, too. David Geffen, who was now a real player in the Democratic Party (and a *real* real player when it came to funding cultural institutions), was bored by my intellectuality and my Jewish concerns. I surmise that he was content that I had stopped our awkward telephone conversations and our quick lunches. I think he thought I was irrelevant. But I didn't think I was irrelevant. But I didn't want to go with the flow the way people were telling me. I'd heard this before—before the Palmer House—and it never worked: mistakes accrued, and infantilizing people never helped. And I wasn't one to go along, get along.

I wasn't where I'd been ten years ago. I was distant from Harvard. From the *New Republic*. From political power. And even personally things were breaking apart because I was getting a divorce. But I was still saying what I thought needed to be said. I still had my voice.

I don't like to talk about the end of things with Anne. I still wear the wedding ring. She was my helpmate, I was hers. She helped me get the *New Republic*; I helped her found the Family Center. She is the mother of my kids. We had, as people say, our "troubles." But I don't think that's what caused our split. I think it was me. As things slipped away, as the ups and downs got more unpredictable—the problems at the magazine, the rancor over Iraq, my alienation from American society—I got more distant, harsher. The shift brought out what I'd learned from my father, what I'd spent a lifetime stepping around: the outbursts and eruptions I resorted to when I felt cornered. Occasionally there would be leakages, but the defense mechanisms I'd developed dealing with him had mostly stayed dormant. Now, whatever tectonic plates I'd forced into place, the ones that made generosity my main impulse, were starting to separate.

In many ways, I was who I was at fifteen: I was smart; there was a force in me that everybody sensed; I had general intelligence spread over a wide range; and I'd managed to put all the drives and interests into a collection of pursuits that spanned the personal and professional. I never had to adapt, to tighten. I got to indulge my passions. I got to be emotional, not transactional, and to justify my likes and dislikes without much rational thinking. I got to take risks. I'd give you all of my attention even though I knew it might end up unreciprocated. And I was happy to live that life. I was happy to be disconcerting and answer only to myself. I was happy to love people without conditions, or many conditions, and to act on that love. There's a lot of tenderness in me: it's easy, a friend once told me (this was after I'd talked him through his second divorce), to get into the loam of my heart.

But that meant other things, too. It meant I could be hurt. It meant that the grudges I bore, for myself and for other people, weren't about transactions—they were emotional. And it meant that, as the grudges and disappointments started to pile up, I got more frantic and felt like I had less time. After 2000, I started to lose people, people I loved or who shaped me, for the first time, in a rush: Adam Ulam in 2000; Emily Cohen and Donny Cohen (no relation) in 2001; David Riesman in 2002; Pat Moynihan, Frank Manuel, and Simcha Dinitz in 2003; Gene McCarthy in 2005; and Eve Curie in 2007. The coordinates of the world I'd lived in my whole life were starting to wink out, fade away. I was the elder now. But what, exactly, was I leaving behind?

I repressed most of this. I kept batting the change away. I kept acting, which was an instinct and a trap. A lot of what I'd made for myself had come because I hadn't thought too much. I'd held things at a distance. If I'd have thought too much, been too self-conscious, in a world where I was a smart but not brilliant Jewish boy from the Bronx, I wouldn't have been able to act. Now, as the room to act in public life got narrower, as the disappointments and frustrations mounted, my defenses shifted into place, and they started to interfere with my marriage and my professional life.

The two of us together, Anne and me, had a kind of magic. We wanted to experience life. We wanted to give to others. Our home, our dinner table, was almost a salon; it took a lot of time and thought—and nerves, early on—to bring it off properly. Yo-Yo told me once that people would study our methods for years to see why they were so fantastic. I was a little bit surprised to hear this, but the secret, I told him, was this: a party is not a Rolodex; it's a product of a lot of real relationships. We cared about relationships, and we loved each other for feeling that way about the world.

As things finally broke down between us, people who were part of that world we'd built together saw us coming apart and tried to help. Yo-Yo, who knew a little about my father, told me he wanted to spend the day with me, go to the Bronx, and walk with me to where I'd gone with my father to collect rent from his tenants. But he couldn't penetrate my wall. It wasn't something I would let down.

In 2005 Anne and I stopped living together; in 2007 we formally separated; and in 2009 the divorce was finalized. The financial parts dragged out—the settlement was hard to reach. When the paperwork was finalized, Anne came over to 20 Larchwood, where I still lived (she had bought a new house in Cambridge—an old house, really) and brought with her a CD she'd made of some of our favorite pieces. We turned on "Valse Triste" by Sibelius and danced around the living room. Later that night she left. And then I was alone. Really alone. Anne and I had spent thousands of hours, even after our troubles, in therapy, talking through things—over email, over the phone. Now I had no one to talk to who knew me that way. And that led me toward other outlets for expressing how I felt.

I turned to an outlet that would have been hard for me to imagine before: I became a blogger. It was a mistake.

Blogging, short for web-logging, involved writing fast takes on the news of the day. At the time, fifteen years ago, it was seen as a harbinger of the future of journalism, accelerated by the internet to respond to events as they happen. These days, Twitter has made blogging look quaint.

At the *New Republic*, we were suspicious of blogs and fast takes: we thought they implied a lack of thought. On the other hand, one of the most popular blogs was Andrew Sullivan's *Daily Dish*, which I thought captured his elegant in-the-moment-ness pretty well. I figured if he could do it so could I. I was feeling distant from the magazine anyway; I wanted to stretch my muscles, to freestyle a little. So I started a blog on the *New Republic* website called *The Spine*, which gives you an idea of how I saw myself right then.

On its face, me blogging was a nutty idea. I didn't know the first thing about technology, about television, about popular culture. My kids always told a story about me from this period: me, on a plane from Washington to New York, diverted for the weather, and a sort of strange-looking man sitting next to me. During the delay, we started talking. He asked me what I did, I said I ran the *New Republic*. He said he had read the *New Republic* when he studied at the London School of Economics: he thought it was sort of between *The Spectator* and the *New Statesman*, and I thought that was a smart observation. We talked for the next couple of hours as we waited for the plane to take off. I didn't ask him much about himself, which was unusual; instead we talked politics and history and we parted without exchanging information. But a few days later David Geffen called me up and said, "You know that guy you sat next to on the plane?" and I said, a little surprised, "Well, sure, how do you know about it?" And he said, "You idiot, that was Mick Jagger." And I said, "Mick who?" Which goes to show, if there was a popular mainstream, I was outside it.

But in another way, blogging fit. It was a sort of extension of what I did as a teacher, and at the *New Republic* staff meetings, and on phone calls or over lunches or dinners. I would test out ideas, off the cuff, cut myself off midstream, and switch to a new topic. It felt natural, and it seemed to work by the new online metrics: sometimes my pieces got the highest readership on the site. I meandered a lot: there'd be a reference to Mitt Romney, then a circling back to the New York City school uprisings of 1965, and then a swerve to an old Yiddish joke. But it was me. And this was what I told my friends who were a little concerned when they heard I'd loosed myself online: it was a substitute (I know this is pathetic) for the pillow talk Anne and I had had—a letting off of steam.

Most of the sharpest points I made on the blog were about Israel, which was much on my mind. As other things in my life cracked up or fell away, I came back to my Jewishness. As things got less familiar, I doubled down on what I thought to be most true. I felt more alone, maybe even more corrupt: I'd broken my marriage, split my family. I went to the one thing that I knew, had always known, wasn't corrupt. I went to my people.

I had reason to feel that Israel needed me: the disrepute the foreign policy establishment had brought on itself through Iraq had coupled with almost a decade of stalemate between Israel and the Palestinians to make Israel a prime journalistic target for people who'd never liked the Jewish state anyway. The early rivulets—Judt's piece, Walt and Mearshimer's book—had widened and spread. Claire Messud, James Wood's wife, was writing pieces in *The Guardian* and the *Boston Globe* highlighting the Palestinian plight. Starting in 2006, Nicholas Kristof began a mounting critique from the heights of his prime *New York Times* real estate. Attacks came from the fringes: Max Blumenthal, Sidney Blumenthal's son, captured a video of a couple of drunk Jews on Birthright saying racist things and posted it on YouTube under the title "Feeling the Hate in Jerusalem on the Eve of Obama's Cairo Address." Until then, I'd never heard of YouTube. Even Andrew Sullivan was criticizing Israel: he had gone from cheerleader for the War on Terror in 2001 to an ardent believer that America's Israel policy was somehow connected to the neocons' mistakes. Everybody had supported the neocons in the beginning; now they were looking for scapegoats.

I'd always ridden on the edge, tried to say things that were as provocative as I could, in substance and in style, but always telling the truth. And I bristled at edits: most people were afraid to give them to me. Or they weren't paying attention. Leon was preserving the literary section; Frank had battles elsewhere. So, I wrote what I wanted. Oftentimes I wasn't making arguments anymore; I was making noise, less interested in persuading people and more in throwing punches. If Max Lerner had been there, he would have told me that I needed to make my arguments in full. If Frank Manuel had been there, he would've told me my sloppiness was starting to obscure, not illuminate. They would've told me what I was writing now wasn't humanism all down the line: it was humanism up against a wall.

I scored one big victory in this period, but it wasn't on the blog. It was in the *New Republic*. When the UN-commissioned Goldstone Report on the Gaza War of late 2008 and early 2009 got not just the conclusions but the stakes of the conflict blatantly wrong, I got Moshe Halbertal, who'd helped draft the army's ethics code, to write a response in the *New Republic*. I'm still proud of having commissioned an indictment by a genuinely humane man about the distorting function of the international community, of the lies that get told, and the agendas that get advanced, under the cover of the international community's commitment to representing even the most undemocratic countries and groups. As Moshe wrote,

In Goldstone's account of the history that led to the war, for example, Hamas is basically described as a legitimate party that had the bad luck to clash with Israel. The bloody history of the movement—which, since the beginning of the Oslo accords, was determined to do everything in its power, including the massacre of civilians, to defeat the peace process—is not mentioned.

The Israeli reader who actually experienced the events at the time remembers vividly that Hamas terrorists murdered Israeli men, women, and children all over Israel while a peace process was underway. Hamas was doing all this in accordance with its religious ideology, which is committed to the destruction of Israel and is fueled by Iranian military and financial support. In the supposed context that the report analyzes, there is no mention of Hamas's role and its ideology as reflected in its extraordinary charter, which calls for the destruction of Israel and the genocidal killing of Jews.

It was so devastating that Goldstone recanted. Even if he didn't say he recanted because of Moshe Halbertal—he didn't say he recanted because of anybody—he recanted all the same.

But the trend in the commentariat was against Israel. And in June of 2010, another former editor besides Andrew Sullivan joined the crowd: Peter Beinart.

I'd always known Peter was vain. But now I thought he might be the most self-absorbed person I'd ever met. Partly this is social psychology of a recognizable ethnic sort: when your Jewish mother loves you much too much, you spend your life trying to recreate the love. Partly it's social psychology of a more complex kind. If you come up straight through the best institutions, if you never really step outside of Cambridge in any real way, you think you're on a set course. If something disturbs that course, you panic because you've never imagined life any other way.

What had disturbed Peter's course was Iraq: the war he'd championed in his first big gig at the *New Republic* when he was thirty-one. He'd spent seven years trying to sort it out, writing one book lamenting our failure in Iraq and another urging liberals to get tough. Now he came out in the *New York Review of Books* with an article titled "The Failure of the American Jewish Establishment," a straightforward attack on the elders:

> *Particularly in the younger generations, fewer and fewer American Jewish liberals are Zionists; fewer and fewer American Jewish Zionists are liberal. One reason is that the leading institutions of American Jewry have refused to foster—indeed, have actively opposed—a Zionism that challenges Israel's behavior in the West Bank and Gaza Strip and toward its own Arab citizens. For several decades, the Jewish establishment has asked American Jews to check their liberalism at Zionism's door, and now, to their horror, they are finding that many young Jews have checked their Zionism instead.*

My read of the years after 2000 is different. I think an establishment, which was supportive of Israel, stumbled in Iraq even as the peace process between Israelis and Palestinians broke down, and I think these converging realities allowed anti-Israeli one-world or hard-Left voices, from George Soros to Noam Chomsky, an opportunity to press their case. I think young people coming up in the midst of the Establishment failure, just like in the sixties, knew which side they were on—or thought they knew.

The subtext was clear enough to one who knew how to read it: a renunciation of the fathers—me, Leon, the *New Republic*, and maybe some others I'm not aware of. It was one of two articles Peter ever wrote for the *Review*, both critical of Israel. He hasn't written for them since, which to me means the *Review* used and then discarded him, which is just like them and has a sort of perverse justice to it. I don't want to say the article hurt, it didn't really, but it was jarring. Ten years earlier, I'd thought Peter would be writing, with me behind him, directly for the Gore White House, strengthening Zionism, strengthening pluralism, and strengthening the American center. Look what happened instead.

❊ ❊ ❊

That summer of 2010, the one after my divorce, was a sour one. I was living alone at 20 Larchwood. I wasn't teaching anymore. I had a social circle, but it had gotten older and was more spread out. Politically, I was alienated from my friends. Henry Rosovsky kept telling me, more and more upset, that I couldn't generalize the way I was generalizing on my blog.

Now I had a center-Right contingent of allies. Fouad, in the aftermath of Iraq, was embattled, on the defensive, and consumed with troubles of his own—troubles of health that would lead to his death. But there was Niall Ferguson and Pierpaolo Barbieri, an Argentine Catholic interested in ideas and finance who worked with Niall. Pierpaolo is a pious man, and that draws me: he now runs a hugely successful Argentine financial app that both George Soros and I are invested in and is a man on the move. But he still goes to church every morning, if only for a moment.

There was also Rory Stewart. One night, John Kerry was going to appear at my house in Cambridge for dinner—this was a period when we were talking—and that day I ran into Al and asked him over. So there they were, the former vice president and the head of the Senate Foreign Relations Committee. But they weren't the main attractions. Rory was there that night too, and nobody knew as much about Iraq and Afghanistan as him. Rory's a tiny, wiry guy, very sharp, and always knows when people are bullshitting. He has authority. And what he said about Iraq always circled back to the same thing: nobody who made decisions knew what was happening on the ground.

None of these newer friends or interesting moments was a substitute for the people I'd been with for forty years. I'd grown up on the Left, and now I had lost the Left. And I'd lost a lot of other things, too. That was a reality that no passing feeling could shake. I needed something fresh.

I decided to go to Israel in the fall to teach at Bialik-Rogozin, a public school located in a poor area of Tel Aviv that I'd heard about from Israeli friends. I thought teaching kids who really needed it would somehow revivify things. I submitted myself to three job interviews and was hired to teach English language usage to ninth graders. We would read autobiographies: Frederick Douglass, Isak Dinesen, and Booker T. Washington. It was a kind of relief; it felt like I was slipping back into an old rhythm.

I was going to leave Cambridge after an event at Harvard that I wanted to attend: the fiftieth anniversary of the founding of the Social Studies program. All my old colleagues and comrades were coming back, and I found out in early September that a circular had been sent around urging people to donate to what would be a new scholarship: the Martin Peretz Undergraduate Research Fund. The signatories ranged from Bill Ackman, Michael Alter, and Jamie Gorelick to Juan Carlos Zarate, Sherry Turkle, and Ed Zwick.

August finished. September started. The donations crept up to $700,000. I made sure my kids would be in Cambridge at the end of the month: it would be an event, the kind of thing I loved. I made plans for Israel. And I kept blogging.

On Saturday, September 4, I woke up and went through the online papers—my normal routine. I read the papers I hated first because they were the ones guaranteed to raise the bile in my throat, and I still liked that feeling: it made me feel that I was in the thick.

That day, the bile rose higher than usual at an article, nominally a piece of reportage, genteelly deploring poll results that showed New Yorkers had a "sadly wary misunderstanding of Muslim-Americans…Asked whether they thought Muslim-Americans were 'more sympathetic to terrorists' than other citizens, 33 percent said yes, a discouraging figure, roughly consistent with polls taken since Sept. 11, 2001. Thirty-one percent said they didn't know any Muslims; 39 percent said they knew Muslims but not as close friends."

This made me want to scream. It had absolutely nothing to do with life as it is really lived. Determining that Muslims were unknown to parts of the New York population wasn't the same as determining that the New York population was necessarily racist: Muslims were proportionally a small part of New York, many of them were immigrants, and immigrants especially tend to collect in their own groups and mind their own business. And living in "the most diverse and cosmopolitan" city in America was a special point of pride, but not everyplace had to be that way. I was happy that New York was so diverse, but with diversity of population comes diversity of opinion.

It was the Obama era in freeze-frame: the arrogance, the one-size-fits-all rationalizations of people who had never really gotten beyond the constructed theories of the upper-middle class and the Ivy League. They weren't like my generation of meritocracy. Not at all. They were the trend I'd first seen with Clinton's New Democrats taken to its logical—but to me, not imaginable—conclusion: if the world didn't meet their idealism, the world was at fault.

Even the above is more cogent than what I actually wrote. I would have done better to have gone to the root of what had made me angry. But I didn't. I didn't dig deep, just like Frank Manuel had told me I didn't. Instead I ignored the actual content of the article and hit on an easy target, an old passion: the willful blindness of the Western press to human rights abuses in the Muslim world.

> *Why do not Muslims raise their voices against... planned and random killings all over the Islamic world? This world went into hysteria some months ago when the Mossad took out the Hamas head of its own Murder Inc.*

> *But, frankly, Muslim life is cheap, most notably to Muslims.... So, yes, I wonder whether I need honor these people and pretend that they are worthy of the privileges of the First Amendment which I have in my gut the sense that they will abuse.*

I didn't think much of the column in the days after. My readers knew me; they knew I'd be honest about the thoughts I had at three o'clock in the morning—that was part of my appeal. But not everyone was such a fan. On September 12, Nick Kristof, who I had recently insulted quite eloquently on my blog ("But in what else does Kristof deal than...*dicta*?"), published his Sunday *Times* essay. He titled it "Is This America?" and he led off with me:

> *Thus a prominent American commentator, in a magazine long associated with tolerance, ponders whether Muslims should be afforded constitutional freedoms. Is it possible to imagine the same kind of casual slur tossed off about blacks or Jews? How do America's nearly seven million American Muslims feel when their faith is denounced as barbaric?*

There were only 2.5 million Muslims in the United States in 2010, but never mind. The column was a condemnation, a condemnation read by millions of people, and others agreed with him, loudly, in a chorus: Eric Alterman at *The Nation*; James Fallows at *The Atlantic*; and Jack Shafer, the media critic at *Slate*. Some of these people, Alterman for example, had hated me for years. Andrew Sullivan defended me. Henry Louis Gates defended me. A petition started circling for Harvard not to accept money my students were raising for the fund.

The controversy wouldn't die down, mostly because of the internet. Many of my writings were now online, and people dug into them, looking for more offense, which they found. Somebody set up a site, Peretz Dossier, and listed the worse comments I'd made in a long career of saying whatever I wanted. The condemnations mounted: an old nemesis, Todd Gitlin, in the *New Republic Online*, said "the life of the mind is not the life of the spleen." Alan Gilbert, who I'd vaguely known in the early days of the Social Studies program, said "If the tradition of the Jews is to stand for internationalism and against bigotry, Marty is not a Jew." *The Economist* said the conflict mattered because it "delineate[d] the boundaries for acceptable discourse in America." And Ta-Nehisi Coates at *The Atlantic*, a rising star among a younger generation, criticized the magazine for its approach to race.

On September 17, I wrote a post called "Atonement," a rather embarrassed apology for my "wild and wounding language, especially hurtful to our Muslim brothers and sisters." I said that I "allowed emotion to run way ahead of reason, and feelings to trample arguments."

It wasn't enough. And few were brothers and sisters anymore. The *Harvard Crimson* reported on September 20 that "five student support groups joined to send an open letter to senior administrators in the Committee of Degrees in Social Studies, encouraging the committee not to honor Peretz at its fiftieth-year anniversary celebration." Now, the committee and the university had to decide how to respond to the petition not to take the money. We sat in Drew Faust's office, and I knew how it would go when she said, worriedly, "But Nick Kristof is one of our most respected public intellectuals." I think she wished no one had started a fund in the first place. But in the last week it had increased by 30 percent, so there was clearly support for me. Drew could have said something presidential about how ill-chosen comments and a record of service are different things—that you can honor one without endorsing the other. But she didn't. She sat on her hands and didn't really take a stand.

On September 24, there was a dinner in my honor at the Harvest restaurant in Cambridge. Friends and family were there: Bill Ackman told me he'd never seen so many people from so many different professions at such a high level in one room.

At eight or nine, going in to the hall where the speeches would be, was when I first saw the protestors with signs: "'Muslim Life is Cheap'" and "Marty Peretz is a Racist Rat." Some of them were old and looked like the people who'd collected around Stuart Hughes rallies; others were obviously students. They were facing away from the building, so I got into the hall without being noticed. Michael and Judy Walzer met me inside with concerned faces and the events commenced. Two hours later, we left by a side exit for lunch. The crowd, which had grown to forty or so people with signs, hadn't gone away, and this time they spotted us and surrounded our cohort as we walked across Harvard Yard.

You can see a video of it online: "A Party for Marty." I'm wearing a white jacket and pants and a dark shirt; I look a little surprised. They're chanting: "Harvard, Harvard shame on you, honoring a racist fool." Michael and I are talking; Judy's walking, looking straight ahead. Fifty-one years earlier I'd walked across Harvard Yard for the first time, elated that Protestant America had let me in, even if William Yandell Elliot had insulted me. Now I was walking across the same yard, and they were calling me a racist fool.

We got to lunch, where there were to be more speeches, and the keynote was by Robert Paul Wolff, the adviser to Tocsin, who'd left Harvard when he wasn't promoted forty years before. I don't think we'd spoken in all that time, but he ended his speech with an attack on me and the fund that my students raised for me. It was an example of Harvard as an "imperial power" in higher education. The money, he said, "stinks."

After lunch I left. This was the most painful episode in my public life—worse than the Palmer House, worse than anything. A fifty-one-year career at Harvard, and I was leaving as Nathan Pusey, my contributions dismissed, and my positions reviled.

A week or so later, I left for Israel. It was a relief. The school was in a poorer section of Tel Aviv. The students were young, and most of them from difficult backgrounds. Some of them had come from terrible places, war-torn African countries. Sometimes they did the reading, other times not. They were, for all the toughness of their backgrounds, more optimistic than me, brighter. They wondered why I always made them read sad books—why, for example, I obsessed over Frederick Douglass's autobiography. "Can you imagine how you could be stripped of your humanity if you were denied the things that made you you?" I asked them when we read it. I didn't know if they could.

CHAPTER SIXTEEN

Logjam, 2011–2020:
Universalists v. Tribalists v. Socialists,
Obama v. Trump v. the Squad

I came back to America in the spring of 2011, faced with the necessity of selling the *New Republic*. Money was an issue behind the sale, but it wasn't the only issue. I had come to the conclusion that people weren't listening to what we said: we had to fight for the right to be heeded, and I was sick of spending money on it. "I am exhausted," is what I told *New York Magazine* in a profile they did on me in the wake of the mess at Harvard. And it was true. I felt like it was all over.

The magazine's backers, Larry and Bill, supported by Gerry, Michael, Richard, and Leon, started looking for somebody with the pockets to pick up where they'd left off, and late that year they told me they were talking to Chris Hughes, one of the Facebook founders, who'd been roommates with Mark Zuckerberg at Harvard. They were an odd group, these kids who captured the internet: they didn't come from very specific traditions or histories. I didn't know any of them as students. Hughes was the one in the group who knew how to socialize and had managed their public relations. This meant, when we met, that I didn't dislike him and that he said all the right things about the importance of argument and debate. He was a pleasant man—and I don't really mean that as a compliment. Shallow, I guess, is the word.

He seemed to me to be looking for a way to spend his money and a magazine was just one place. Later, he spent heavily on his boyfriend's failed congressional race, an effort that included investing millions in a house in a rural district to legitimize the run and that resulted in a sixty-thousand-vote loss.

I also had a small instinct that he wasn't up to the task intellectually. He had been head of technology for Obama's 2008 campaign, which was not reassuring. I had a feeling the *New Republic* was going to be carried away by this new culture I didn't like or understand, this culture of numbers, technology, and pop ideology that Chris Hughes represented and the Obama White House played very ably.

When I sold the magazine to Chris, it was a metaphorical passing of the torch. In 1974, I'd bought the magazine from good-intentioned liberal types; now I was selling it to new money technocrats. And, when he assumed control in January 2012, Chris did what I'd done when I bought the magazine: he fired the current editor, Richard Just, who was terrific, and replaced him with his pick— in this case, Frank Foer, for Frank's second run as editor. (Leon continued to edit the back of the book: he had already replaced me in Washington as the eminence of the magazine.) From there, Chris shaped the magazine to match his fashion.

The cover of the first rebranded issue of the Hughes era of the magazine, which ran a year later, in January 2013, announced its new top-down approach with an interview—Barack Obama. We had never, in thirty-seven years, led with an interview with a president. We made it a rule not to interview high-ranking Washington officials. We were a magazine that punched in the elite, but we weren't a stenographer for power, and we thrived by being almost the opposite: even our allies we would take on.

By this point, I couldn't criticize the magazine in the *Times* or the *Post*: it was a period, after the collective media censure of late 2010, when I was unofficially in disrepute. And I didn't have much connection to press my case internally at the *New Republic*. Leon and I spoke, but Frank Foer and I no longer did, for reasons I still don't understand. But the *Wall Street Journal* would take me, and in February 2013, I wrote a piece for the Opinions section called "The New New Republic: I don't recognize the magazine I used to own.

We were liberal but not narrowly partisan," in which I said exactly that. My usual supporters agreed with me—but it didn't have any effect on the magazine. I hadn't expected it to.

I was on the sidelines, and I watched as the next few years brought the fulfillment of the worst possibilities of the politics I'd seen building for twenty years: a war between the Democrats, now fully the party of universals, and the Republicans, now fully the party of the tribe. This was made clear to anyone who hadn't been paying attention by the election of Donald Trump. But the causes of Trump's election had accreted for years before him even as its consequences are still reverberating years after. That's the way I understand the Trump phenomenon—how an increasingly unhumanized technocracy made it possible. The things this man has done...

In 2013, Michael Walzer retired from *Dissent*, which he had inherited, intellectually anyway, from Irving Howe. He passed the reins to Michael Kazin, whom I had known since freshman seminar and the University Hall takeover. Walzer was, as always, a loyal friend, and at his retirement dinner from *Dissent*, he asked—insisted—that I speak. This was my disgrace period, and in a way, it was a validating moment for our friendship. In another way, it was sad. Michael's scrupulousness with regard to fact and his support of the liberal center as a necessary precondition for the flourishing of the decent Left weren't things I saw much of anymore. The *New Republic* had gone managerial technocrat; now *Dissent* was moving hard Left—more signs that the center as we'd known it had ceased to exist.

That November, the *New Republic* had its one-hundredth year anniversary dinner with Bill Clinton, of all people, as the featured speaker. I wasn't invited, but I heard later it was an uncomfortable evening because the worm was already in the apple at the magazine. My backers had sold to Chris, hoping he'd take their strategy: run a minimized operation and build on it by investing more online, hire a few online writers, tweak the digital aspect, and hire a few star journalists. But this was the strategy of forty- and fifty-year-olds, people with a history of investments who'd made money in the trenches. Chris was not yet thirty. He'd gotten rich with astonishing speed, and his enthusiasms outpaced reality. In the beginning, he seemed to realize it was a vanity project, and he vainly poured a million a year back into the magazine, built a new headquarters in New York and a new library for Leon, hired a bunch of new writers, and expected revenues to materialize. When they didn't, he grew impatient, and he doubled down on what he knew: he brought some Silicon Valley people in to make the magazine an "integrated media company." They wanted to—I don't kid—"break shit." It was managerial governance on steroids: they didn't even bother to pretend, like W. Edwards Deming, that the voices of the workers mattered. A month after the anniversary dinner, Leon, Frank, most of the senior staff, and almost all of the contributing editors resigned. Larry Grafstein told me later that he said to Chris: "You alienated the world's largest collection of polemicists."

A couple of months later, for the first new issue since the resignations—they missed an issue or two in between because there was no one left to work—the magazine put out a cover story by Jeet Heer titled "The New Republic's Legacy on Race: A historical reflection." It was a hit piece—Chris Hughes's gloss on the magazine in my era. The cover picture was a can of white paint, so everyone would know what to expect inside. According to Heer, during my tenure, the magazine published mostly right-wing blacks or black-bashing pieces; supported the Clinton welfare reform bill, some of the provisions of which made black poverty and prison rates worse; and stood in the way of social progress, on the wrong side of the identity wars.

I would have argued that Shelby Steele was different than Glenn Loury who was different than Wynton Marsalis who was different than Stanley Crouch who was different than Skip Gates, all of whom we published. *The Bell Curve* had been a question, to me, of the free exchange of ideas. Clinton's welfare and crime bill were necessary for his reelection, since he was negotiating with a Republican congress. And when it came to the identity wars, we had asked big, contentious questions in service of practical democratic politics. I would also have argued that Heer's piece used race to distract from the real issue at the magazine right then: the bloodbath Chris had unleashed in the Republic of Letters with his managerial pretensions a few months before. But who wanted to listen?

Still, I thought I had something valuable to say in the way of an accounting of my public life. People might not like where we were as Americans, and they might not like me or the hand I'd played in helping to get us here. But I had some idea, some set of experiences, that showed how the last half century had played out. I'd sold the Cambridge house and moved to New York. I'd gotten an office, shipped down my old files, and was looking for the first time in my life backward. I was having conversations with Anne about writing a memoir.

Meantime, what I heard of the new *New Republic* was not encouraging and not surprising: profits were not materializing. Seems like "break shit" wasn't a strategy that applied to the world of ideas or those who trafficked in those ideas. In early 2016, Chris Hughes sold the magazine to Win McCormack, who was my actual first tutee in 1962. I liked him well enough, a leftist with literary inclinations. He came from money, and you could tell he didn't have a lot of urgency about anything. I wasn't quite sure what he'd been doing for forty years, but it was clear enough who his friends were. He hired Nita Lowey's old opponent, Ham Fish V, who was later fired for manhandling a number of women, to be his publisher. Pretty soon I was getting emails offering *New Republic* cruise trips to Cuba and Iran. It was like reading *The Nation*.

In the end, Win turned out to be a moderate: he didn't make the magazine doctrinaire, he brought in conservative voices like Christopher Caldwell who added intellectual diversity, and he didn't make the magazine a voice against Israel. Maybe that was a bow to his old professor or to longtime readers of the magazine. For sure it was an improvement over Hughes: an old-fashioned, gentle Left rejoinder to the unhumanized technocracy of the Facebook Democrats.

❋ ❋ ❋

In the political sphere, the Obama White House drove the agenda: there were no rejoinders as yet to its top-down technocracy and confident managerialism. In 2010, when Republicans recaptured the House, limiting Obama's room for domestic maneuver, he turned his interest to foreign policy. In the Middle East, he was determined to correct for what he saw as the flaws of the Bush administration with "a new beginning" predicated on rapprochement with Iran. This, for me, was another testament to the limitations of high universalist ambitions, an effort to make reality conform to the austere principles that increasingly guided Democratic thinking.

By this point, to anyone noticing, the reality of Iran's moves in the Middle East was clear. It was opposing the "Great Satan" by contracting with Russia for missiles and arms, sponsoring Hamas in the Gaza Strip, and exercising de facto control in Lebanon through the Iranian-backed Lebanese Armed Forces, which allowed Hezbollah, also backed by Iran, to operate in Lebanon undisturbed. It was sending operatives as far as Venezuela for rapprochements with Hugo Chávez and Nicolás Maduro. It was making moves toward ties with China. And by 2013, through its backing of Syrian dictator Bashar al-Assad, another Russian client, it was functionally sponsoring the Syrian genocide.

After Bashar al-Assad put down the Arab Spring demonstrations in a series of massacres, a vicious civil war broke out between the minority Alawite Shia rulers and a mostly Sunni population. In the late summer of that year, Assad used sarin gas on Syrian resistance forces in a Damascus suburb: a clear violation of norms of war for one hundred years. It was a step over any ethically accepted form of conflict, reminiscent of the trenches of the First World War and the Holocaust—something that had to be deterred or the language of human rights would become a scrim for whatever crimes authoritarians chose to commit. I had hope for a response now that Samantha Power was ambassador to the UN. Leon was talking to her a couple of times a week, urging action. Bernard-Henri Lévy was talking to President François Hollande in France. And, initially, Obama backed a retaliatory strike on Assad.

The night before planes were supposed to hit Assad, BHL had actually gotten a text from Hollande saying the planes would fly the next morning. But Obama cancelled the strike, drawing back from his vaunted red line. And that was it. The slaughter continued and over four hundred thousand Syrians have died—two or three times worse than anything in Iraq. Perhaps five million more were driven out of the country, creating a refugee problem that has reached all the way to Europe.

UN Ambassador Power had said in *A Problem from Hell*, her book on the repeated failures to prevent genocide, "What is most shocking about America's reaction...is not that the United States refused to deploy US ground forces...What is most shocking is that US policymakers did almost nothing to deter the crime."

When it came to *this* American abdication of responsibility, Samantha kept her head down and didn't resign. Of course, no high official had resigned over a principled policy disagreement since 1980, when Cy Vance left Carter's administration over its handling of the Iran hostage crisis. Official shame was a thing of the past: that wasn't the way the new generation, the achievers, did it. I was so disappointed in her. She had written the book, and now she was fronting for an administration that had failed in exactly the ways she'd laid out. Experienced as I was seeing people and causes not turn out the way I wanted, I couldn't believe it.

Having avoided alienating Iran over Syria, Obama appointed a Chas Freeman prototype—unknown enough to escape attention, powerful enough to manage the ground—to make a peace deal happen. Robert Malley was Jewish, and a type of Jew I recognized: a believer in higher one-world ideals who used historical injustice to justify them. He was a childhood friend of Tony Blinken in Paris, though Malley's background was very different. His father was a participant in the Algerian struggle for independence and the editor of the political magazine, *Afrique Asie*, which promoted Castro and Arafat in its pages. The younger Malley first surfaced with a piece in the *New York Review of Books* on the Camp David Summit of 2000, making the case that Barak and Clinton hadn't laid the groundwork sufficiently to engage Arafat. In 2009, he was booted from his advisory role on the Obama campaign when it was "discovered" that he had been "engaging" with representatives of Hamas when he worked at the Soros-funded International Crisis Group as its Mideast point person. Six years after that, in 2015, the administration appointed him National Security Council coordinator for the Middle East, Africa, and the Gulf Region.

The new threat Malley had to confront was the Islamic State, radical Islamists who had proclaimed a new caliphate in the large areas of Iraq and Syria they captured with breathtaking speed in the mid-2010s. They were street thugs of messianism, marrying little girls off wholesale to their fighters; they seemed to have come out of nowhere, and they forced Malley into a de facto alliance with Assad and his Iranian allies. By 2016, the Islamic State was defeated, the US had a new peace deal with Iran, hundreds of thousands were dead in Syria, Iraq was further destabilized, the Lebanese government was in increasing chaos, and Saudi Arabia was at war with Iranian proxies in Yemen. And Iran, along with its allies Russia and China, had a stronger hand in the region. This wasn't, couldn't have been, what Obama predicted. But it was of a piece with his style of governance: one-size-fits-all solutions that created unexpected problems.

Hefty weapons transactions continued, the largest in the history of their relationship, but Israel was out of favor in Washington. With their policy toward Iran and Syria, Obama and Malley shifted the strategic ground toward Israel's historic enemies. Meantime, John Kerry, secretary of state under a president who shared his universalist aspirations, made the case that Israel was as much responsible for tensions with the Palestinians as the Palestinians themselves because Netanyahu's government would not discourage settlements by Israeli nationalists in the West Bank and Gaza. I had opposed some of the outlier settlements, though I didn't see them as a major cause of the current impasse. But Kerry made them equal—or greater than equal—to the Palestinian leadership's endemic corruption, its weakness in the face of Hamas, and its refusal to accept five serious peace offers over forty-five years. In a speech at the Brookings Institution, a video of which made the Twitter rounds, Kerry was explicit: "There will be no advance and separate peace with the Arab world without the Palestinian process and Palestinian peace. Everybody needs to understand that. That is a hard reality."

This was the Obama diagnosis for Middle Eastern problems, a position hardened by a universalist disdain for a world of peoples and particularities and by a Left belief in the need to atone for what they saw as past American injustices. It shifted the way Israel got talked about among many liberal Democrats and accelerated the zero-sum aspect of American politics at large. The poster child for these changes was Ben Rhodes, who sold Obama's eventual Iran nuclear deal to Congress and the public. He argued that American Jews who opposed Obama's policies were acting out of a persecution complex, a pathology. They had, as he said in his memoir, "internalized the vision of Israel constantly under attack." This more-in-sorrow-than-in-anger condemnation of Israel became the line among Democrats; the dismissal of opponents as psychotic or absurd was of a piece with the way Rhodes conducted the campaign for the nuclear deal. "We created an echo chamber," he told David Samuels in the *New York Times*. "[The experts] were saying things that validated what we had given them to say.... In the absence of rational discourse, we are going to discourse the shit out of this. We had test drives to know who was going to be able to carry our message effectively, and how to use outside groups...So we knew the tactics that worked.... I mean, I'd prefer a sober, reasoned public debate, after which members of Congress reflect and take a vote. But that's impossible."

This was the voice of the Democratic Party—no longer my Democratic Party—rejecting the possibility of rational discourse in American political life and embracing top-down political force instead. Twenty years ago, Hillary Clinton had told opponents of her healthcare plan that she would "crush" them. Now the Obama administration was repeating the mantra: Agree with us, they were saying, or we'll "discourse the shit" out of you.

A backlash was coming. "Exhibit A" as far as I was concerned was that old New York huckster Al Sharpton, now Obama's advisor and ambassador to the black community, the role Jesse Jackson had fulfilled under Bill Clinton. He was no longer fat, he wore three-piece suits, and he dined at the Regency, which is the breakfast headquarters of the near billionaire Jewish set. Toxic politics had stopped working, so he'd changed—he got respectable. But what good was he doing for the black community, actually, apart from appearing on CNN and preaching shibboleths about injustice and diversity? The bigger piece of proof that the Democrats didn't see signs of trouble ahead was their admiration of Hillary Clinton, whom everyone was waiting to get elected president. The Obama administration was turning into the Clinton administration in waiting.

In one way it was odd that, with all the problems in the country at large, the Democrats chose Hillary and somehow expected her to win the election. For all of her "evolution" from communitarian leftist to foreign policy establishmentarian, her approach to politics never changed: she governed top down, following academic or Washington wisdom, and was always surprised by any sort of backlash to that style. In another way, the party choosing Hillary made sense. If Ben Rhodes was any indication, the Democrats were more top down now, too, addicted to their conventional wisdom that had evolved through the Clinton and then Obama White Houses to become a rationalist disease. But I never deluded myself that institutions staffed by people so insulated could maintain public trust.

The first sign of the backlash to the Establishment was on the Democratic side, among the young, whose issues had changed: Black Lives Matter. The Dreamers. Transgender advocacy. The dominant tone was suspicion of structures—financial, governmental, and institutional—that a younger generation felt were out of control. It was a mirror perception of the voters on the other side, who, in 2008, had supported Sarah Palin's vice presidential nomination and who were dissatisfied with Mitt Romney in 2012. I thought the issues themselves were scrims for something deeper, some sense the young had that the institutions weren't doing their jobs, that the world was getting unmanageable, and it was unclear what the future held for them. Identity politics was the easiest way to express that sense and protect against it.

There was also Bernie Sanders. A decade earlier, he had been a figure on the margins, a Vermont socialist who'd visited the USSR on his honeymoon and worked on a Communist kibbutz in Israel. Now he was mounting a surprisingly serious and effective challenge to Hillary for the Democratic presidential nomination. Sanders was also a sign to me that the top-down approach was not resonating for essential parts of their base.

More of the signs, though, came from the Right.

Bibi Netanyahu's supporters called him Bibi Melech Yisrael, and with his fourth election victory in early 2015, he was looking like "the King of Israel." Since 1993, Barak, Sharon, and Ehud Olmert had made substantive, concrete offers to the Palestinians for peace: each time, even after the Oslo Accords, violence against Israelis followed. A rough sense had developed among Israelis: compromise gets us nowhere; the Palestinian leadership won't deal. High-minded universalist condemnation only made Israelis angry—and Bibi knew it.

The night of the Brexit vote, in June 2016, I had a party at a New York restaurant, and the smart money among the financiers and academics at the table was that the people who voted for Brexit hadn't known what they were voting for. I didn't think that was true at all. I thought they were choosing the nation-state—the construct that was realer and more familiar—over the lame, universalist proposal of the EU.

After Donald Trump became the de facto Republican nominee for president, having demolished the ordinary politicians in the Republican field, I had a sense that this impulse was operating in America, too. Later that summer, Marc Granetz took me to lunch, and he said that he thought Hillary would win. It was surprising to hear Marc repeating the common wisdom because he usually doesn't do that. I thought it was testament to how common that wisdom was. And so, on an instinct, I asked the waiter who he was voting for: Trump. Then I asked another server: Trump. Then, when we left, I asked the maître d': Trump. And these were New Yorkers!

I remembered what I had said about Trump thirty years before when I sent Fran Lebowitz my letter: "Lord, what this man has done to New York." Now he'd come fully into his own as a tribal hustler riding a history of controversy, outrage, and outright lies against an establishment people increasingly didn't believe in. He was the antithesis of respectability: he refused to play by the rules, which seemed not to apply to him anyway. Sex scandals and revelations of financial misdeeds seemed to bounce right off him. He bypassed the media gatekeepers by harnessing the disruptive new technology of Twitter, a bully pulpit he used not to preach universals like peace and brotherhood but to utter primal screams.

Trump's was a coarse, money-powered populism that didn't solve problems, just inflated anger. It was the opposite of a humanized technocracy even if it was the natural response to an un-humanized one. He took over the Republican Party and made it his creature over the objections of serious, decent conservatives like John McCain and Mitt Romney. When Charles Krauthammer, having opposed Trump to his last breath, died in 2018, it was a symbol to me of the end of something—and of how far the party had fallen.

The Republicans had never been my party, so I mainly saw Trump as a lesson to Democrats, a tribal backlash to their arrogant elitism and one-worldism. When Hillary lost, they didn't take it as a sign of the limits of their rationalist vision—they took it as an existential threat. Never considering their own appeal to voters might want a rethink, that history was no longer looking the way they liked it, they declared "resistance" against the elected president. They ginned up an investigation into Russian links to Trump's campaign. The much-hyped report by special prosecutor Robert Mueller failed to produce a smoking gun. But House Democrats who had retaken the speaker's gavel in 2018 impeached Trump for an unrelated shakedown of the president of Ukraine. Few understood the labyrinthine game of claims and counterclaims that seemed to me too hard to prove and too hyperbolically prosecuted. I had never trusted certain kinds of hysteria on my own side, not since the nuclear politics of the sixties, and this hysteria was worse.

The "resistance" also took the form of a series of reform movements powered by anger this country hadn't seen since the sixties, as the Democrats made common cause with the rising young socialist and identitarian progressives to fight the Trumpian threat.

The first front in that war came very close to home.

* * *

Male celebrity abuse of power was already in the news. But when Donald Trump became president in spite of his recorded and documented mistreatment of women, investigating these abuses became a priority, a cause. It looked to me like an establishment reeling from Trumpism was trying to find a way to fight it. A million angry women descended on Washington just after the inauguration. That fall, investigations by the *New York Times* and the *New Yorker* exposed Harvey Weinstein's predations, an exposure that started an avalanche of revelations about other men. Caught in the #MeToo

avalanche was Leon Wieseltier, who was working on a new magazine, *Idea*, to be put out by Steve Jobs's widow, Laurene Powell Jobs,
a philanthropist in her own right. The magazine was scheduled to
come out at the end of October 2017: a renaissance for him, for our
version of liberalism, and for serious thought in Washington, D.C.
in the age of tribal reaction. But it wasn't to be.

Leon is an intellectual who is also a man of the senses—it was
a commitment of his, part of his throwing off of the kippah. It
wasn't a fake commitment, not at all. But it was not a commitment
many people get to make. When you're as much of a genius as Leon,
you get to live in a fantasy world, at least for a while, and people I
trusted already could see the problems this caused. Anne, who was
both more loving and more disciplined than I was, kept telling me
to rein him in.

Leon's public troubles began when Michelle Cottle, who had
worked at the *New Republic* for several years and is now on the
editorial board of the *New York Times*, started questioning Leon's
past behavior. Cottle may have actually fobbed off the origins of the
Wieseltier accusations on someone else, an anonymous somebody
who actually may be herself. This was the email that opened the
matter, forwarded later to Leon:

> *hey gorgeous Odd Q. With the Weinstein fueled fury
> on workplace harassment was perhaps inevitable
> Leon's shenanigans would bubble up. An ex-TNR...
> has asked many of us to contact women who came
> through there over the years to say that she is orga-
> nizing an anonymous support group of sorts...and if
> interested...xo, mmc.*

Soon after the accusations broke, Cottle wrote an article for
The Atlantic on Leon titled, a bit pompously, "Leon Wieseltier:
A Reckoning." Cottle didn't leave me out of her arraignment of
the *New Republic*. She coyly asserted that I had "a reputation as a
scorching sexist (a tale for another day), and the magazine was seen
as something of a boys' club." So, what is the "tale for another day"?
Men? Women? It's bullshit.

I believe Cottle thought she would kill him or at least damage
him for good, and she did damage him. Leon was minutes away

from launching his new magazine, and there was great anticipation of the appearance of this vigorous, brainy, and beautiful publication, when Mrs. Jobs pulled the plug on him. Copies of the magazine were already in boxes, ready to be shipped. She simply had them destroyed or discarded and no one ever saw it. She didn't suspend Leon and replace him with Adam Kirsch, his assistant literary editor at the *New Republic* and then his deputy for the new journal, or with any number of brilliant women who might have done a creditable job. It was wiped off the intellectual memory stream—and at the time nobody said anything.

The Trump phenomenon made darlings of Alexandria Ocasio-Cortez, Ilhan Omar, Rashida Tlaib, and Ayanna Pressley—the four representatives, elected from safe Democratic districts after waging aggressive primaries, who were anointed "the Squad" when they arrived in the House in January 2019. They came to represent for me the worst of the anti-Trump politics—a repeat of the Palmer House, except now on a much, much, much larger stage.

They identified with the left wing of the party: Ocasio-Cortez was put up to run by Justice Democrats, a newer and harder-edged version of the Democratic Socialists of America, which saw its own membership surge after Trump. Like Trump, they wielded Twitter as a weapon, oftentimes against members of their own party. They accused moderate House Democrats who opposed their plans—the Green New Deal, Medicare for All—of being racist, sexist, and corporatist, and they worked to primary them in 2020. They were vocally anti-Israel on the grounds of Palestinian oppression. They reminded me of H. Rap Brown, Stokely Carmichael, and Carl Oglesby—racial politics married to radical socialistic politics. But the frightening difference was that their brand was eagerly taken up by the powers-that-be, the powers-that-are: *Saturday Night Live* cast them in flattering lights, while the *New York Times* and the *New Yorker* wrote profiles about them. My favorite congressmen, moderates like Josh Gottheimer and Ritchie Torres, elected in the same year, didn't get anything like that sort of coverage.

The leading issue beyond #MeToo or socialist policy proposals became race—and the Establishment responded with the same enthusiasm. Writing in *The Atlantic*, primarily for upper-middle-class readers, Ibram X. Kendi declared that every instance of a racial disparity is evidence of racism, a societal malady, a cancer, to be treated by antiracist institutional policies—a position echoed by Black Lives Matter at protests across the country. This racialism came with the ridicule of whites with the purpose of degrading them: it was the opposite of Josephine Baker's salt-and-pepper crowd. It was full of sloganeering that did not look at the real problems in neighborhoods: for example, gentrification and absentee fathers that even Barack Obama commented on, or the economic effects of finance that William Julius Wilson wrote about. It was full of rhetorical devices and that only made people angry at individuals—poor whites, police officers—who couldn't produce results.

But even worse than the shift in social issues was the shift in culture. During the Trump era, the people in charge of addressing issues of public concern bought into the zero-sum rhetoric. When I donated $2,500 to Bernie, in the hopes that he would beat Hillary in the 2016 primary, I found myself on dozens of paranoid and sensationalist email lists, including Blue State Digital, which advised me: "DON'T delete this email; DON'T turn off your computer; DON'T check Facebook," and instead to "drop everything you're doing right now and donate just $5 to help us pass the 'For the People Act.'" It was a pure distillation of cocooned moral fervor, and not just the kind to be found on Facebook, Twitter, or email chains, which I didn't look at, but also in the *New York Times* Opinion pages, which I did.

In 2020, in the midst of the racial protests, James Bennet, a *New Republic* alumnus, was dismissed as editor of the *New York Times* Opinion page. His crime: publishing an opinion piece by Senator Tom Cotton of Arkansas, a Republican and Trump supporter, arguing for the government to impose martial law on cities that could not get their protests under control—a piece he hadn't read before its publication. A controversial argument? To be sure. But whatever happened to a diversity of opinion? It's out with the trash at the *New York Times*.

There are, however, some positive trends in journalism. Leon started another publication, *Liberties, a Journal of Culture and Politics*, to fight for the liberal idea in a time when it is being pressed from all sides. "Accept the truth," says Maimonides on the preface page, "from whoever utters it." The truth is that Leon may have been disrespectful to women, but he has also respected them and their work. The new journal features contributions from Martha Nussbaum, Helen Vendler, and Nobel laureate Louise Glück, among many others.

Tablet, which Alana Newhouse founded in 2009 with her husband David Samuels, has become more political in recent years and has maintained many of the *New Republic*'s values. It is, even by our definition, a Jewish magazine: the political analysis of Bernard-Henri Lévy, Jeffrey Herf, and Jamie Kirchick share space with matzah recipes. Tony Badran, a Maronite from Lebanon, writes everything I believe—and the *Times* editorial board won't say—on Middle East politics. Michael Lind has crafted a complex liberal critique of racial entitlements. Lee Smith wrote effectively against Obama's universalist approach to the Middle East, though he has become more than a bit nutty and paranoid since the Trump election. Bari Weiss started at *Tablet*. She wrote things, most of which I agreed with, for the *New York Times* before she quit on principle in solidarity with James Bennet.

And they aren't the only ones. Bret Stephens spent the Trump years at the *Times*, making the lonely case against tribalism, universalism, and progressivism. John McWhorter now writes for the *Times*, too, offering a weekly or biweekly antidote to easy identity politics and humane commentary on culture besides.

✳ ✳ ✳

In 2018, right before the Squad came to Congress, long before the resistance to them began, Anne and I attended a kind of reunion of the Eugene McCarthy presidential campaign at the West Side apartment of Peter Yarrow to raise money for the film Mary Beth was making about Gene. I saw a lot of the old faces there. It made me realize how long ago it all was. The hopes we had seemed so distant now.

Really, in one way, the event gave me the creeps: all of the righteous people at that sing-along, full of good will, with almost no interest in or awareness of how America had changed.

But, in another way, the event made me think: 1968 was another period of logjam—my party split, threats from the ground and the Establishment, no political place to call home, and the reactionary Right cresting to the White House. If we could get out of it then—well, we could get out of it now.

Vantage Point, 2022: Where to Next?

And we did get out of it—sort of, though not necessarily to a better place.

COVID-19 was more than a meteor that cleaved a decade: it was a once-in-a-century event, the biggest global catastrophe we've faced since the Second World War and possibly, like that war, a realigning one.

Two years ago, things still seemed predictable, even suddenly hopeful, for people like me. In March 2020, after four years of up-and-down turmoil under Trump, the Democrats put their most centrist candidate on offer: Anne's and my candidate for the United States Senate seat from Delaware in 1972, Joe Biden, whose nomination was an implicit vindication of the assumptions of centrist Democrats like me. An old-fashioned son of organized labor, a glad-handing politician who made his name over almost forty years in the Senate, catapulted to the nomination over Bernie Sanders by the votes of black Americans in the South—Biden was proof positive that the radicalism promoted by the identitarian socialists and the rationalism promoted by the austere universalists were as unrealistic as we'd thought. The Democratic Party, contra Sanders and the Squad on one hand and Obama and Soros on the other, was showing that people voted based on moderate promises and older ties, not utopian visions and sterile universals.

This March 3, Super Tuesday, was before the pandemic—before lockdown, before George Floyd's death and the subsequent riots and protests in major American cities, before the vaccine mandate wars, before Trump's "Stop the Steal," before the thwarted coup in the US Capitol, and before controversies about the power of Facebook, Twitter, and Google in the American electoral process. Not since my childhood, with the attack on Pearl Harbor and the American victory in 1945, the revelation of the *churb'n* in that same year, and the creation of the state of Israel in 1948, has history moved so fast—not even in the late sixties, the time whose early hopes and subsequent reversals shaped my perspective of the politically possible.

Where it's left us now is strange to me: it's accelerated trends I'd seen from the top of society in ways I'd never expected. The widespread distrust that started with the failure in Iraq and then accelerated with the financial crisis, global economic competition, Trump, and COVID has made tribalism and leftism the most potent political draws in a country that people like me had faith would never, ever, ever be drawn in those directions. For my father, capitalism and democracy in a land of immigrants could smooth out anything; I've lived long enough to see that they might have their limits.

The Biden presidency is an attempt to cope with these forces. I don't have faith that it can. I don't have doubts, exactly, but I don't have certainty.

❋   ❋   ❋

Internationally, the administration is trying to strike a middle ground between Trump and Obama. Under the guidance of Secretary of State Tony Blinken, it is taking a harder stance toward China than Obama did when it comes to diplomatic alliances and tariffs, and it has appointed Rahm Emanuel as ambassador to Japan, a key post in any project of combating Chinese influence. The United States is sending billions of dollars in aid to Ukraine to support its counteroffensives against the Russian invasion. While it is true that the administration set out to allow Iran back into the nuclear deal, the 2022 protests in response to the murder of Mahsa Amini by the morality police have put those negotiations on pause, and I'm hopeful that the United States will continue with a tougher attitude toward the regime. In Afghanistan, the Biden administration's withdrawal reminded a lot of people of Saigon and the Vietnam War; it reminded me of those who got no honor, even from me, for arguing for a responsible withdrawal from a war gone wrong. Now my friends and I are the ones who argued for a responsible exit. Overall, this is American leadership in a more straitened age. But it's still leadership I can recognize from the postwar tradition in which I came up. It recognizes, however obliquely and selectively, the power of the nation and of the tribe, and the power of evil in the world. It's not one size fits all.

George Soros, once considered by the Clinton White House a nation-state unto himself, is no longer. The *New York Times* recently ran a story, "George Soros is Making Changes at his Foundation While he Still Can," that was a kind of coda to his twenty-five-year project. Soros, the article said, was making severance payments to many of his philanthropies to focus on fighting the nationalist, tribal backlash that has made him—and his foundation—persona non grata in his native land of Hungary and has made Eastern Europe not one open society but dozens of distinct nationalities. What the article didn't say is that Soros himself helped cause the tribal backlash and, in the process, he has proven the limits of his own vision: the open society and the open market that came with it, what we call neoliberalism or globalization, is not a beneficial thing when it's pushed to its extremes—when it means the denuding of the nation-state or of national identity. What we're seeing now, politically, is what comes from that extreme push. I wonder sometimes how Soros feels. But then I return to my schadenfreude.

Meantime, Soros's great avoidance, the state of Israel, is proving the power of the democratic nation-state. One of the few benefits of Trump's election was that his foreign policy in the Middle East, under the de facto minding of his son-in-law, Jared Kushner, was a clear improvement over Obama's. I met Kushner a long time back and didn't much like him. He asked me for money for the Harvard Chabad and didn't bother to hide his annoyance when I said no. But I figured he'd be tougher, more clear-eyed, about the Middle East than the previous administration's movers, and I said as much to the

New York Times after the election. About this I was correct. Kushner deserves credit for seeing the regional opportunities that John Kerry and Obama ignored. The Palestinian issue has been made irrelevant to Israel's position in the Middle East. As the Iranian threat loomed, the Sunni states, led by Saudi Arabia, were more amenable to Israel as a bulwark against Iran, and in 2020 the United Arab Emirates and Bahrain became the third and fourth countries to open diplomatic relations with Israel since 1948. There are more to come, and Kerry's gamble, his arrogant statement in 2016 about the necessity of a Palestinian peace before a peace with the Arab states, was proven wrong in less than four years. The Chas Freemans and the Jim Bakers of the world, and David Ignatius, Thomas Friedman, and the other Washington wise men of the generation after mine, have had twenty or thirty years of analysis rendered irrelevant by facts on the ground.

Domestically, things are trickier; and this is a trickiness that has had—and certainly will continue to have—implications for America abroad.

The disruptions at home scare me not because they're the same as the disruptions of the late sixties, which formed my political consciousness, but because they're different. Like in 1968, a vast tribal Right rebels against postwar liberalism; like in 1968, a socialistic Left rebels against it from the other side. But the Right is much angrier, more atomized, and more distrustful, than it has ever been: Trump's sallies against the deep state and his mixed policies on vaccines are not signs of rebellion against the institutions—they're signs of total alienation from them. And the Left has a greater presence in the institutions than it has ever before: Bernie Sanders and Alexandria Ocasio-Cortez are writing budget policy.

These radicalisms are fighting over an America that is much more vulnerable to them than it has been in the past for a simple and sweeping reason: all of the old, supporting structures people like me came up with have been thrown away. The Biden campaign really tells this story: it was an old Democratic campaign—southern black moderates and Midwestern blue-collar voters were led by a nearly eighty-year-old pol from Scranton—but it's the last of those campaigns. The institutions that defined them, which can support real, sustained activism about problems faced by people that demand pragmatic solutions, are slivering away. The churches and the unions that powered civil rights, and the voters themselves who found meaning in them, are receding, almost gone. (Some of my friends tell me there is a renaissance brewing among the unions, but I'm not so sure. We'll have to wait and see.) In their place is a nationalized, media-ized, financialized, and atomized America, the one David Riesman, Nat Glazer, and Dan Bell warned us about but whose consequences are different than any of us imagined. Trump is the spokesperson for an entire class of people who feel marginalized and left behind in this strange society, the Squad speaks for groups who feel equally at sea, and the consequences of the unrest they foment on this new America, an America without traditional institutional guardrails, will be something we haven't yet seen.

Meantime, the institutions that still exist, the national ones, haven't caught up to the problem. I know that from what I see in those places I once called home—the places my tribe and generation helped build in order to make American society better, more humane. They are falling short.

Harvard has returned to its roots training ministers for a theocracy. It's not just giving awards to Colin Kaepernick. Any number of emails that I read from the Mahindra Humanities Center—Homi Bhabha's creation whose funder comes from a family known for, according to Homi, "the cosmopolitan ethos of its business ventures"—or from the Theological Seminary or from one or another associate dean, confirm the obvious: racial justice, environmentalism, global cooperation, cosmopolitanism, the "global reach of the humanities" (another Homi phrase) are the ways to the future. Fifty years ago, we didn't have an associate dean of social justice, and we didn't commit to a "global reach," even if we hoped for the humanities to spread. Certainly positions this vague and aims this universal don't help bridge the gap between experts and ideologues, and certainly they don't help future leaders connect their intellect with their experience to form their values. They just assure them that virtue comes from saying the right words. And the people who come out of this environment are much more susceptible to moralisms of the rationalists and increasingly of leftists than the people who came before.

The Washington establishment, which the *New Republic* once poked and prodded, has as its venerable institutions Brookings and *The Atlantic* (now owned by Laurene Jobs). They have not so much arguments as symposiums among the respectable, even as, from the steps of Capitol Hill, Marjorie Taylor Greene fulminates against the deep state and the Squad fulminates against white capitalists. The Biden White House is ignoring the problems of our society and culture, too: the disruptors are writing policy, with a handful of moderates villainized as threats to democracy in the pages of the *New York Times* for asking for bipartisanship and less than two trillion-dollar spending bills.

I'm still following a trajectory I've been on since the McCarthy campaign got stranded between superior, crazy forces in Chicago and caught between the partly corrupted Establishment and the increasingly irresponsible disenfranchised. This time the choice is easy, at least for me, because the radicalisms of the disenfranchised are so radical. But the choice is still not encouraging: I am tired of all of the promises of the politics I supported that I thought were real. Still, I cannot think that the present dispensation—the progressive dispensation and its Trumpian alternative—is the future.

In this position, you do what you know how to do. I know how to humanize the technocracy: that's what almost forty years at the *New Republic* and almost fifty at Harvard were about for me. After my flirtations with radicalism in the sixties, I committed to work through, though not always to agree with, the national institutions—government, finance, universities, and the media. I've lived most of my life on the faith that drove this work and the faith that came from it: faith that a humanized technocracy—made up of smart people who came through and eventually ran the institutions my generation and tribe helped expand—could make the country better, could save it from extremes. There are places I've fallen short, and places I've succeeded.

On the negative side of the ledger:

Domestically, I regret not recognizing the plight of the black underclass in the pages of the *New Republic*. The same effects of the consumer culture, the culture without traditional institutions or community guardrails, that I saw impacting blacks in the nineties is happening to poor whites now. Still, nobody's talking about it: we're talking innate racist psychologies among whites instead. I wish I could've given more of a platform to people like William Julius Wilson who talked about trends like the fall of industry and the rise of a multiracial underclass clearly, to lay down markers for what was just beginning thirty years ago. But, as Frank Manuel said, I'm a skimmer not a plumber. And I don't regret trying to address the problem because I believe you must name something before you solve it. But sometimes when you do that you get burned—and you burn others.

Internationally, I don't have regret for what I've said about Israel and the Middle East—for the way I've said it, maybe, but not for my underlying positions. I've always supported a two-state solution, at least in theory. But the Palestinians say they want it also—and they have sabotaged all the reasonable proposals offered to them. The truth is that most of the Middle East was distorted by the Ottomans, the British, and the French, and those distortions have locked the region into choices between false leaders and civil wars, false nationalisms and total disorder. The Palestinians are the example that never goes away. Iraq is the example writ large.

Domestically and internationally, I regret Iraq. But regret is not a big enough word for something where more than three thousand of your countrymen and one hundred thousand Iraqis were killed. I regret that the war was so divisive, so mismanaged, that it helped precipitate the disillusion and disorder we now see in American society. And I regret that the *New Republic* didn't see the potential for this mismanagement—not only because we believed the intelligence about weapons of mass destruction, but because Iraq played into all of the causes I believed in.

On the positive side of the ledger:

Domestically, I am proud that we brought the reality of the AIDS epidemic, and the idea of gay marriage, to a polity that wanted nothing to do with either, right on the cusp of the period in which AIDS deaths rose to their highest levels and just as American culture was about to bring gay men and women into society. We anticipated the politics of this issue—and, with Andrew as our editor, contributed to the cultural shift. I am proud that we didn't go with either easy Democratic or Republican talking points when it came to race and that we pressed on this issue that is so complex and has so many facets—from the black (and now white) underclass to the unending issue of affirmative action among the elite—and weren't afraid to push our side to recognize and argue with points of view they would otherwise dismiss. Publishing *The Bell Curve* cost me reputationally, but I would do it again, both as an issue of freely exchanging ideas and as a warning of the tribal backlash that eventually came from Democrats ignoring tribal realities. And I am proud that we stood up against the Clinton healthcare plan, which to me was the biggest potential domestic policy disaster in my lifetime. That kind of top-down managerialism is a mockery of humanized technocracy. I'm not proud of the way we did it—Betsy McCaughey's article should have been modified. But the Clintons pushed without regard to fact or dissent—and we pushed back, and we published dissents, too.

Internationally, I am proud that the *New Republic* made Communism and its suppressions of nationalities issues when, in the 1980s, the Establishment, and especially the Democratic Party, wanted to ignore it. And I'm proud that our pushing America to focus on the reality of a world of peoples abroad made a dent in Washington, D.C., right before the breakup of the Soviet Union created a new world where many of these peoples needed America's help. We saw what happened when we held back from helping in Kurdish Iraq and Rwanda and Syria—and in Biafra before all of these, though I may be one of the few who remembers. We saw what happened when we intervened, in Bosnia and Kosovo. I'm proud to have pushed America to help, and to have sometimes succeeded. And I'm proud to have published the book, *A Problem from Hell*, that became *the* book on American responsibility in a world of genocides. Even if its author later disappointed me, the book stands as a testament to not just our successes but also to our failures—failures that the fiction of the international community, bolstered by the Democrats' universalist fixations, helped make possible.

Finally, I am proud of the leaders I backed: Gene McCarthy and Al Gore changed America for the better throughout their political lives, and Ehud Barak almost did the same in Israel. They were incrementalists, not universalists or radicals; they were educated, thoughtful, and experienced; and they believed in improvement and individuality while respecting the power of difference and the force of tribalism and the reality of darkness. These three people point to the root of my faith in a humanized technocracy. I started my life as a man of causes. But what all of these causes have in common are the people I mentored, hired, and promoted to fight for them, alongside and above me—the people whom I've argued with and who have in turn argued and fought to improve the world. They are the people who make my faith a reality.

My faith is a very Jewish one, though my life is testimony of many more people than Jews holding it: that the solutions to our problems lie in debate, learnedness, cultivation, and honest differences among smart, talented, committed people. It was the key to such success as I had, and it was the key to the humanized technocracy I fought to build. Now, we're in an age of disjuncture, where the wrong people are fighting for the wrong causes and where out-of-touch managers, tribalists, and socialists set the terms of our politics. Changes in American life—the migration of radicalism to the national institutions as society at large has lost its mediating institutions—have simply, enormously, unimaginably raised the stakes of their beliefs.

But I have faith that we'll get through and beyond this—most of all, above all, because of the people I've taught, the people I've fought with, promoted, and encouraged. They've shown me what can be done in this country, for this country. I know they, and those like them, can do that again.

That, in the end, is the ground on which I'll stand or fall.

INDEX

ACKNOWLEDGMENTS

Daniel Bellow did a large part of the difficult work of editing this manuscript, cutting some of my most treasured words and adding some of his own—and it is much better for his efforts. I should add that Matthew Wolfson was a collaborator more than an assistant during the years-long writing process. He argued me out of several positions and enhanced many others. In the later stages, Benjamin Kravitz's editorial instincts, which were always shrewd, and literary touch, which was always graceful, gave this book exactly what it needed. A friend of mine, the writer Adam Plunkett, contributed his fresh perspective on Martin Luther King Jr. and the civil rights movement. For this I am grateful.

Thanks also goes to Adam Bellow, Aleigha Kely, and everyone at Post Hill Press for guiding this manuscript to publication with such diligence.

Michelle Ajami, Leon Wieseltier, and Miguel Wright read versions at various stages of completion, as did Gerald Peretz, Anne Peretz, Evgenia Peretz, and Jesse Peretz. I have done my best to heed their advice, which I always cherish.